DISCOURSES OF RŪMĪ

DISCOURSES
OF RŪMĪ

✻

A. J. ARBERRY

SAMUEL WEISER
New York
1972

© A. J. Arberry 1961
First Published 1961
by John Murray
Fifty Albemarle Street London
First American Edition 1972

SAMUEL WEISER INC.
734 Broadway
New York, N. Y. 10003

Library of Congress Catalogue Card No. 77-184563

ISBN 0-87728-179-3

Printed in U.S.A. by
NOBLE OFFSET PRINTERS, INC.
NEW YORK 3, N. Y.

To the memory

of my teacher and friend

REYNOLD ALLEYNE NICHOLSON

1868–1945

the supreme interpreter

of Rūmī

CONTENTS

PREFACE

Jalāl al-Dīn Rūmī (1207-1273) has long been recognised as the greatest mystical poet of Islam, and it can well be argued that he is the supreme mystical poet of all mankind. Yet his prose utterances have hitherto lain neglected, and have only been rescued from the obscurity of forgotten manuscripts in recent years. The eminent Persian scholar of mysticism, Professor Badī' al-Zamān Furūzānfar, published in 1952 a masterly edition of Rūmī's *Discourses* which I have now translated, drawing freely upon the editor's valuable annotations. In my version I have sought to be as faithful to the original as could be contrived, endeavouring to reproduce the actual style of Rūmī as he uttered these impromptu conversations.

This is not an easy book to read, but I believe that its study will prove richly rewarding, both for its own sake and for the light which it frequently throws upon Rūmī's poetry. It is in fact not too much to say, that the *Discourses* are a necessary introduction to the understanding of the poems. I am most grateful to the publishers for undertaking this book, and for the care which they have lavished upon it. My hearty thanks are also due to the Trustees of the Spalding Trust, who advanced a generous grant towards the costs of production.

A. J. ARBERRY

INTRODUCTION

The discourses of Jalāl al-Dīn Rūmī, Muslim saint, mystic and poet of the thirteenth century, here translated for the first time out of the original Persian, must be allowed to rank amongst the most remarkable documents of religious literature. Before describing and discussing their contents, it will be useful to summarise the history of the tumultuous times in which their author lived, an age of hitherto unparalleled violence and catastrophe; for it is only by recapturing the daily circumstances of the man who here speaks out of his heart to all humanity, that one can fairly measure the greatness of his spirituality and truly assess the sublimity of his detachment from the world of matter and events.

Jalāl al-Dīn Muḥammad, son of Bahā' al-Dīn Valad of Balkh, was born on 30 September 1207. His father, whose full name was Muḥammad ibn Ḥusain al-Khaṭībī al-Bakrī al-Balkhī, claimed direct paternal descent from Abū Bakr, the first caliph of Islam; on his mother's side he is said to have been of the local ruling house of the Khvarizmshahs, established about 1080 by a Turkish slave but none the less royal in its pretensions for all that, but this side of his lineage can be safely disregarded as legendary. Bahā' al-Dīn Valad came of stock long esteemed in Khurasan as experts in theology and canon law; the province, for all its remoteness from the heartland of Islam, had for centuries been a leading centre of Muslim learning and piety, and had produced notable schools of both philosophy and mysticism. In 1207 Khurasan was flourishing under the rule of the powerful and ambitious 'Alā' al-Dīn Muḥammad Khvarizmshah, who had just captured Balkh the previous year from the Ghurids and would shortly master all Persia and Afghanistan and aspire to even greater dominion until halted by forces far more terrible than his own.

Bahā' al-Din himself was born about 1148 of a father who was also a noted scholar and divine. Brought up in the traditional atmosphere of Sunni orthodoxy, he acquired such a reputation as a teacher and preacher that he had conferred upon him the title Sultan of the Ulema. He was additionally a Sufi mystic, thus following in the footsteps of the great Muḥammad al-Ghazzālī of Tus (died 1111) whose rigorous attacks on the philosophers had seriously undermined the influence of Avicenna and virtually put an end to free speculation in eastern Islam. It was, however, to al-Ghazzālī's more ecstatic brother Aḥmad (died 1123), author in Persian of a subtle metaphysical essay on Divine Love, that Bahā' al-Dīn traced his spiritual descent. This combination of profound theological and theosophical learning won for him high repute as a religious preceptor and lends peculiar charm to his sermons and meditations, a large volume of which has recently for the first time become available in print. This book, called *Ma'ārif* ('Gnoses'), afterwards fascinated and greatly influenced his son.

A not unexpected *odium theologicum* brought Bahā' al-Dīn into collision with his contemporary Fakhr al-Dīn al-Rāzī (born 1149), an outspoken critic of al-Ghazzālī and a skilful champion of scholasticism whose numerous and voluminous writings deserve far more attention than they have received hitherto. Echoes of the hostility between these two men, competitors for royal favour, are to be found in Bahā' al-Dīn's *Ma'ārif* and are loudly and exaggeratedly repeated by the Persian biographers. It is commonly asserted that Fakhr al-Dīn was the cause of the Khvarizmshah's turning against the Sufis, so that he drowned Majd al-Dīn Baghdādī, a prominent member of the circle to which Bahā' al-Dīn himself belonged, in the river Oxus. It is further alleged that Fakhr al-Dīn's enmity led to Baha' al-Dīn's precipitate flight from Balkh; this report, however, involves an anachronism, for Fakhr al-Dīn died in 1210 whereas Bahā' al-Dīn did not flee until 1219, and then under very different compulsion. For in that year the Mongol hordes under Chingiz Khān, storming down from the north-east, stood poised to ravage Balkh, a fearful holocaust which followed the city's surrender in 1220. Those who would and could ran headlong before the wrath to come; amongst the many thousands who preferred martyrdom was the aged Najm al-Dīn Kubrā, founder of the Kubraviya Order of dervishes.

A graphic description of terrible events from which Bahā' al-Dīn and his young son so narrowly escaped has been given by another famous Sufi, a disciple of Majd al-Dīn Baghdādī and Najm al-Dīn Kubrā, who ran from those regions not long after Bahā' al-Dīn himself.

2

'It was in the year 1220,' he writes, 'that the God-forsaken army of the Tartar infidels, may God forsake and destroy them, gained the mastery over those territories. The confusion and slaughter, the devastation and leading into captivity, the destruction and conflagration that followed at the hands of those accursed creatures were such as had never before been witnessed in any age, whether in the lands of heathendom or Islam. How could slaughter ever be vaster than this that they wrought from the gate of Turkistan to the gate of Syria and Rum, wherein they laid waste so many cities and provinces, so that in one city alone—Raiy, where I myself was born and brought up—it has been estimated that 700,000 mortals were slain or made captive.' Where was any country to be found in which true believers still dwelt, uncontaminated by the blight of heresy and fanaticism, under the protection of a just and religious king? In every place Dāya asked this question, and always he was given the same answer—in Rum, those provinces of what is now Asiatic Turkey which were still ruled over by the western branch of the once immensely powerful Saljuq House. It was to Rum therefore that Dāya betook himself, whither he had already been preceded by Bahā' al-Dīn.

At the time of the flight Jalāl al-Dīn was a boy of twelve, already well grounded in his father's learning and piety, old enough to remember in after years his childhood environment, reminiscences of which are to be found scattered here and there in his discourses. Bahā' al-Dīn made his way first to Nishapur, all too soon to share the horrible fate of Balkh, and there called upon the venerable poet and mystic Farīd al-Dīn 'Aṭṭār, another pupil of Majd al-Dīn Baghdādī. Farīd al-Dīn recognising in Jalāl al-Dīn the signs of spiritual greatness, presented him with a copy of his *Asrār-nāma* ('Book of Secrets'), an important poem of the mystical life which Rūmī studied deeply and from which he was delighted in later years often to quote. From Nishapur the fugitives pressed on to Baghdad, which still had some thirty-eight years of grace before Hūlāgū Khān would reduce the splendid capital city of Islam to a bloody shambles. They stayed in the metropolis only three days, being in a hurry to make the pilgrimage to Mecca. There is a pretty story that whilst in Baghdad Bahā' al-Dīn predicted the imminent downfall of the caliphate, but not too much credence need be given to this typical piece of hagiography.

The rites of the pilgrimage duly completed, Bahā' al-Dīn now led his spiritually refreshed party to Syria. A veil of obscurity covers the next period of the wanderers' adventures, but it is possible that the poet and hagiographer Jāmī (died 1492) was correct in saying that they stopped for four years in Arzanjan, a pleasant town in the province of Armenia having a considerable Christian population. Presently Bahā' al-Dīn moved on to Laranda, a township some thirty-five miles to the south-east of Konia. There he arranged a marriage between his son Jalāl al-Dīn, now eighteen years old, to Gauhar Khātūn, daughter of one Lālā of Samarqand, presumably a member of the fugitive party. To this union a son was born in 1226 named Sultān Valad, who would later compose a poetical biography of his father and in all likelihood edited his scattered discourses. From Laranda Bahā' al-Dīn was invited by the Saljuq ruler to remove to his capital Konia, where he took up honourable appointment as preacher and teacher. In this office he died in 1230.

Konia, the ancient Iconium which St Paul thrice visited, and according to one Arab legend the resting-place of Plato's bones, had been in Muslim hands since about 1070 when the Saljuqs in their fiery prime wrested Anatolia from Byzantium. Well inland and some 5,000 feet above sea level, chosen as their capital by the Saljuqs of Rum, the city escaped recapture during the Crusades though the tide of battle ebbed and flowed not very far away. At the time of Bahā' al-Dīn's arrival Konia had recently been adorned with a new royal palace and citadel; the great mosque founded by Kai-Kā'ūs I had been completed in 1220 by his successor Kai-Qubād I (reigned 1219–1236), whose invitation it was that brought Bahā' al-Dīn and his family to the Saljuq capital. We may therefore picture the young scholar Jalāl al-Dīn, stepping into his father's religious offices on the latter's death, as entering upon a sort of metropolitan life, preaching before the monarch and teaching the sons of the local notables, which must have recaptured for him the memory of Balkh in its prosperity.

Presently there arrived in Konia a new refugee who had of old been closely associated with Bahā' al-Dīn and his family in Balkh. Burhān al-Dīn Muḥaqqiq, who is said to have been one of Jalāl al-Dīn's teachers in those halcyon days, had fled from Balkh to his native Tirmidh during the first Mongol onslaught; now, hearing of the security and charity

4

offered to learned and pious Persians by the ruler of Rum, he came to join his former friend only to find that he had been dead a year. He therefore devoted himself to the spiritual advancement of Jalāl al-Dīn, and during the ensuing nine years initiated him into the high mysteries of the Sufi way and doctrine. In this period Jalāl al-Dīn, at the direction and in part in the company of Burhān al-Dīn, journeyed into Syria and studied at Aleppo and Damascus. After some seven years' further education during which t me he can hardly have failed to meet the great Andalusian mystic and theosophist Ibn 'Arabī (he died at Damascus in 1240), Jalāl al-Dīn returned to Konia where Ghiyāth al-Dīn Kai-Khusrau II was now on the throne. Shortly afterwards he learned that Burhān al-Dīn had died in Caesarea, whither he proceeded to take possession of his teacher's books and papers, doubtless including the manuscript discourses (Ma'ārif) which are as yet unpublished.

From 1240 to 1244 Jalāl al-Dīn taught and preached in Konia, wearing the traditional turban and gown of orthodox religious scholars. Konia had hitherto seemed a long way from the Mongol hordes; but now they were upon the eastern borders of Asia Minor, Erzerum capitulated to them, and in 1243 the defeat of Kozadagh reduced the Saljuq of Rum to the paltry status of a tribute-paying vassal. Jalāl al-Dīn, however, still stood outside these tremendous events. He seemed destined for a career of modest distinction as an expositor of the faith and the sacred law. Presently he might be applying himself to writing a commentary on the Koran, or collecting choice Traditions of Muhammad, or publishing his elegant sermons. Certainly nothing seemed less likely than that he would turn poet. As he tells us in one revealing passage in his discourses, the trade of poet was held in little esteem amongst the religious in his native Khurasan, and 'I am affectionate to such a degree that when these friends come to me, for fear that they may be wearied I speak poetry so that they may be occupied with that. Otherwise, what have I to do with poetry? By Allah, I care nothing for poetry, and there is nothing worse in my eyes than that. It has become incumbent upon me, as when a man plunges his hands into tripe and washes it out for the sake of a guest's appetite, because the guest's appetite is for tripe.'

In 1244, when he was already thirty-seven years old and therefore well established in the religious society of Konia, Jalāl al-Dīn went through a profound emotional and spiritual experience which changed the course of his life. In that year a wandering dervish called Shams al-Dīn, a native of Tabriz seemingly of artisan origin, suddenly arrived in the Saljuq capital and attracted attention by the wildness of his demeanour. The story of how Jalāl al-Dīn reacted to his first encounter with the mysterious stranger and of the subsequent episodes of their passionate attachment fills many pages in the books of the hagiologists. Here it will suffice to quote the late Professor R. A. Nicholson's summary of the events of those four tremendous years.

'Jalāl al-Dīn found in the stranger that perfect image of the Divine Beloved which he had long been seeking. He took him away to his house, and for a year or two they remained inseparable. Sulṭān Valad likens his father's all-absorbing communion with this "hidden saint" to the celebrated journey of Moses in company with Khaḍir (Koran, XVIII 64–80), the Sage whom Sufis regard as the supreme hierophant and guide of travellers on the Way to God. Meanwhile the Mevlevi disciples of Rūmī, entirely cut off from their Master's teaching and conversation and bitterly resenting his continued devotion to Shams al-Dīn alone, assailed the intruder with abuse and threats of violence. At last Shams al-Dīn fled to Damascus, but was brought back in triumph by Sulṭān Valad, whom Jalāl al-Dīn, deeply agitated by the loss of his bosom friend, had sent in search of him. Thereupon the disciples "repented" and were forgiven. Soon, however, a renewed outburst of jealousy on their part caused Shams al-Dīn to take refuge in Damascus for the second time, and again Sulṭān Valad was called upon to restore the situation. Finally, perhaps in 1247, the man of mystery vanished without leaving a trace behind.'

The intense excitement of these adventures transformed Jalāl al-Dīn from the sober divine into an ecstatic wholly incapable of controlling the torrent of poetry which now poured forth from him. To symbolise, it is said, the search for the lost Beloved, now identified with Shams al-Dīn, he invented the famous whirling and circling dance of his Mevlevi dervishes, performed to the accompaniment of the lamenting reed-pipe and the pacing drum. Night was turned into day in the long mystical orgy, and from time to time under the impact of the passionate moment Jalāl al-Dīn uttered extempore brief quatrains or extended lyrics which his disciples hastily transcribed and committed to memory.

6

To confess the human source of his inspiration, he very often introduced into his lyrics the name of Shams al-Dīn as though he were the poet; at other times he signed his verses with the soubriquet Khāmūsh, the Silent, a reference to the ineffable nature of the mysteries. Thenceforward, and for the remainder of his days, Jalāl al-Dīn residing in his madrasa presided over his own Dervish Order, the Mevlevīs, surrounded by an ever growing circle of disciples, visited by the greatest in the land who were eager to consult his wisdom, and thus enjoying, or at any rate occupying, a position of wide influence in the now declining Saljuq kingdom. The discourses are a record of many of the discussions which he led during those famous years.

Ghiyāth al-Dīn Kai-Khusrau II died in 1245 leaving three sons, and a testament appointing as his successor the youngest, 'Alā' al-Dīn, seven-year-old child of the Georgian princess Tamara. The powerful vizier of the late king, Shams al-Dīn Iṣfahānī, had a preference for the eldest of the three, 'Izz al-Dīn, whose mother was the daughter of a Greek priest; but Rukn al-Dīn, the middle of the trio, attended the convention at which Kuyuk was proclaimed Great Khan of the Mongols and returned with the coveted title Sultan of Rum, to purchase which he undertook to pay heavy tribute and to execute the vizier and his associates. This was duly effected in 1249. In 1251 Kuyuk was succeeded by Mangu Khān, who now recognised the three brothers as a triumvirate. Presently 'Alā' al-Din was murdered on his way to pay homage to the Great Khan, while 'Izz al-Dīn Kai-Kā'ūs II, who had thrown Rukn al-Dīn into prison, found himself embattled against the Mongol Baiju and constrained to take refuge with Theodore Lascaris in 1256. In those days Mongol soldiery occupied Konia and demolished its fortifications but spared the inhabitants, according to the hagiographer Aflākī out of high regard for Jalāl al-Dīn. Rukn al-Dīn was freed and 'Izz al-Dīn obliged to accept him as equal partner of the Saljuq throne. In 1257, however, 'Izz al-Dīn was discovered to be boldly conspiring with the Egyptian Mamluks to resist Hūlāgū Khān, about to take and massacre Baghdad; he had to run for his life, which continued in precarious exile down to 1280.

Rukn al-Dīn was thus free at last to assume, of course under Mongol patronage, sole rule of Rum. The real authority, however, was exercised by his prime minister, the Parvāna Mu'īn al-Dīn, who allowed his master to wear the diadem from 1257 to 1267 and then arranged his execution. Baiju himself had promoted Mu'īn al-Dīn to the chancellorship in 1256, and for twenty years he was the actual ruler, as Mongol vassal, of Anatolia. He extended his liberal patronage to Jalāl al-Dīn, and it seems clear from the discourses, not a few of which are addressed to him personally, that he sincerely admired the Sufi master-poet. Jalāl al-Dīn died in 1273, and was thus spared the sorrow of witnessing the downfall of his puissant protector. For in 1277 a party of Turk noblemen, in secret league with Baibars of Egypt, planned to rebel against the Mongol overlords and to join forces with the heroic Mamluk in Caesarea. However, the conspirators lost courage; the suspect Parvāna fled with the boy Sultan Kai-Khusrau III; he was taken into custody by Abāqā Khān, put to death, and then eaten.

So much at least of the tangled historical background is necessary to the understanding of the circumstances attending Jalāl al-Dīn's later years. The discourses show him as fully conscious of the tense drama of political events, which they do much to illuminate. Their value as a primary source of history is thus considerable; but this, of course, is merely incidental to their importance as first-hand documents illustrating the mystical doctrine of Jalāl al-Dīn, and throwing light upon his thought processes. During the years covered by the discourses Jalāl al-Dīn, who after Shams al-Dīn's disappearance had attached his affection successively to Salāḥ al-Dīn Farīdūn Zarkūb and, on Zarkūt's death about 1261, to Ḥusām al-Dīn Ḥasan, occupied a large part of his time with composing the *Masnavi*, his famous six-volume verse miscellany of the mystical life, available to English readers in R. A. Nicholson's luminous translation.

The *Masnavi*, which contains many passages of poetry of the highest order of excellence, is a notoriously difficult work to read and understand; not only, or even not so much on account of the intricacy and unfamiliarity of the doctrines therein enunciated, but still more because of the casual looseness, not to say anarchy, of its construction. Anecdotes of prophets and saints and legends of all sorts and conditions of men and women are well-nigh inextricably intertwined with long didactic passages abounding in learned and otherwise obscure allusion. The *Discourses* are now seen to be composed, if that is the right term, in very similar fashion and to be in no small measure the raw materials

8

out of which the great poem was fashioned; and it has become abundantly evident that they, like the *Masnavi*, represent the impromptu outpourings of a mind overwhelmed in mystical thought, the multifarious and often arresting y original and beautiful images welling up unceasingly out of the poet's overflowing unconscious. The title by which the discourses are traditionally known, *Fihi mā fihi* ('In it what is in it'), a quotation from a poem of the mystic Ibn 'Arabī, has been explained by some as meaning, 'There is to be found in *this* book what is contained in *that* book,' that is, the *Masnavi*. But publication of the *Ma'ārif* of Bahā' al-Dīn Valad has now enabled us to see that in his *Discourses* the son was also following in his father's footsteps; and we were already aware from other sources that Jalāl al-Dīn studied his father's writings assiduously, so much so that the jealous Shams al-Dīn of Tabriz took him to task. When the latter's *Maqālāt* become available in print, they will prove likewise to have been an important source for the *Discourses*.

Further comment on the contents of the *Discourses* will be found in the notes appended to this volume, where summaries of each are provided together with explanations of the allusions and references. The translation, made as literal as could be contrived (and the original is by no means easy always to understand), has been based upon the fine and erudite edition (Teheran, 1952) of Professor Badī' al-Zamān Furūzānfar, whose learned and authoritative annotations have been fully consulted. This work is intended as a memorial to my own teacher and initiator into the Sufi mysteries, Reynold Alleyne Nicholson, and represents the first stage of an extensive exploration of the life and writings of Jalāl al-Dīn Rūmī, surely the greatest mystical poet in the history of mankind.

DISCOURSES

I

The Prophet, on whom be peace, said: The worst of scholars is he who visits princes, and the best of princes is he who visits scholars. Happy is the prince who stands at the poor man's door, and wretched is the poor man who stands at the door of the prince.

People have taken the outward sense of these words to signify that it is not right for a scholar to visit a prince, lest he should become amongst the worst of scholars. That is not their true meaning, as they have supposed. Their meaning is rather this: that the worst of scholars is he who accepts help from princes, and whose welfare and salvation is dependent upon and stems from the fear of princes. Such a man first applies himself to the pursuit of learning with the intention that princes should bestow on him presents, hold him in esteem, and promote him to office. It was therefore on their account that he consented to better himself and converted from ignorance to knowledge. When he became a scholar, he was disciplined by the fear of them and was subject to their control. Willy-nilly, then, he comports himself in conformity with the way which they have mapped out for him. Consequently, whether it is the prince who formally visits him or he goes to visit the prince, he is in every case the visitor and it is the prince who is visited.

When, however, the case is otherwise, when the scholar has not become qualified with learning on account of princes but rather his learning from first to last has been for the sake of God; when his way and work have been upon the path of rectitude because it is in his nature so to comport himself and he cannot do otherwise—just as a fish can only live and thrive in water—such a scholar is subject to the control and direction of reason. All men living in his time are held in check by the awe of him and derive succour from the reflection of his radiance, whether they are aware of the fact or no. If such a scholar goes formally to visit the prince, it is himself who is visited and the prince is the visitor, because in every case the prince takes from him and receives help from him. That scholar is independent of the prince. He is like the light-giving sun, whose whole function is giving and dispensing universally, converting stones into rubies and cornelians, changing mountains of earth into mines of copper and gold and silver and iron, making the earth fresh and verdant, bestowing upon the trees fruits of diverse kinds. His trade is giving: he dispenses and does not receive. The Arabs have expressed this in a proverb: 'We have learned in order to give, we have not learned in order to take.' Hence it is they who are in all circumstances the visited, and the princes who are the visitors.

It comes into my mind at this point to comment on a verse of the Koran, although it is not related to the present discourse. However, this thought comes now into my mind and I will express it so that it may go on record. God most High says:

> *O Prophet, say to the prisoners in your hands:*
> *'If God knows of any good in your hearts*
> *He will give you better than what has been taken*
> *from you, and He will forgive you; surely*
> *God is All-forgiving, All-compassionate.'*

This verse was revealed under the following circumstances. The Prophet, God bless him and grant him peace, had defeated the unbelievers, slaying and plundering and taking many prisoners whom he had fettered hand and foot. Amongst the prisoners was his uncle 'Abbās, may God be well pleased with him. They were weeping and wailing all the night through in their chains and helpless humiliation and had given up all hope of their lives, expecting the sword and slaughter. The Prophet, upon whom be peace, looked at them and laughed.

'Did you see?' the prisoners exclaimed. 'He has the attributes of a man after all. That claim of his, that he was superhuman, was contrary to the truth. There he is; he looks at us and sees us prisoners in these chains and fetters, and rejoices. So it is with all men governed by their passions—when they get the victory over their enemies and see them vanquished to their will, they rejoice and make merry.'

'Not so,' answered the Prophet, God's blessings be upon him, perceiving what was in their hearts. 'Far be it from me that I should laugh because I see my enemies vanquished to my will, or because I see you come to grief. It is for this reason that I rejoice, indeed I laugh, because I see with the inward eye that I am dragging and drawing a people by main force, by collars and chains, out of the fiery furnace and black smoke of Hell unto Paradise and Ridwan and the Eternal Garden of Roses; while they lament and cry aloud, saying, "Why are you drawing us out of this pit of destruction into that rose-bower and place of security?" So laughter overcomes me. For all that, inasmuch as you have not yet been given the vision to discover and behold this that I say, God commands me: "Say to the prisoners: First you gathered together your hosts and mustered much might, trusting completely in your virtue and valour and panoply. You said amongst yourselves, so we will do; we will conquer the Muslims so, and will vanquish them. You did not see One Omnipotent who is more powerful than yourselves, you did not know of One All-forceful above your force. So inevitably all that you planned to do turned out opposite to your designs. Even now that you are in fear, you have not repented of your old distemper; you are in despair, and do not see One Omnipotent over you. Therefore it behoves you forthwith to behold My might and strength, and to know yourselves to be vanquished to My will, so that all things may be made easy for you. Do not despair of Me, even in your present fear; for I am able to deliver you out of this fear and to make you secure. He who is able to produce out of a white bullock a black bullock is also able to bring forth out of a black bullock a white bullock.

> *He makes the night to enter into the day*
> *and makes the day to enter into the night.*
> *He brings forth the living from the dead,*
> *and brings forth the dead from the living.*

Now, in this present state when you are prisoners, break not of hope of My Presence, that I may take you by the hand, for

> *of God's comfort*
> *no man despairs, excepting the people*
> *of the unbelievers."*

Now God most High declares : ' O prisoners, if you turn again out of your former ways, beholding Me alike in fear and hope and beholding yourselves as vanquished to My will in all circumstances, I will deliver you out of this present fear. I will likewise restore to you all the property that has been plundered from you and has become lost to you, nay, many times as much, and better than that. Moreover I will grant you absolution, and conjoin felicity in the world to come with prosperity in this world."

'I have repented,' said 'Abbās. 'I have returned from my former ways.'

The Prophet, God's blessings be upon him, said, 'God most High demands of you a token of this claim you now make.'

> Easy it is to boast of love,
> But other is the proof thereof.

'In Allah's name, what token do you demand?' asked 'Abbās.

'Give of the properties that remain to you for the army of Islam, that the army of Islam may be strengthened,' answered the Prophet. 'That is, if you have truly become a Muslim and desire the good of Islam and Muslimdom.'

'Prophet of God, what remains to me?' demanded 'Abbās. 'They have taken everything in plunder, leaving me not so much as an old reed-mat.'

'You see,' said the Prophet, God's blessings be upon him, 'you have not become a righteous man. You have not given up your old ways. Tell me, how much property have you got? Where have you hidden it? To whom have you entrusted it? In what place have you concealed and buried it?'

'God forbid!' exclaimed 'Abbās.

'Did you not entrust so much property specifically to your mother?' the Prophet retorted. 'Did you not bury it under such and such a wall? Did you not enjoin your mother in detail, saying, "If I return, you will hand it back to me; and if I do not return safely, you will expend so much upon such and such an object, and give so much to So-and-so, and so much is to be for yourself"?'

When 'Abbās heard these words he raised his finger in token of complete acceptance of the Faith.

'Prophet of God,' he said, 'truly I always thought that you were

16

under the special favour of heaven like the ones of old, kings such as Haman, Shaddad, Nimrod and the rest. Now that you have spoken these words I know of a truth that this favour is of the world beyond, divine and of the Lord.'

'Now you have spoken truly,' said the Prophet, God's blessings be upon him. 'This time I have heard the snapping of the girdle of doubt which you had within you, and the noise of that snapping has reached my ears. I have an ear hidden within my inmost soul, and with that hidden ear, I hear whenever any man breaks the girdle of doubt and polytheism and unbelief, and the sound of that breaking reaches the ear of my soul. Now it is true for a fact that you have become a righteous man and professed the Faith.'

The Master said in explanation of the foregoing I have spoken thus to the Amir Parvāna for this reason, that in the beginning you came forward as the champion of Muslimdom. 'I make myself a ransom,' you said. 'I sacrifice my reason, deliberation and judgement that Islam may survive and its followers multiply, so that Islam may remain secure and strong.' But inasmuch as you put your trust in your own judgement, not having God in sight and not recognising that everything proceeds from God, God therefore converted that very means and endeavour into a means bringing about the diminishment of Islam. Having made common cause with the Tartars, you are giving them assistance so as to destroy the Syrians and the Egyptians and to ruin the realm of Islam. God therefore made that very means which would have secured the survival of Islam into the means of its diminishment.

In this situation, turn your face to Almighty God, for things are in a parlous state. Bestow alms, to the end that God may deliver you out of this evil state of fear; and break not off hope of Him, even though He has cast you down out of such a state of obedience into such a state of disobedience. You saw that obedience as proceeding from yourself, and therefore it was that you fell into this disobedience. Now, even in this present state of disobedience, break not off hope, but turn to God in humble petition. He who disclosed disobedience out of your former obedience is also able to disclose obedience out of your present disobedience. He is able to grant you repentance, and to furnish the means whereby you may labour again for the increase of Muslimdom, and prove a tower of strength to Islam. Break not off hope, for

of God's comfort
no man despairs, excepting the people
of the unbelievers.

My object in speaking thus (the Master explained) was that the Parvāna should understand the matter aright, and in this situation give alms and humble himself to God. He has fallen out of an exceedingly high state into a low state; yet even in this present state he may have hope. God most High is a great deviser; he shows forth fair forms, but in the maw of them are evil forms, lest a man should say in the delusion of his conceit, 'A good idea and a good action took shape in me and displayed itself.'

If everything were in truth as it appears to be, the Prophet, endowed as he was with a vision so penetrating, so illumined and illuminating, would never have cried, 'Lord, show me things as they are.' 'Thou showest a thing as fair, and in reality it is ugly; Thou showest a thing as ugly, and in reality it is lovely. Therefore do Thou show us every thing just as it is, that we may not fall into the snare and that we may not go astray perpetually.' Now your judgement, however good and luminous it may be, is certainly not better than the Prophet's judgement. He used to speak in this fashion; so do you now not put your trust in every idea and every notion. Be ever humble and fearful before God.

This (the Master concluded) was my object. The Parvāna applied this verse and this interpretation to his own plans, saying, 'This hour when we move forward the legions we must not put our reliance in them; and if we are defeated, then in that time of fear and impotence we must likewise not break off hope of Him.' He applied my words to his own design, and my object was as I have stated.

2

Someone was saying: Our Master does not utter a word.

I said: Well, it was the thought of me that brought this person to my presence. This thought of me did not speak with him, saying, 'How are you?' or 'How are things with you?' The thought without words drew him hither. If the reality of me draws him without words and transports him to another place, what is so wonderful in that? Words are

18

the shadow of reality and the branch of reality. Since the shadow could draw, how much more the reality!

Words are the pretext. It is the element of congeneity that draws one man to another, not words. If a man should see a hundred thousand miracles and expositions and divine graces, if there is no element of congeneity in him connecting him with the prophet or the saint concerned, then all those phenomena will be profitless. It is that element which keeps him agitated and restless. If there were no element of amber in a straw, the straw would never move towards the amber. This congeneity between them is a hidden and not a visible thing.

It is the thought of a thing that brings a man to that thing. The thought of the garden brings him to the garden, the thought of the shop brings him to the shop. Within these thoughts, however, is a secret deception. Do you not see how you will go to a certain place and then repent of having done so, saying, 'I thought that it would be good. It was not so'? These thoughts then are like a shroud, and within the shroud someone is hidden. Whenever the thoughts vanish from the scene and the realities appear without the shroud of thought, there is a great commotion. Where such is the case, there remains no trace of regret. When it is the reality that draws you, there is nothing there other than the reality. It would be that same reality which drew you hither.

Upon the day when the secrets are tried.

What occasion is there then for me to speak?

In reality that which draws is a single thing, but it appears to be numerous. Do you not see how a man is possessed by a hundred different desires? 'I want vermicelli,' he says. 'I want ravioli. I want halwa. I want fritters. I want fruit. I want dates.' He enumerates these and names them one by one, but the root of the matter is a single thing: the root is hunger, and that is one. Do you not see how, when he has had his fill of one thing, he says, 'None of these things is necessary'? So it is proved that it was not ten or a hundred things but one thing that drew him.

And their number
We have appointed only as a trial.

This 'number' of creatures is a trial appointed by God. They say,

'This man is one and they are a hundred'—that is, they say the saint is one and mankind are many, a hundred and a thousand. This is a great trial. This view and this thought that makes a man see them as many and him as one is a great trial.

> *And their number*
> *We have appointed only as a trial.*

Which hundred? Which fifty? Which sixty? A people without hands and feet, without mind and soul, quivering like a magic talisman, like quicksilver or mercury—call them if you will sixty or a hundred or a thousand, and this man one, but on the contrary the truth is that they are nothing, whereas he is a thousand and a hundred thousand and thousands of thousands.

> Few in the numbering, many in the charge.

A king had given a single soldier a hundred men's rations of bread. The army protested, but the king said within him, 'The day will come when I will show you, and you will know why I did this.' When the day of battle arrived they all fled from the field, and that soldier alone fought. 'There you are,' the king said. 'It was for this purpose.'

It behoves a man to strip his discriminative faculty of all prejudices and to seek a friend in the Faith. Faith consists in knowing who is one's true friend. When, however, a man has spent his life in the company of people who lack discrimination, his own discriminative faculty becomes feeble and he is unable to recognise that true friend of the Faith.

You have nurtured this substance in which there is no discrimination. Discrimination is that one quality which is hidden in a man. Do you not see that a madman possesses hands and feet but lacks discrimination? Discrimination is that subtle essence which is within you. Day and night you have been occupied with nurturing that physical substance without discrimination. You put forward as a pretext that that subsists through this. Yet this likewise subsists through that. How is it that you have devoted all your energies to looking after the physical substance, and have entirely neglected the subtle essence? Indeed, the physical subsists through the other, whereas the other is by no means dependent upon the physical for its subsistence.

That light which shines abroad through the windows of the eyes and

ears and so forth—if those windows did not exist, it would nevertheless shine through other windows. It is just as if you had brought a
lamp in front of the sun, saying, 'I see the sun by means of this lamp.'
God forbid! If you do not bring the lamp, still the sun will show itself:
what need is there of a lamp?

It behoves us not to break off hope of God. Hope is the head of the
road to security. If you do not travel upon that road, at least guard the
head of that road. Do not say, 'I have done crooked things'; choose
the way of straightness, and no crookedness will remain. Straightness
is like the rod of Moses, and those crookednesses are as the tricks of
Pharaoh's magicians: when straightness comes, it will swallow up all
those tricks. If you have done evil, you have done it to yourself;
how should your wickedness reach out to affect God?

> The bird that perched on yonder mount,
> Then rose into the sky—
> Tell me, what gain was there to count?
> What lost the mount thereby?

When you become straight, all those crookednesses will disappear. So
beware, do not break off hope.

The danger of associating with kings consists not in the fact that
you may lose your life: one must lose one's life in the end, whether it
be today or tomorrow matters not. The danger arises from the fact that
when kings enter upon the scene and the spell of their influence gains
strength, converting so to speak into a dragon, the man who keeps
company with them and lays claim to their friendship and accepts
money from them will inevitably speak in accordance with their wishes.
He will receive their evil views with the utmost attention and will not
be able to gainsay them.

That is where the danger lies, in that it leads to the detriment of the
true faith. When you cultivate their interest, the other interest, which
is fundamental to the good life, becomes a stranger to you. The more
you proceed in that direction, the more this direction, where the Beloved dwells, turns away from you. The more you make your peace
with worldly men, the more the Beloved is angry with you. 'Whosoever assists an oppressor, God gives him power over him': your

'going in his direction' renders you subject to this rule. Once you have gone in that direction, in the end God gives him power over you.

It is a pity to reach the sea, and to be satisfied with a little water or a pitcher-full from the sea. After all there are pearls in the sea, and from the sea myriads of precious things may be produced. What worth is there in taking water? What pride can intelligent men have in that, and what will they have accomplished? Indeed, the world is a mere foam-fleck of that Sea; its water is the very sciences of the saints; where is the Pearl itself? This world is but foam full of floating jetsam; but through the turning about of those waves and the congruous surging of the sea and the constant motion of the billows that foam takes on a certain beauty.

> *Decked out fair to men is the love of lusts—*
> *women, children, heaped-up heaps of gold*
> *and silver, horses of mark, cattle*
> *and tillage. That is the enjoyment of*
> *the present life.*

Since therefore God has called it *decked out fair*, it is not truly beautiful; rather its beauty is a borrowed thing, coming from else-where. It is false coin gilded; that is to say, this world which is a fleck of foam is false coin, valueless and without worth, but we have gilded it so that it is *decked out fair to men*.

Man is the astrolabe of God; but it requires an astronomer to know the astrolabe. If a vegetable-seller or a greengrocer should possess the astrolabe, what benefit would he derive from it? With that astrolabe what would he know of the movements of the circling heavens and the stations of the planets, their influences, transits and so forth? But in the hands of the astronomer the astrolabe is of great benefit, for 'He who knows himself knows his Lord.'

Just as this copper astrolabe is the mirror of the heavens, so the human being—*We have honoured the Children of Adam*—is the astrolabe of God. When God causes a man to have knowledge of Him and to know Him and to be familiar with Him, through the astrolabe of his own being he beholds moment by moment and flash by flash the manifestation of God and His infinite beauty, and that beauty is never absent from his mirror.

God has servants who cloak themselves in wisdom and gnosis and grace; though other men have not the vision to behold them truly, yet out of the excess of jealousy these servants cloak themselves, even as Mutanabbī says:

> Figured silks they wore, not their bodies to beautify
> But to guard their beauty against the lustful eye.

3

The Parvāna said: Night and day my heart and soul are intent upon serving God, but owing to my preoccupations with Mongol affairs I am not able to discharge that service.

The Master replied: These works too are work done for God, since they are the means of procuring peace and security for Muslimdom. You have sacrificed yourself, your possessions and your body, to bring their hearts to a point that a few Muslims are occupied peaceably in obeying God's will. So this too is a good work. God has inclined you towards such good work, and your exceeding ardour is a proof of Divine favour; just as when this inclination flags it is a sign of the denial of Divine favour, God most High not willing that such a momentous good should be realised by means of such a man, so that he should earn the right to that reward and high preferment.

Take the case of a hot bath. Its heat derives from the fuel utilised in the stove, such as dry hay, firewood, dung and the like. In the same way God most High discovers means which, though to outward appearance evil and nasty, yet in reality are the instruments of the Divine favour. Like the bath, the man fired by such means becomes hot and promotes the benefit of all the people.

At this point some friends arrived. The Master excused himself, saying: If I do not attend to you and do not address you or ask after you, this is really a mark of respect. Respect for any thing is what is appropriate to the occasion. When a man is at prayer he should not enquire after his father and brother or make a fuss of them. His in-attention to his friends and kinsmen while engaged in prayer is the very acme of attention and courtesy, since he does not on their account break away from his religious performance and absorption and does not become distracted. In that way they do not lay themselves open to Divine punishment and reproach. It is therefore the acme of attention and courtesy when he has guarded against what would involve them in Divine chastisement.

Someone asked: Is there any way nearer to God than prayer?

He replied: Also prayer, but prayer which is not merely this outward form. This is the 'body' of prayer, since formal prayer has a beginning and an end; and everything which has a beginning and an end is a 'body.' The words *Allahu akbar* are the beginning of formal prayer, and its end is the salutation 'Peace.' Similarly the profession of faith is not merely the formula uttered on the tongue, for that formula too has a beginning and an end. Every thing which is expressed in words and sounds and has a beginning and an end is 'form' and 'body'; its 'soul' is unconditioned and infinite, and has neither beginning nor end.

Moreover this formal prayer was invented by the prophets. Now our Prophet, who invented the Muslim prayer, spoke as follows: 'I have a time with God when I am not contained by any prophet sent by God, neither by any angel set near to God.' Hence we realise that the 'soul' of prayer is not this 'form' alone. Rather it is a complete absorption, a state of unconsciousness excluding and not finding room for all these outward forms. Gabriel himself, who is pure reality, is not contained therein.

It is related of our Master, the Sultan of the Learned, Pole of the World, Bahā' al-Ḥaqq wa'l-Dīn (God sanctify his great soul), that one day his companions found him in a state of complete absorption. The hour of prayer arriving, some of his disciples called out to our Master, 'It is time for prayer.' Our Master did not heed their words, so they rose up and occupied themselves with the prayer.

Two disciples, however, bore the Shaikh company and did not stand up to pray. Now one of the disciples who was praying was named Khvājagī. It was shown to him clearly in his inward heart that all those companions who were at prayer were standing behind the imam with their backs turned on Mecca, whereas the two disciples who had borne the Shaikh company had their faces turned towards Mecca. Inasmuch as the Shaikh had passed away from the sense of personal identity so that his self no longer remained, having been consumed in the Light of God—'Die before you die'—he (the inward voice explained) had become the Light of God.

24

Whoever turns his back on the Light of God and faces the wall of the prayer-niche has assuredly turned his back on Mecca. For God's Light is the 'soul' of the Mecca-ward direction. After all, these people who turn their faces to Mecca—it was the Prophet who made the Kaaba to be the place of turning in prayer for all the world. How much the more is He the place of turning, for whose sake Mecca was appointed.

The Prophet, God's blessings be upon him, once reproached a friend, saying, 'I called you. How is it that you did not come?' The friend replied, 'I was occupied with prayer.' The Prophet said, 'Well, did I not call you?' The friend answered, 'I am helpless'

The Master said: It is good if you are helpless all the time and at every moment, and see yourself helpless in the state of capacity just as in the state of incapacity. For above your capacity there is a greater Capacity, and you are vanquished to God's will in every state. You are not divided into two halves, now capable and now helpless. Pay regard to His Capacity, and know yourself to be helpless always, without hand and foot, poor and utterly incapable. What indeed is the plight of feeble man, seeing that lions and tigers and crocodiles, all are helpless and tremble before Him? The heavens and the earths likewise are helpless and subject to His decree.

He is a mighty Emperor. His Light is not as the light of the moon and the sun, in the presence of which a thing abides in its place. When His Light shines forth unveiled, neither heaven remains nor earth, nor sun nor moon; nothing remains but that King.

A certain king said to a dervish. 'In the moment when you are granted revelation and propinquity in the Court of God, remember me.'

The dervish answered, 'When I come into that Presence and the light of the sun of that Beauty shines upon me, I shall no more remember myself. How then should I remember you?'

When, however, God has chosen out a servant and caused him to be utterly absorbed in Him, if any man takes him by the skirt and makes a request of him, even without that worthy mentioning him before God and representing his need God fulfils his request.

It is related that there was once a king who had a favourite and highly confidential servant. Whenever that servant set out for the royal palace, people who had a request to make presented him with their histories and their letters, begging him to submit them to the king. He would place the documents in his wallet. On coming into the king's presence he could not endure the splendour of his beauty, and would fall down dumbfounded. The king would then in a loving manner put his hand into his purse and pocket and wallet, saying, 'What has this dumbfounded servant of mine, who is utterly absorbed by my beauty?' In this way he found the letters and would endorse the petitions of every man and then return the documents into the wallet. So he would attend to the needs of every one of them, without that servant ever submitting them, in such manner that not a single one was rejected; on the contrary their demands were granted many times over, so that they attained far more than they had asked for. But in the case of other servants who retained consciousness, and were able to present and indicate to the king the histories of people in need, out of a hundred affairs and a hundred needs only one perchance would be fulfilled.

4

Some one said: Here is something I have forgotten.

The Master said: There is one thing in this world which must never be forgotten. If you were to forget everything else, but did not forget that, then there would be no cause to worry; whereas if you performed and remembered and did not forget every single thing, but forgot that one thing, then you would have done nothing whatsoever. It is just as if a king had sent you to the country to carry out a specified task. You go and perform a hundred other tasks; but if you have not performed that particular task on account of which you had gone to the country, it is as though you have performed nothing at all. So man has come into this world for a particular task, and that is his purpose; if he does not perform it, then he will have done nothing.

> *We offered the trust to the heavens and the earth*
> *and the mountains, but they refused to carry it*
> *and were afraid of it; and man carried it. Surely*
> *he is sinful, very foolish.*

'We offered that trust to the heavens, but they were unable to accept it.' Consider how many tasks are performed by the heavens, whereat the human reason is bewildered. The heavens convert common stones into rubies and cornelians; they make mountains into mines of gold and silver; they cause the herbs of the earth to germinate and spring into life making a veritable Garden of Eden. The earth too receives the seeds and bears fruit; it covers up blemishes; it accepts and reveals a hundred thousand marvels such as can never be told in full. The mountains too give forth all those multifarious mines. All these things they do, yet that one thing is not performed by them; that task is performed by man.

And We honoured the Children of Adam.

God did not say, 'And We honoured heaven and earth.' So that task which is not performed by the heavens and the earth and the mountains is performed by man. When he performs that task, 'sinfulness' and 'folly' are banished from him.

If you say, 'Even if I do not perform that task, yet so many tasks are performed by me,' you were not created for those other tasks. It is as though you were to procure a sword of priceless Indian steel such as is to be found only in the treasuries of kings and were to convert it into a butcher's knife for cutting up putrid meat, saying, 'I am not letting this sword stand idle, I am putting it to so many useful purposes.' Or it is as though you were to take a golden bowl and cook turnips in it, whereas for a single grain of that gold you could procure a hundred pots. Or it is as though you were to take a dagger of the finest temper and make of it a nail for a broken gourd, saying, 'I am making good use of it. I am hanging the gourd on it. I am not letting this dagger stand idle.' How lamentable and ridiculous that would be! When the gourd can be perfectly well served by means of a wooden or an iron nail whose value is a mere farthing, how does it make sense to employ for the task a dagger valued at a hundred pounds?

God most High has set a great price on you, for He says:

God has bought from the believers their selves
and their possessions against the gift of Paradise.

27

The poet says:

> You are more precious than both heaven and earth:
> What can I more? You know not your own worth.

> Sell not yourself at little price,
> Being so precious in God's eyes.

God says, 'I have bought you, your moments, your breaths, your possessions, your lives. If they are expended on Me, if you give them to Me, the price of them is everlasting Paradise. This is your worth in My sight.' If you sell yourself to Hell, it is yourself you will have wronged, just like the man who hammered the dagger worth a hundred pounds into the wall and hung a jug or a gourd upon it.

To return: you put forward your excuse, saying, 'I expend myself upon lofty tasks. I am studying jurisprudence, philosophy, logic, astronomy, medicine and the rest.' Well, for whose sake but your own are you doing all these things? If it is jurisprudence, it is so that nobody shall steal a loaf out of your hands or strip you of your clothes or kill you, in short it is for your own security. If it is astronomy, the phases of the sphere and its influence upon the earth, whether it is light or heavy, portending tranquillity or danger, all these things are connected with your own situation and serve your ends; if the star is lucky or unlucky, it is connected with your own ascendant and likewise serves your own ends. When you consider the matter well, the root of the whole business is yourself; all these other things are but branches of yourself.

If these things, which are a branch of yourself, are so multifarious and comprise so many marvels, phases and worlds both wonderful and without end, consider what phases you may pass through, who are the root! If your branches have their ascensions and descensions, their lucky and unlucky aspects, consider what may transpire to you who are the root, what ascension and descension in the world of spirits, what luck and unluck, what profit and loss! Such a spirit possesses this property and produces that; such a one is suitable for such a task.

For you there is other food, besides this food of sleep and eating. The Prophet said, 'I pass the night in the presence of my Lord, He giving me to eat and drink.' In this lower world you have forgotten that heavenly food, being occupied with this material sustenance. Night and day you are nourishing your body. Now this body is your horse, and this lower world is its stable. The food of the horse is not the food of the rider; the rider has his own kind of sleeping and eating and taking enjoyment. But because the animal and the bestial have the upper hand over you, you have lagged behind with your horse in the stable for horses and do not dwell in the ranks of kings and princes of the world eternal. Your heart is there, but inasmuch as the body has the upper hand you are subject to the body's rule and have remained its prisoner.

Even so when Majnūn was making for Lailā's dwelling-place, so long as he was fully conscious he drove his camel in that direction. But when for a moment he became absorbed in the thought of Lailā and forgot his camel, the camel which had a foal in a certain village profited of the opportunity to return in its tracks and came to that village. On coming to his senses Majnūn found that he had gone back a distance of two days' journeying. For three months he continued on his way thus. Finally he exclaimed, 'This camel is the ruin of me!' So saying, he jumped off the camel and continued on foot, singing:

My camel's desire is behind me, and my desire is before:
She and I are at cross purposes, and agree no more.

The Master said: Saiyid Burhān al-Dīn Muhaqqiq, God sanctify his lofty spirit, declared: Someone came and said, 'I heard your praises sung by So-and-so.' Burhān al-Dīn replied: 'Wait until I see what sort of a man he is, whether he is of sufficient rank to know me and to praise me. If he knows me only by word of mouth, then he does not truly know me. For these words do not endure; these syllables and sounds do not endure; these lips and this mouth do not endure. All these things are mere accidents. But if he likewise knows me by my works and if he knows my essential self, then I know that he is able to praise me and that that praise belongs to me,'

This is like the story they tell of a certain king. This king entrusted his son to a team of learned men. In due course they had taught him the sciences of astrology, geomancy and so forth so that he became a complete master, despite his utter dullness of wit and stupidity.

One day the king took a ring in his fist and put his son to the test. 'Come, tell me what I am holding in my fist.'

'The thing you are holding is round, yellow and hollow,' the prince answered.

'Since you have given all the signs correctly, now pronounce what thing it is,' the king said.

'It must be a sieve,' the prince replied.

'What?' cried the king. 'You gave correctly all the minute signs, such as might well baffle the minds of men. Out of all your powerful learning and knowledge how is it that this small point has escaped you, that a sieve cannot be contained in the fist?'

In the same way the great scholars of the age split hairs on all manner of sciences. They know perfectly and have a complete comprehension of those other matters which do not concern them. But as for what is truly of moment and touches a man more closely than all else, namely his own self, this your great scholar does not know. He pronounces on the legality or otherwise of every thing, saying, 'This is permitted and that is not permitted, this is lawful and that is unlawful.' Yet he knows not his own self, whether it is lawful or unlawful, permissible or not permissible, pure or impure.

Now these attributes of being hollow and yellow, inscribed and circular, are merely accidental. Cast the object into the fire, and none of them will remain. It will become its essential self, purified of all these attributes. So it is with the 'signs' they give of any thing, whether science, act or word; they have no connexion with the substance of the thing, which alone continues when all these 'signs' are gone. That is how it is with their 'signs'; they speak of all these things, expound them, and finally pronounce that what the king has in his fist is a sieve, since they have no knowledge at all of that which is the root of the matter.

I am a bird. I am a nightingale. I am a parrot. If they say to me, 'Make some other kind of sound,' I cannot. Since my tongue is such as it is, I cannot speak otherwise; unlike one who has learned the song of the birds. He is not a bird himself; on the contrary, he is the enemy of the birds and their fowler. He sings and whistles so that they may take him for a bird. Order him to produce a different kind of note and he is able to do so since that note is merely assumed by him, and is not truly his own. He is able to make other notes because he has learned to rob men of their household goods and to show a different kind of linen filched from every home.

5

He said: How gracious it was of our Master to honour me in this manner. I never expected, and the thought never entered my mind, that I should be worthy of such an honour. By rights I should have been standing night and day with hands folded in the ranks and company of his servants and attendants. Now I am not worthy even of that. How gracious it was!

The Master said: That is all because you have such lofty aspirations. The higher and greater your rank and the more you are occupied with important and exalted affairs, the more you consider yourself to have fallen short of your lofty aspirations and are not satisfied with what you have achieved, reckoning that you have many other obligations. Though my heart was always intent on serving you, for all that I wanted to pay you formal honour as well. Form too possesses great importance, its importance residing in the fact that it is associated with substance. Just as a thing fails if it lacks a kernel, so too it fails without a skin. If you sow a seed in the earth without its husk, it fails to germinate, whereas if you bury it in the earth with its husk it does germinate and becomes a great tree. So from this viewpoint the body too is a great and necessary principle, and without it the task fails and the purpose is not attained. Yes, by Allah! The principle is the reality in the eyes of him who knows the reality and has become a reality. The saying, 'Two inclinations in prayer are better than the world entire and all that is in it,' does not apply to everyone. It is true only of the man to whom the failure to perform two inclinations means more than the world entire and all that is in it. To miss two inclinations is for him harder to bear than to lose the empire of the world which is entirely his.

A dervish once entered the presence of a king. The king addressed him, 'O ascetic.'

'You are the ascetic,' the dervish answered.

'How should I be an ascetic,' the king demanded, 'seeing that the whole world belongs to me?'

'Ah, you see things the opposite of what they are,' replied the dervish. 'This world and the next and all that there is to possess, these all belong to me. I have seized the whole world. It is you who have become satisfied with a mouthful and a rag.'

Whithersoever you turn, there is the Face of God.

That is a 'face' which runs and extends infinitely and for ever. True lovers have sacrificed themselves for the sake of that 'face'; they look for no compensation. The rest of men are like cattle.

The Master said: Though they are cattle, yet they are deserving of favour. Though they are in the stable, yet they are acceptable to the Lord of the stable. If He so desires, He transfers them from this stable and brings them into His private pen. So in the beginning when man was non-existent God brought him into existence, then transferred him from the pen of existence into the world inanimate, then from the pen of the world inanimate into the vegetable, then from the vegetable to the animal, then from the animal to man, then from man to angel, and so *ad infinitum.* Therefore He manifested all these things to the end that you may be sure that He has many such pens loftier one than the other.

You shall surely ride stage after stage:
then what ails them, that they believe not?

God revealed this present world in order that you may acknowledge the other stages which yet lie ahead. He did not reveal it so that you should disbelieve and say, 'This is all that there is.' A master craftsman demonstrates a craft and an art in order that the apprentices may have faith in him, and acknowledge and believe in the other arts which he has not yet demonstrated. A king bestows robes of honour and presents and lavishes kindness on his subjects so that they may look forward to receiving other gifts from him and may hang hopefully upon future purses of gold. He does not give them these things for them to say, 'This is all that there is. The king is not going to confer any other blessings,' and so make do with that amount. If the king knows that any subject is going to say that and take that for granted, he will never confer any blessing whatsoever upon him.

The ascetic is one who sees the hereafter, while the worldling sees only the stable. But the elect ones of God who have true knowledge see neither the hereafter nor the stable. Their eyes are fixed on the first thing, and they know the beginning of every matter. When the expert sows wheat he knows that wheat is going to grow; in short, he sees the end from the beginning. So it is with barley and rice and so forth; since he sees the beginning his eyes are not fixed on the end; the end is known to him in the beginning. Such men are rare. Those who see the end are of the middling kind; while those who are in the stable are the cattle.

It is pain that guides a man in every enterprise. Until there is an ache within him, a passion and a yearning for that thing arising within him, he will never strive to attain it. Without pain that thing remains for him unprocurable, whether it be success in this world or salvation in the next, whether he aims at being a merchant or a king, a scientist or an astronomer. It was not until the pains of parturition manifested in her that Mary made for the tree:

> *And the birthpangs surprised her by*
> *the trunk of the palm-tree.*

Those pangs brought her to the tree, and the tree which was withered became fruitful.

The body is like Mary. Every one of us has a Jesus within him, but until the pangs manifest in us our Jesus is not born. If the pangs never come, then Jesus rejoins his origin by the same secret path by which he came, leaving us bereft and without portion of him.

> The soul within you is needy, the flesh without is well fed:
> The devil gorges to spewing, Jamshid lacks even for bread.
> See now to the cure of your soul while Jesus is yet on earth;
> When Jesus returns to heaven all hope of your cure will have fled.

6

These words are for the sake of that person who is in need of words in order that he may understand. But as for the man who understands without words, what need has he of words? The heavens and earth indeed are words to him who understands aright, being themselves engendered by words, namely *Be! and it is.* The man therefore who hears a low sound, what need has he of shouting and screaming?

An Arabic-speaking poet once came into the presence of a king. Now the king was a Turk, and did not even know Persian. The poet had composed in his honour some brilliant verses in Arabic and had brought these with him. When the king had taken his seat on the throne and the courtiers were all present and duly stationed, commanders and ministers each in his place, the poet rose to his feet and began to recite his poem. At every passage meriting applause the king nodded his head, while at every passage provoking astonishment he looked amazed; similarly he took note of every passage expressing submission. The courtiers were astounded.

'Our king did not know a word of Arabic,' they murmured amongst themselves. 'How is it that he nodded his head so appositely? He must have known Arabic all these years and kept it secret from us. If we have ever uttered any incivilities in Arabic, then woe betide us!'

Now the king had a favourite slave. The courtiers therefore assembled together and gave him a horse and a mule and a sum of money, and engaged to present him with as much again.

'Just inform us whether or no the king knows Arabic,' they said to him. 'If he does not, how was it that he nodded just at the right places? Was it a miracle? Was it divine inspiration?'

Finally one day the slave found his opportunity. The king was out hunting, and he perceived that he was in a good humour because much game had been taken. He therefore asked the king point blank. The king burst out laughing.

'By Allah, I don't know Arabic,' he said. 'As for my nodding and applauding, I knew of course what his object was in composing that poem and so I nodded and applauded.'

So it was realised that the root of the matter was the object in view; the poem itself was merely the branch of that object. If it had not been for the object, the man would never have composed that poem.

If the object is kept in view, duality vanishes. Duality characterises the branches: the root is one. So it is with the Sufi shaikhs. Though to outward form they are of various kinds and differ widely in their states and acts and words, from the standpoint of the object it is one thing only, namely the quest of God.

Take the case of the wind. When it blows through a house it lifts

34

the edge of the carpet, and the rugs all flap and move about. It whisks into the air sticks and straws, ruffles the surface of the pool until it looks like a coat of mail, sets trees and twigs and leaves a-dancing. All those states appear distinct and different, but from the standpoint of the object and root and reality they are one thing only inasmuch as they are all set in motion by the one wind.

Someone said: I have been remiss.

The Master replied: When this thought enters a man's mind and he reproaches himself, saying, 'Ah, what am I about, and why do I do these things?'—when this happens, it is a sure proof that God loves him and cares for him. 'Love continues so long as reproof continues': one reproves friends, but one does not reprove a stranger.

Now there are degrees in kind of such reproof. When a man is hurt by it and is thus made aware of it, that is a proof that God loves him and cares for him. But if the reproof flows over him and does not hurt him, then this is no proof of love. When a carpet is beaten to get rid of the dust, men of sense do not call that a 'reproof'; but if a man beats his own child and darling, then that is called a 'reproof' and is a proof of love. Therefore so long as you perceive pain and regret within yourself, that is a proof that God loves you and cares for you.

If you perceive a fault in your brother, the fault which you perceive in him is within yourself. The learned man is like a mirror in which you see your own image, for 'The believer is the mirror of his fellow believer.' Get rid of that fault in you, for what distresses you in him distresses you in yourself.

He went on: An elephant was led to a well to drink. Perceiving himself in the water, he shied away. He supposed that he was shying away from another elephant, and did not realise that it was from himself that he shied away.

All evil qualities—oppression, hatred, envy, greed, mercilessness, pride—when they are within yourself, do not pain you. When you perceive them in another, then you shy away and are pained. A man feels no disgust at his own scab and abscess; he will dip his affected hand into the broth and lick his fingers without turning in the least squeamish. But if he sees a tiny abscess or half a scratch on another's hand, he shies away from that man's broth and has no stomach for it whatever. Evil qualities are just like scabs and abscesses; when they are within a man himself he is not pained by them, but when he perceives them even to a small degree in another he is pained and disgusted.

Just as you shy away from your brother, so you should excuse him if he shies away from you and is pained. The pain you feel is his excuse, because your pain comes from perceiving those faults, and he perceives the same faults. 'The believer is the mirror of his fellow believer': that is what the Prophet said, he did not say, 'The unbeliever is the mirror of the believer.' The unbeliever does not possess that quality, for he is not a mirror to another and only knows what he sees in his own mirror.

A certain king was seated dejected on the bank of a river. The generals were nervous and afraid of him. His face would not clear up by any means whatsoever. Now he had a jester whom he treated as a great favourite. The generals engaged with him that if he should make the king laugh they would give him a certain sum. The jester therefore approached the king, but despite all the efforts the fellow made the king did not so much as look at him, so that he might make a face and cause the king to laugh. The king kept staring into the river and did not lift his head at all.

'What do you see in the water?' the jester asked the king.

'I see a cuckold,' the king replied.

'King of the world,' the jester said, 'your slave is also not blind.'

So it is in your own case. If you see something in your fellow which pains you, after all he also is not blind; he sees exactly what you see.

In God's presence two I's cannot be contained. You say 'I' and He says 'I': either do you die before Him, or He will die before you, so that duality may not remain. But as for God's dying, that is both impossible and inconceivable; for He is the Living, the Immortal. So gracious is He, that if it were at all possible He would die for your sake, so that duality might vanish. Now since it is not possible for Him to die, do you die so that He may reveal Himself to you and so that duality may vanish.

Tie two birds together, and despite their congeneity and the fact that their two wings have been changed to four they will not fly. That is because duality persists. But if you tie a dead bird to a living bird it will fly, because duality no longer remains.

36

The sun is so gracious that it would gladly die before the bat. But as that is not possible the sun says, 'O bat, my grace is universal. I desire to favour you too. So do you die, since it is possible for you to die, so that you may partake of the light of my glory and be metamorphosed out of your bathood and become the Simurgh of the Mount Qaf of propinquity.'

There was a servant of God who had the power to destroy himself for the sake of a friend. He prayed to God for such a friend, but God did not accept his petition. 'I do not wish that you should see him,' came a voice. That servant of God persisted, and would not refrain from his petition, saying, 'O God, Thou hast implanted this desire for him, and it does not depart out of me.' Finally a voice came saying, 'Do you desire that this should come to pass? Sacrifice your self, and become nothing. Do not tarry, and depart out of the world.' 'Lord, I am well content,' that servant cried. So he did: he gambled away his life for the sake of that Friend, so that his desire was accomplished.

If a servant of God can possess such grace as to sacrifice such a life, one day's portion of which is worth the life of all the world from first to last, shall not the Creator of grace also possess this grace? It would be absurd to suppose otherwise. But since it is not possible for Him to pass away, at least do you pass away.

A bore came and sat himself down above one of the great saints. The Master said: What difference does it make to them whether they are above or below the lamp? If the lamp seeks to be on high, it does not seek that for its own sake. Its purpose is to be of benefit to others, so that they may enjoy their share of its light. Otherwise, wherever the lamp may be, whether below or above, it is the lamp, which is the Sun Eternal. If the saints seek worldly rank and elevation, it is for this purpose: they desire to snare the worldlings, who have not the vision to behold their true elevation, in the trap of worldly rank so that they may find their way to that other elevation and fall into the trap of the world to come.

In like manner the Prophet, God's blessings be upon him, did not conquer Mecca and the surrounding lands because he was in need of that. He conquered them in order that he might give life and vouchsafe light to all men. 'This is a hand which is accustomed to give, it is not accustomed to take.' The saints beguile men in order to bestow gifts on them, not in order to take anything from them.

When a man lays a trap and by cunning catches little birds in his trap so as to eat them and sell them, that is called cunning. But if a king lays a trap so as to capture an untutored and worthless hawk which has no knowledge of its own true nature, and to train it to his own forearm so that it may become ennobled and taught and tutored, that is not called cunning. Though to outward seeming it is cunning, yet it is known to be the very acme of rectitude and bounty and generosity, restoring the dead to life, converting the base stone into a ruby, making the dead sperm into a man and far more than that. If the hawk knew for what reason men seek to capture it, it would not require any bait; it would search for the trap with soul and heart and would fly on the king's hand.

Men pay regard only to the outward significance of the words of the saints and say, 'We have heard plenty of this. Our hearts are stuffed full of words of this kind.'

And they say, 'Our hearts are uncircumcised.'
Nay, but God has cursed them for their unbelief.

The unbelievers would say, 'Our hearts are a foreskin for words of this kind. We are stuffed full of them.' God most High answers them, 'God forbid that they should be full of them! They are full of whisperings and vain conceits, they are full of evil and doubt, nay, they are full of cursing.'

Nay, but God has cursed them for their unbelief.

Would that they were empty of those ravings! Then they would be open to receive these words. But they are not open to receive them; God has set a seal upon their ears and eyes and hearts. Their eyes see things other than as they truly are; they see Joseph as a wolf. Their ears hear things other than as they truly are; they count wisdom for gibberish and raving. Their hearts have been transformed into a lodging for whisperings and vain conceits. A winter's tangle of dark shapes and vain conceits has possessed them; they are congealed with ice and frost.

God has set a seal on their hearts and on their hearing,
and on their eyes is a covering.

38

How likely is it indeed that they should be full of these true words? They have never caught so much as a whiff of them; they have never heard them in all their lives, neither themselves nor those in whom they glory, nor their miserable household. It is a pitcher which God most High shows to men. To some He shows it full of water, and they drink of it till they are sated; but to some He shows it empty. What thanks shall the latter sort render for the pitcher? He renders thanks for it to whom God shows this pitcher full.

When God most High fashioned Adam out of earth and water— 'He kneaded the clay of Adam forty days'—He fashioned his body complete and perfect. For some while he remained thus upon the earth. Then Iblis, God's curse be upon him, came down and entered Adam's body. He went about all his veins and examined them, and perceived those veins and sinews to be full of blood and diverse humours.

'Ah!' he exclaimed. 'It would not be surprising if this were the Iblis whom I saw at the foot of the Throne was to be manifested. If Iblis exists, he must be this.'

And peace be upon you.

7

The son of the Atabeg entered.

The Master said: Your father is always occupied with God. His faith is overmastering, and reveals itself in his words. One day the Atabeg said: The Rumi infidels have urged me to give my daughter in marriage to the Tartars, so that the religion may become one and this new religion which is Muslimdom may disappear. I said: Why, when has this religion ever been one? There have always been two or three, and war and fighting have always gone on between them. How do you want me to make the religion one? It will be one only in the next world, at the resurrection. As for this present world, here it is not possible, for here each one has a different desire and design. Here unity is impossible; it will be possible only at the resurrection, when all men will be one and will fix their eyes on one place, and will all have one ear and one tongue.

In man are many things. There is mouse, and there is bird. The bird carries the cage upwards, while the mouse drags it downwards. A hundred thousand different wild beasts are together in man, except that they are proceeding to the point when the mouse will renounce its mousehood and the bird its birdhood and all become one. For the objective is neither above nor below; when the objective becomes manifest, it will be neither above nor below.

A man has lost something. He keeps on seeking left and right, in front and behind. When he has found that thing he no more seeks above or below, left or right, before or behind, for he becomes tranquil and collected. Similarly, on the resurrection day all men will be one of eye and tongue and ear and understanding. When ten men share a garden or a shop in common their speech is one, their concern is one, their preoccupation is with one thing, since their objective has become one. So on the resurrection day, since the affair of all will be with God, they will all be one in this real sense.

In this world every man is preoccupied with a separate affair. One is in love with women, one is in love with wealth, one is engaged in acquiring possessions, one in acquiring knowledge. Every single one of them believes that his cure, his joy, his pleasure and his repose consist in that one thing. And that is a Divine mercy. When he proceeds thither and seeks, he does not find; so he returns. When he has tarried for a little he says, 'That joy and mercy must be sought after. Perhaps I have not sought well. I will seek again.' When he seeks again, still he does not find. So he continues, until such time as Mercy shows its face without a veil. Then he knows that that was not the right way.

But God most High has certain servants who are like that even before the resurrection: they see truly. 'Alī, God be well pleased with him, said: 'Even were the veil removed, I would not be increased in certain faith.' That is to say, 'When the body is removed and the resurrection appears, my certain faith will not become greater.' The like of this is a group of people on a dark night, within a house, at prayer: they have turned their faces in every direction. When day comes they all turn themselves about, save for that one man who through the night was facing towards Mecca: why should he turn himself about? For all are now turning towards Him. So those special servants of God keep their faces towards Him even in the night and have turned their faces away from all else. Hence with regard to them the resurrection is already manifest and present.

40

There is no end to words, but they are imparted according to the capacity of the seeker.

Naught there is, but its treasuries are with Us,
and We send it not down
but in a known measure.

Wisdom is like the rain. In its store it is unlimited, but it comes down according to what the occasion requires, in winter, in spring, in summer, in autumn, always in due measure, greater and less; but there whence it descends, there it is unbounded. Druggists put sugar or drugs in a screw of paper; but the sugar is not the amount which is in the paper. The stocks of sugar and the stocks of drugs are unlimited and unbounded; how are they to be contained in a piece of paper?

Certain men uttered taunts, saying, 'Why does the Koran come down upon Muhammad word by word? Why not chapter by chapter?' Muhammad (God's blessings be upon him) answered, 'What do these fools say? If it were to come down upon me all at once I would dissolve and vanish away.'

For he who is truly apprised of a little understands much; of one thing, many things; of one line, whole volumes. It is like when a company of men are seated listening to a story, but one of them knows all the circumstances, having been present at the event. From a single hint that man understands it all; he turns pale and crimson, changes from state to state. The others understand only as much as they have heard, for they are not apprised of all the circumstances. But he who is apprised understands much from the amount that he hears.

To return: when you come to the druggist he has sugar in abundance. But he sees how much money you have brought and gives accordingly. By 'money' is here meant resolution and faith. The words are imparted according to one's resolution and faith. When you come seeking sugar, they examine your bag to see what its capacity is, then they measure out accordingly, one bushel or two. But if a man has brought strings of camels and many bags, they order the weighmen to be fetched.

So one man comes along whom oceans do not satisfy; another man finds a few drops enough, and more than that would be harmful to him.

41

This applies not only to the world of ideas and sciences and wisdom. It is true of every thing. Property, gold, mines—all are unbounded and infinite; only they are imparted according to the capacity of the individual, since he would be unable to support more and would be driven mad. Do you not see how Majnūn and Farhād and the other famous lovers took to mountain and desert for the love of a woman when they were loaded with passion beyond their power to control? Do you not see how Pharaoh, when empire and wealth were showered upon him excessively, laid claim to divinity?

Naught there is, but its treasuries are with Us.

'Naught there is, whether good or evil, but treasures of it unlimited are with Us and in Our treasuries, but We send only according to the capacity appropriate.' Yes indeed: this person has faith, but he does not know what his faith is in. In the same way a child has faith in bread, but he does not know what thing he has faith in. So with all things that grow: a tree turns yellow and dry of thirst, but it does not know what thirst really is.

The substance of man is like a flag. He first sets the flag fluttering in the air, and then sends troops to the foot of that flag from every direction as God alone knows—reason, understanding, fury and anger, forbearance and liberality, fear and hope, states without end and qualities unbounded. Whoever looks from afar sees only the flag, but he who beholds from close at hand knows what essences and realities reside in it.

Someone came in and the Master said: Where have you been? We have been longing to see you. Why have you kept away?

The man replied: So things conspired.

The Master said: We for our part have been praying that this conspiracy of things might change and cease to be. A conspiracy of things that produces separation is an improper conspiracy. Yes, by Allah, it too comes from God, only in relation to God it is good. It is a true saying, that all things in relation to God are good and perfect, only in relation to us it is not so. Fornication and purity, not praying and prayer, unbelief and Islam, polytheism and unitarianism—with God all these are good; in relation to us fornication and thieving, unbelief and polytheism are bad, while unitarianism and prayer and good works in relation to us are good. But in relation to God all are good.

A king has in his realm prison and gallows, robes of honour and wealth, estates and retinue, feasting and making merry, drums and flags. In relation to the king all these things are good. Just as robes of honour are the perfect ornament of his kingdom, so too gallows and slaying and prison are the perfect ornament of his kingdom. In relation to him all these things are the perfect ornament; but in relation to his people how should robes of honour and the gallows be one and the same?

8

Someone asked what there was that was superior to prayer. One answer is what I have already said, that the 'soul' of prayer is better than prayer, as I then explained. The second answer is that faith is better than prayer.

Prayer consists of five times' performance, whereas faith is continuous. Prayer can be dropped for a valid excuse, and may be postponed by licence: there is this other advantage which faith has over prayer, that faith cannot be dropped for any excuse and may not be postponed by licence. Again, faith without prayer is beneficial, whereas prayer without faith confers no benefit. Another point: the prayer of hypocrites and the prayer of every religion is of quite a different kind, whereas faith does not change in any religion; its states, its locus and the rest are invariable.

There are also other differences; according to the attractive power of the listener they become evident. The listener is like flour in the hands of a dough-maker; words are like water, which is sprinkled on the flour according to what is required in the circumstances. The poet says:

> 'Mine eye is fixed on another; what shall I do?'
> 'Complain of yourself, for that eye's light is you.'

'Mine eye is fixed on another'; that is, it is seeking another listener apart from you. 'What shall I do? For that eye's light is you': because you are with yourself; you will not have escaped from yourself until your light is a hundred thousand times you.

There was once a skinny person, feeble and contemptible as a sparrow, exceedingly contemptible to behold, so much so that even contemptible forms looked on him with contempt and gave thanks to God, though before seeing him they used to complain of their own contemptible form. For all that he was very rough in his speech and bragged enormously. He was in the court of the king, and his behaviour pained the vizier; yet for all that he swallowed it down. Then one day the vizier lost his temper.

'Men of the court,' he shouted, 'I picked this creature out of the gutter and nourished him. By eating my bread and sitting at my table and enjoying my charity and my wealth and that of my ancestors he became somebody. Now he has reached the point of saying such things to me!'

'Men of the court,' cried the man, springing up in his face, 'and nobles and pillars of the state! What he says is quite true. I was nourished by his wealth and charity and that of his ancestors until I grew up, contemptible and ignominious as you see me. If I had been nourished by someone else's bread and wealth, surely my form and stature and worth might well have been better than this. He picked me out of the gutter; all I can say is, *O would that I were dust.* If someone else had picked me out of the gutter, I would not have been such a laughing stock.'

The disciple who is nourished at the hands of a man of God has a clean and chaste spirit. But he who is nourished at the hands of an impostor and a hypocrite and learns the science from him is just like the man in the foregoing story, contemptible and feeble, weak and with no way out, unable to make up his mind about anything, deficient in all his senses.

> *And the unbelievers—their protectors are*
> *idols, that bring them forth from the light*
> *into the shadows.*

In the composition of man all sciences were originally commingled, so that his spirit might show forth all hidden things, as limpid water shows forth all that is under it—pebbles, broken sherds and the like—and all that is above it, reflected in the substance of the water. Such is its nature, without treatment or training. But when it was mingled with earth or other colours, that property and that knowledge was parted from it and forgotten by it. Then God most High sent forth prophets and saints, like a great, limpid water such as delivers out of darkness and accidental coloration every mean and dark water that enters into it. Then it remembers; when the soul of man sees itself unsullied, it knows for sure that so it was in the beginning, pure, and it knows that those shadows and colours were mere accidents. Remembering its state before those accidents supervened, it says:

This is that wherewithal we were provided before.

The prophets and the saints therefore remind him of his former state; they do not implant anything new in his substance. Now every dark water that recognises that great water, saying, 'I come from this and I belong to this,' mingles with that water. But the dark water that does not recognise that water and deems it other than itself and not of its own kind takes refuge with the colours and shadows, so that it mingles not with the sea and is even farther off from mingling with the sea. It was for this reason that the Prophet said: 'Those spirits which recognise one another associate together, and those which recognise not one another fall into variance.' It was on this account that God declared :

Now there has come to you a Messenger from among yourselves.

That is to say, the great water is congener of the little water, and is of itself and its own substance. That which deems it not of itself, that failure to recognise springs not of the water itself but is an evil associate of the water. The reflection of that associate impinges upon such a water, and the water does not know whether its shying away from the great water, and the sea, springs from itself or from the reflection of that evil associate, so closely are they mingled together. In like manner mean clay does not know whether its inclination towards clay springs from its own nature or from some fault mingled with its character.

Know that every line of poetry that they adduce, every tradition, every verse of the Koran, is like a pair of witnesses bearing testimony, apprised of various kinds of testimony; they bear witness in every situation according to the nature of the situation. In the same way there are two witnesses to the bequest of a house, two witnesses to the sale of a shop, two witnesses to a marriage; they bear witness according to the nature of every case at which they are present. The form of the testimony is always the same; it is its meaning that differs. I pray that God may cause these words to be of benefit to us and you alike. 'The colour is the colour of blood, and the scent is the scent of musk.'

9

We said: The man had the desire to see you. He kept saying, 'I wish I could have seen the Master.'

The Master said: He does not see the Master at this moment in truth because the desire which filled him, namely that he might see the Master, was a veil over the Master. So he does not see the Master at this moment without a veil. So it is with all desires and affections, all loves and fondnesses which people have for every variety of thing— father, mother, heaven, earth, gardens, palaces, branches of knowledge, acts, things to eat and drink. The man of God realises that all these desires are the desire for God, and all those things are veils. When men pass out of this world and behold that King without these veils, then they will realise that all those were veils and coverings, their quest being in reality that One Thing. All difficulties will then be resolved, and they will hear in their hearts the answer to all questions and all problems, and every thing will be seen face to face.

It is not God's way to answer every difficulty singly, but by one answer all questions will be made known all at once and the total difficulty will be resolved. In the same way in winter every man puts on warm clothes and a leather jacket and creeps for shelter from the cold into an oven, into a warm hollow. So too all plants, trees, shrubs and the like, bitten by the venomous cold remain without leaves and fruit, and store and hide their goods and chattels inwardly so that the malice of the cold may not reach them. When spring in a single epiphany answers their requests, all their various problems, whether they be living, springing or lying fallow, will be resolved, and those secondary causes will disappear. All will put forth their heads, and realise what was the cause of that misery.

God has created these veils for a good purpose. For if God's beauty should display itself without a veil, we would not have the power to endure and would not enjoy it. Through the intermediary of these veils we derive succour and benefit.

You see yonder sun, how in its light we walk and see and distinguish good from bad and are warmed. The trees and orchards become fruitful, and in the heat of it their fruits, unripe and sour and bitter, become mature and sweet. Through its influence mines of gold and silver, rubies and cornelians are made manifest. If yonder sun, which through intermediaries bestows so many benefits, were to come nearer it would bestow no benefit whatsoever; on the contrary, the whole world and every creature would be burned up and destroyed.

When God most High makes revelation through a veil to the mountain, it too becomes fully arrayed in trees and flowers and verdure. When however He makes revelation without a veil, He overthrows the mountain and breaks it into atoms.

And when his Lord revealed Him to the mountain
He made it crumble into dust.

Someone interposed the question: Well, is there not the same sun too in the winter?

The Master answered: Our purpose here was to draw a comparison. There is neither 'camel' nor 'lamb.' Likeness is one thing, comparison is another. Although our reason cannot comprehend that thing however it may exert itself, yet how shall the reason abandon the effort? If the reason gave up the struggle, it would no more be the reason. Reason is that thing which perpetually, night and day, is restless and in commotion, thinking and struggling and striving to comprehend, even though He is uncomprehended and incomprehensible.

Reason is like a moth, and the Beloved is like a candle. Whensoever the moth dashes itself against the candle, it is consumed and destroyed, But the moth is so by nature, that however much it may be hurt by that consuming and agony it cannot do without the candle. If there were any animal like the moth that could not do without the light of the candle and dashed itself against that light, it would itself be a moth; whilst if the moth dashed itself against the light of the candle and the moth were not consumed, that indeed would not be a candle.

Therefore the man who can do without God and makes no effort is no man at all; whilst if he were able to comprehend God, that indeed would not be God. Therefore the true man is he who is never free from striving, who revolves restlessly and ceaselessly about the light of the Majesty of God. And God is He who consumes man and makes him naught, being comprehended of no reason.

IO

The Parvāna said: Before the Master arrived on the scene, our Master Bahā' al-Dīn excused himself to me, saying, 'The Master has so ordained that the Amir should not come to visit him and put himself to trouble. I am subject to various states: in one state I speak and in another I do not speak, in one state I attend to the affairs of other men and in another state I withdraw and go into retreat, whilst in yet another state I am utterly absorbed and distraught. I would not wish that the Amir should come when I am in a state of being unable to be amiable to him, when I am not free to counsel him and converse with him. It is therefore better that when I am free and able to attend to my friends and do them some good, I should go out and visit my friends.'

The Amir went on: I answered our Master Bahā' al-Dīn, saying, 'I do not come here in order that our Master may attend to me and converse with me. My purpose in coming is so that I may have the honour of being amongst the company of his servants.' One of the things that has just now happened is that our Master was preoccupied and did not show himself until he had kept me waiting for a long time. This was so that I might realise how difficult and disagreeable it is if I keep good Muslims waiting when they come to my door and do not quickly admit them. The Master has made me taste the bitterness of that and has given me a lesson, so that I may not act like that with others.

The Master answered: That is not so. On the contrary, my keeping

48

you waiting was the acme of lovingkindness. It is related that God most High declares: 'O my servant, I would answer your petition and complaint forthwith, were it not that the voice of your complaint is sweet in my ears. My answer is delayed to the end that you may complain abundantly, for the voice of your complaint is sweet in my ears.'

For example, two beggars have come to the door of a certain person. One is much sought after and beloved, whilst the other is greatly hated. The master of that house says to his slave, 'Give that hated one a piece of bread quickly and without delay, so that he may quickly go abroad from my door.' To the other beloved beggar he makes promises, saying, 'The bread is not yet baked. Wait patiently until the bread is properly cooked and baked.'

My greater desire is to see my friends and to gaze my fill upon them, and they on me. For when many friends have seen very well into one another here below, when they come to be raised up in the other world, having become very familiar indeed they will quickly recognise one another. Knowing how they were together in the world of mortality, their reuniting will be with joy.

For a man all too quickly loses his friend. Do you not see how in this mortal world you have become the friend and darling of some person, and he is a very Joseph of beauty in your eyes, then on account of a single shameful action he vanishes from your sight and you lose him completely? That Joseph-like form is changed into a wolf, and the very same one you saw formerly as Joseph you now see as a wolf, for all that his actual form has not been changed but is still the same as you formerly saw it. By that one accidental motion you lost him. To-morrow, when the mustering of men is re-enacted and this present essence is changed into another essence, since you never knew that person well and never penetrated thoroughly into his essence how are you going to recognise him?

The lesson to be learned from this is that men must see one another very well indeed. They must overpass the good and bad qualities which are present temporarily in every man, and must enter into the other's very essence, seeing exceedingly clearly that these qualities which men bestow upon one another are not their original qualities.

The story is told of a man who said, 'I know that fellow very well. I

49

will give his distinguishing mark.' The others said, 'Pray do.' The man said, 'He was a muleteer of mine. He had two black cows.' People talk in this same fashion. 'I consider So-and-so my friend. I know him.' Every distinguishing mark that they give is just like the story of the two black cows. That is not his distinguishing mark, and that mark is of no use whatever.

So one must overpass the good and evil in a man and enter into his essence, to see what essence and substance he possesses. That is truly seeing and knowing.

It astonishes me how some men say, 'How do saints and lovers of God play at love in the eternal world beyond space and form and time? How do they derive help and strength? How are they affected?' After all, are they not engaged night and day in that very thing? This person who loves a certain person and derives help from him—after all, he derives from him help and grace, kindness and knowledge, recollection and remembrance, happiness and sorrow. All these belong to the infinite world; yet moment by moment he derives help from these abstractions and is affected by them. This does not however surprise the doubters; yet they are amazed how the saints should be lovers in the infinite world and derive help therefrom.

Once there was a philosopher who denied this reality. One day he became sick and incapacitated, and his illness dragged on a long time. A certain theologian went to visit him.

'What are you seeking?' he asked.

'Health,' the philosopher replied.

'Tell me how this health is shaped,' said the theologian, 'so that I may get it for you.'

'It has no shape. It is indescribable,' said the philosopher.

'If it is indescribable, then how are you seeking it?' the theologian demanded. 'Tell me,' he added, 'what is health?'

'All I know,' answered the philosopher, 'is that when health supervenes there is an access of strength. I become plump and red and white, fresh and blooming.'

'I am asking you about the spirit of health. What is the essence of health?' asked the theologian.

'I do not know. It is indescribable,' said the philosopher.

'If you become a Muslim and turn away from your former views,' said the theologian, 'I will treat you and make you well and bring you back to health.'

The Prophet was asked, God's blessings be upon him, 'Though these truths are inscrutable, can a man derive benefit from them through the mediation of form?' He replied, 'See yonder the form of heaven and earth.'

Through the mediation of this form, derive benefit from that universal reality; inasmuch as you see the changing about of the wheel of the sky, the raining of the clouds in due season, summer and winter and all the transformations of time. You see all these things happening rightly and in accordance with wisdom. After all, what does yonder inanimate cloud know, that it is necessary to rain in due season? You see likewise this earth, how it receives seed and returns yield tenfold. Well, Someone does this; behold that Someone through the mediation of this world, and derive help. Just as you derive help from the body of a man to perceive his reality, even so derive help from the reality of the world through the mediation of the form of the world.

When the Prophet, may God bless him and give him peace, was transported out of himself and spoke, he used to say, 'God says.' From the standpoint of form it was his tongue that spoke; but he was not there at all, and the speaker in reality was God. Having at first perceived himself ignorant and knowing nothing of such words, now that such words are being born from him he realises that he is not now what he was at first. This is God controlling him. The Prophet, may God bless him and give him peace, reported about past men and prophets who lived so many thousands of years before him, and even unto the end of the world, what should come to pass; as likewise about the Throne and the Footstool, the Void and the Plenum. His being was a thing of but yesterday, and a being newly created but yesterday assuredly does not speak of such things. How should a creature born in time give information about the eternal? Hence it became realised that it was not he who was speaking; God was speaking.

Nor speaks he out of caprice.
This is naught but a revelation revealed.

God is wholly free of form and letters; His speech is beyond letters and voice. But He delivers His words by means of any letters and voice and tongue He desires.

Men have fashioned upon the highways, in caravanserais and on the banks of pools, men of stone or birds of stone, and out of their mouths the water comes and pours into the pool. All possessed of reason know that the water does not issue out of the mouth of a stone bird, it issues out of another place.

If you want to get to know a man, engage him in speech. By his words you will know him. If he is an impostor, and someone has told him that by their words men are recognised, and he keeps a watch on his words to the end that he may not be found out, even so in the end he is detected.

This is illustrated by the story of the child and his mother. A child in the desert said to his mother, 'On dark nights a horrible black demon appears to me, and I am terribly afraid.'

'Don't be afraid,' said his mother. 'The next time you see that form, attack it bravely. Then it will become clear that it is nothing but a fantasy.'

'But mother,' said the child, 'what if the black demon's mother has given him similar advice? What shall I do, if she has counselled him, saying, "Don't say a word, so that you won't be exposed"? How shall I recognise him then?'

'Keep silent and yield to him, and wait with patience,' his mother answered. 'It may be that some word may leap from his mouth. Or if it does not leap, it may be that from your tongue some word may leap involuntarily, or in your thoughts some words or some idea may spring up, so that out of that idea or those words you will know him for what he is. For then you will have been affected by him; that is the reflection of him and his feelings that has sprung up inside of you.'

Shaikh Sar-razī, God's mercy be upon him, was seated one day amongst his disciples. One of the disciples had a longing for some roasted sheep's head. The Shaikh signalled, saying, 'You must bring him some roasted sheep's head.'

'How did you know that he wanted some roasted sheep's head?' the disciples asked.

'Because it is now thirty years that no desire has remained in me,' the Shaikh answered. 'I have cleansed and purified myself of all desires and have become clear as an unscratched mirror. When the thought of roasted sheep's head entered my mind and whetted my appetite and became a desire, I knew that that belonged to our friend yonder. For the mirror is without any image of itself; if an image shows in the mirror, it is the image of another.'

A worthy man once shut himself up for a forty days' discipline, seeking after a particular object. A voice came to him, saying, 'Such a lofty object will never be attained by a forty days' discipline. Abandon your discipline, so that the regard of a great saint may fall upon you and your object will be realised.'

'Where shall I find that great one?' the man asked.

'In the congregational mosque,' came the answer.

'In such a throng of people how shall I recognise which man he is?' he enquired.

'Go,' he was told, 'and he will recognise you and will gaze upon you. The sign that his regard has fallen upon you will be that the pitcher will drop from your hand and you will become unconscious. Then you will know that he has gazed upon you.'

He acted accordingly. He filled a pitcher with water and went round the congregation in the mosque like a water-carrier. He was wandering between the ranks of the worshippers when suddenly he was seized with ecstasy. He uttered a loud cry, and the pitcher fell from his hand. He remained in a corner of the mosque unconscious. All the people departed. When he came to his senses he saw that he was alone. He did not see there that spiritual king who had gazed upon him, but he had gained his object.

There are certain men of God who because of their great majesty and jealousy for God do not show themselves openly; but they cause disciples to attain important objects and bestow gifts on them. Such mighty spiritual kings are rare and precious.

We said: Do the great ones come before you?

The Master answered: There is no 'before' left to me. It is a long time now that I have had no 'before.' If they come, they come before that imaged thing they believe to be me. Certain men said to Jesus, upon whom be peace, 'We will come to your house.' Jesus

53

answered, 'Where is my house in this world, and how should I have a house?'

It is related that Jesus, upon whom be peace, was wandering in the desert when a great rainstorm broke. He went to take shelter in the den of a jackal in the corner of a cave, until the rain should cease. A revelation came to him, saying, 'Get you out of the jackal's den, for the jackal's whelps cannot rest on account of you.' He cried aloud, saying, 'Lord, the jackal's whelp has a shelter, but the son of Mary has no shelter, no place where he may dwell.'

The Master said: If the jackal's whelp has a home, yet he has no such Beloved to drive him out of his home. You have such a One driving you out. If you have no home, what does that matter? The loving-kindness of such a Driver, and the grace of such a robe of honour, that you should have been singled out for Him to drive you forth, is worth far and exceedingly more than a hundred thousand thousand heavens and earths, worlds here and beyond, Thrones and Footstools.

He said: The fact that the Amir came and I did not show my face quickly ought not to distress him. His purpose in coming was to pay honour either to me or to himself. If it was to pay honour to me, then the longer he sat and waited for me, the greater the honour to me that ensued. If on the other hand his object was to honour himself and to seek a reward, then since he waited and endured the pain of waiting his reward will be all the greater. On either supposition, his object in coming was realised many times over. So he ought to be delighted and happy.

11

The saying 'Hearts bear witness one to another' refers to a statement or a narration that is not disclosed openly. Else what need would there be for words? When the heart bears witness, what need is there for the testimony of the tongue?

The Amīr Nā'ib said: Certainly the heart bears witness. But the heart plays one part by itself, the ear another, the eye another, the tongue another. There is need of each one, in order that the profit may be the greater.

The Master said: If the heart is totally absorbed, all the other members are obliterated in it and there is no need of the tongue. After all take the case of Lailā. She was not a spiritual being, but corporeal and of the flesh, fashioned of water and clay. Yet passion for her produced such absorption and so utterly seized and overwhelmed Majnūn that he had no need to see Lailā with the eye, no need to hear her words by the voice, for he never saw Lailā apart from himself, so that he cried:

> Your name is upon my tongue,
> Your image is in my sight,
> Your memory is in my heart;
> Whither then shall I write?

So the physical has such power that passion can bring a man into a state in which he never sees himself apart from the beloved. All his senses are absorbed in her, sight, hearing, smell and the rest. No member seeks a share apart, seeing all united and having all present. If each of these members I have mentioned plays its part in full, all are immersed in the experience of that one and seek no share apart. The seeking by the sense of another share apart proves that that one member has not taken its true and complete share. It has enjoyed a defective share and consequently has not been immersed in that share; another sense seeks its share, and all severally seek a share apart.

From the standpoint of reality the senses are a unity, but from the standpoint of form they are separate one from another. When one member is affected by absorption, all the members are absorbed in it. Thus, when a fly flies upwards it moves its wings, its head and all its parts; but when it is immersed in honey, all its parts are alike and not one makes any movement.

The nature of absorption is that the one absorbed is no longer there; he can make no more effort; he ceases to act and to move; he is immersed in the water. Any action that proceeds from him is not his action, it is the action of the water. But now if he strikes out in the water with his hands and feet he is not said to be submerged; if he utters a cry, 'Ah, I am drowning,' this too is not called absorption.

Take the famous utterance, 'I am God.' Some men reckon it as a great pretension; but 'I am God' is in fact a great humility. The man who says 'I am the servant of God' asserts that two exist, one himself and the other God. But he who says 'I am God' has naughted himself and cast himself to the winds. He says, 'I am God': that is, 'I am not, He is all, nothing has existence but God, I am pure non-entity, I am nothing.' In this the humility is greater.

It is this that ordinary men do not understand. If a man renders a service *ad majorem Dei gloriam*, his servanthood is still present there; even though it is for the sake of God, he still sees himself and his own action as well as God; he is not drowned in the water. That man is drowned in the water, in whom no movement, no action remains, all his movements being the movement of the water.

A lion was chasing a deer, and the deer was fleeing from the lion. There were two beings in being, one that of the lion and the other that of the deer. But when the lion caught up with the deer and the deer, being overpowered beneath the lion's clutch, in terror of the lion became unconscious and senseless and collapsed before the lion, in that moment the being of the lion remained alone, the being of the deer was effaced and remained no more.

True absorption is this, that God most High causes the saints to be in fear of Him, but not with the fear of men who are afraid of lions and leopards and oppressors; revealing to them that fear comes from God, and security, pleasure and joy, eating and sleeping—all these are of God. God most High shows to the saint a form particular and sensible to the eye wide-awake and open, the form of lion or leopard or fire, so that it becomes known to him that the form of the lion and the leopard which he beholds in reality is not of this world at all but of the world unseen, imaged forth to him and displayed in mighty beauty. Likewise gardens and rivers, maids of Paradise and palaces, all manner of food and drink, robes of honour, fleet steeds, cities, dwelling-places, and every kind of marvel—he knows that in reality these are not of this world. God displays them and informs them before his eyes. Thus he knows for a certainty that fear comes from God, and security, all comforts and all fine shows.

Now this fear of God does not resemble the fear of men, because it is an object of contemplation and not by proof, since God has shown to him expressly that all things are of Him. The philosopher knows this, but he knows it by proof; and proof is not permanent. That delight which ensues from proof has no permanence, that you should say of the proof that it is delightful and warm and fresh. When the memory of the proof passes, its warmth and delight remain no more.

Thus, a man knows by proof that this house had a builder. He knows by proof that this builder has eyes and is not blind, has power and is not impotent, had being and was not non-existent, was living and not dead, and existed before the house was built. All these things he knows, but he knows them by proof; and proof is not permanent and is soon forgotten. Lovers of God, however, having served the Lord have come to know the Builder and seen with the eye of certainty; they have eaten bread and salt together and mingled one with the other; the Builder is never absent from their apperception and their gaze. Such a man as this passes away in God. In regard to him sin is not sin, crime is not crime, since he is overwhelmed and absorbed in Him.

A certain king ordered his slaves every one to take in his hand a golden cup, because a guest was coming. His favourite slave he also commanded to take a cup. When the king showed his face, that special slave on beholding the king lost control of himself and became distraught, so that the cup fell from his hand and was shattered. When the other slaves saw this they said, 'Perhaps this is what we ought to do'; and they cast down their cups deliberately.

'Why did you do that?' the king reprimanded them.

'He was your favourite, and he did so,' they replied.

'Fools!' the king cried out. 'He did not do that. I did it.'

To outward seeming all those forms were sinful. But that one sin was the very acme of obedience; indeed, it transcended obedience and sin. Of them all the true object was that one slave; the rest of the slaves were followers of the king; hence they are the slaves' followers, since he is the essence of the king, and he wears only the form of slavery. He is full of the beauty of the king.

God most High declares, 'But for thee I would not have created the heavens.' 'I am God' is the same thing, its meaning being, 'I created the heavens for Myself.' This is 'I am God' in another language and another idiom.

Though the words of the great saints differ a hundredfold in form, yet since God is one and the Way is one, how should there be two words? Though in form they appear contrary, in meaning they are one. Differentiation is in the form; in the meaning all is concord.

A prince orders a tent to be stitched. One man twists the rope, another strikes the pegs, another weaves the covering, another stitches, another rends, another sticks in the needle. Though to outward seeming they are diverse and different, from the standpoint of meaning they are united and are doing the same job.

So it is with the affairs of this world. When you look into the matter, all are doing God's service, reprobate and righteous, sinner and obedient, devil and angel. For example, the king desires to prove and make trial of his slaves by various means, so that the constant may be sorted out from the inconstant, the loyal from the disloyal, the faithful from the unfaithful. There is need for a tempter and a provoker, so that the slave's constancy may be established; if there were none, how would his constancy be established? Hence that tempter and provoker is doing the service of the king, since it is the king's will that he should so act. He sent a wind to differentiate between the stable and the unstable, to separate the gnat from the tree and the garden, that the gnat may vanish and the sparrow-hawk may remain.

A certain king ordered a slavegirl to adorn herself and offer herself to his slaves, so that their loyalty and disloyalty might be revealed. Though the girl's action appears outwardly sinful, in reality she is doing the king's service.

These true servants of God have seen themselves in this world not by proof and rote, but face to face and unveiled, that all men, good and evil alike, are obedient servants of God.

Nothing is, that does not proclaim His praise.

Therefore, in regard to them this world itself is the resurrection, in that the resurrection means in reality all serving God and doing no other work but His service. These men perceive this truth even here below, for 'Even were the veil removed, I would not be increased in certain faith.'

The knower, from the linguistic standpoint, is a man of higher degree than the gnostic. God is called the Knower, but must not be called the Gnostic. Gnostic means one who did not know, and then came to know; and this does not apply to God. From the standpoint of common usage however the gnostic is the greater; for gnostic is used to denote one who knows the world, transcending proof, by direct vision and face to face. By usage such a man is called a gnostic.

It has been said, 'The knower is better than a hundred ascetics.' How should the knower be better than a hundred ascetics? After all, the ascetic practises asceticism on the basis of knowledge; asceticism without knowledge is impossible. For what is asceticism? To forsake the world, and to turn one's face to obedience and the world to come. Well, it is necessary to know this world, its foulness and impermanence, to know the charm and permanence and everlastingness of the world to come, and to strive to obey, saying, 'How shall I obey, and what is obedience?' All these things are knowledge. Hence asceticism is impossible without knowledge. Hence the ascetic is both knower and ascetic.

This 'knower' who is better than a hundred 'ascetics' is nevertheless real, only its meaning has not been understood. There is another knowledge which God gives a man after this asceticism and the knowledge which he possessed at first. This second knowledge is the fruit of that knowledge and asceticism. Assuredly such a knower is better than a hundred thousand ascetics.

Let me cite a parallel. A man planted a tree, and the tree bore fruit. Assuredly, the tree that bore fruit is better than a hundred trees that have not borne fruit. For it may well be that the latter trees will never bear at all, since many diseases intervene. A pilgrim who reaches the Kaaba is better than the pilgrim who is still travelling in the desert. There is fear with regard to the latter, whether they will reach the Kaaba or no; whereas the former has really reached the Kaaba. One certainty is better than a hundred doubts.

The Amīr Nā'ib said: He who has not arrived still has hope.

The Master replied: What is the hopeful man compared with him who has arrived? There is a vast difference between fear and security. Why need we speak of such a difference, which is manifest to all? What I am speaking about is security; for there are great differences between security and security. It was in regard to security that Muhammad, God bless him and give him peace, was superior to all the

59

other prophets; otherwise, all the prophets are in security and have transcended fear. But there are stations in security.

> *And We have raised some of them above*
> *others in rank.*

It is possible to give some indication as to the world of fear and the stations of fear; but the stations of security have no indication. In the world of fear every man considers what he shall expend in the way of God. One man expends his body, another his wealth, another his life; one man expends by fasting, another by prayer, another by ten prostrations, another by a hundred. Hence their stages are distinct in form, and can be indicated. In the same manner the stages between Konia and Caesarea are distinct and known: Qaimaz, Uprukh, Sultan, and so forth. But the stages by sea from Antalya to Alexandria are without indication. The ship's captain knows them, but they are not told to landsmen since they are not able to understand.

The Amir said: Even to tell imparts some benefit. Though they may not know everything, still they will know a little and will find out and guess the rest.

The Master replied: Yes indeed, by Allah! A man sits wakeful through the dark night, resolved to travel towards the day. Though he does not know how he shall travel, yet since he is awaiting the day he is near to the day. Another man is travelling by caravan upon a dark night and in a storm of rain. He does not know where he has got, where he is passing, what distance he has covered; but when day comes he will see the result of that travelling and will get somewhere. Whoso labours for the glory of God, though he close both his eyes his labour is not lost.

> *And whoso has done an atom's weight of good shall see it.*

Inasmuch as within he is dark and veiled, he does not see how far he has progressed; but in the end he will know. 'This world is the seed-plot of the world to come.' Whatever he sows here, there he shall reap.

Jesus, upon whom be peace, laughed much; John, upon whom be peace, wept much. John said to Jesus, 'You have become exceedingly secure against the subtle deceits, that you laugh so much.' Jesus replied, 'You have become exceedingly unmindful of the subtle and mysterious and wonderful graces and lovingkindnesses of God, that you weep so much.' One of God's saints was present at this incident. He asked God, 'Which of these two has the higher station?' God answered, 'He who thinks better of Me'—that is to say, 'I am where My servant thinks of Me. Every servant has an image and an idea of Me. Whatever picture he forms of Me, there I am. I am the servant of that picture wherein God dwells; I care nothing for that reality where God dwells not. Cleanse your thoughts, O My servants, for they are My abode and dwelling-place.'

Now make trial of yourself as to weeping and laughter, fasting and prayer, solitude and company, and the rest, which of these is more profitable to you. Whichever state brings you straighter on the road and secures your greater advancement, choose that task. 'Take counsel of your heart, even if the counsellors counsel you.' The truth is within you: compare with it the counsel of the counsellors, and where it accords with that, follow that counsel.

The physician comes to the sick man and questions the inward physician; for within you there is a physician, namely your natural temperament which rejects and accepts. Therefore the external physician questions it: 'Such and such a thing that you ate, how was it? Was it light? Was it heavy? How was your sleep?' From what the inward physician tells him, the external physician makes his prescription. Hence the root of the matter is that inward physician, the patient's temperament. When this physician is feeble and the temperament is corrupt, because of his feebleness he sees things all contrary and gives crooked indications. He says that sugar is bitter, vinegar is sweet. He therefore needs the external physician to succour him, so that his temperament may return to its original balance. After that he shows himself to his own physician and takes his counsel.

Man has a like temperament of the true self. When that is feeble, whatever his interior senses perceive and declare is contrary to the truth. So the saints are physicians who succour a man until his temperament is restored to its right balance and his religion and his heart have gathered strength.

'Show me things as they truly are.' Man is a mighty volume; within him all things are written, but veils and darknesses do not allow him to read that knowledge within himself. The veils and darknesses are these various preoccupations and diverse worldly plans and desires of every kind. Yet for all that he is wrapped in darkness and is veiled by so many veils, he can nevertheless read something and is thereof apprised. Consider when these darknesses and veils are removed, how then he will be apprised and what varieties of knowledge he will discover within him!

After all, all these trades and professions—tailoring, building, carpentry, goldsmithery, science, astronomy, medicine and the rest of men's countless and innumerable callings—all these were discovered from within man, they were not revealed by stones and clods. When it is said that a raven taught man to bury the dead, that too is a reflection of man which impinged upon his brain; man's own inner urge prevailed upon him to do that. After all, the animal is but a part of man: how should the part teach the whole? A man desires to write with his left hand; he takes the pen into his hand, but though his heart is strong his hand trembles as he writes; yet the hand writes at the command of the heart.

When the Amir comes, the Master utters mighty words. The words are never cut off; because he is a master of words, words all the time come to him without interruption.

If in the winter time the trees do not put forth leaves and fruit, let men not suppose that they are not working. They are continually at work. Winter is the season of gathering in, summer is the season of spending. Everyone sees the spending, but they do not see the gathering in. In the same way a person gives an entertainment and spends much upon it; this everyone sees, but no one sees the gathering in and collecting little by little for the sake of the entertainment, no one knows anything of that. Yet the ingathering is the root of the matter, for the expenditure comes out of the income.

With whatever person we are in unison, every moment we have words with him, even when we are silent, in absence and presence alike. Indeed we do battle with the other, and are intermingled; though we strike with our fists one against the other, yet we are speaking to him and are one and in unison. Do not regard that fist, in that fist there are raisins. Do you not believe it? Then open it, and see the difference between raisins and pearls of great price.

Other men speak fine and subtle sayings and high wisdom in verse and prose. The inclination of the Amir thiswards and towards us is not on account of high wisdom and subtle sayings and sermonising. Things of that kind are to be found everywhere, and are by no means in short supply. His loving me and his inclination towards me is not for those things. He sees something else; he sees a light transcending what he sees proceeding from others.

It is related that a certain king summoned Majnūn before him.

'What has happened to you and what has befallen you?' he enquired. 'You have disgraced yourself, forsaken your hearth and home, become wasted and utterly destroyed. What is Lailā? What beauty is hers? I will show you many beautiful and lovely girls, make them your ransom and bestow them upon you.'

When they had been brought to court, Majnūn and the lovely girls were duly introduced. Majnūn kept his head cast down, staring in front of him.

'Well now, lift up your head and look!' the king commanded.

'I am afraid,' Majnūn replied. 'My love for Lailā is a drawn sword. If I raise my head, it will strike it off.'

Majnūn had become so immersed in his love for Lailā. After all, the other girls also had eyes and lips and noses. What then had he beheld in her, to come to such a state?

12

The Master said: I have been longing to call on you, but as I know that you are busy with the interests of the people I have been sparing you the trouble.

The Parvāna said: This duty was incumbent upon me. Now that the emergency has ended, henceforward I will attend upon you.

The Master said: There is no difference. It is all the same thing. You are so gracious that all things are the same to you. How can one speak of troubles? But since I am aware that today it is you who are occupied with good deeds and charities, naturally I have recourse to you.

Just now we have been discussing this question: if one man has a family and another man has none, should one cut away from the former and give to the latter? Literalists say that you cut away from the poor family man and give to the other; when you consider the matter well, he himself in reality is a poor family man. It is the same with the spiritualist who possesses a jewel. He strikes a man and breaks his nose and jaw. Everyone says that the latter is the wronged party. But in reality the wronged party is the one striking the blow; the man doing wrong is he who does not act in his best interests. The one who has been punched and got his head broken is the wrongdoer, and the striker is assuredly the wronged party. Since he is the owner of the jewel, since he is consumed in God, his actions are God's actions. God is not called a wrongdoer.

The Prophet too, God bless him and give him peace, killed and spilled blood and raided; yet they were the wrongdoers, and he was the wronged. For example, an occidental dwells in the occident. An oriental has come to the occident. The occidental is a stranger; but what stranger is he who has come from the orient? For the whole world is but a house, no more. Whether he has gone from this house to that house, or from this corner to that corner, after all is he not in the same house? But that occidental who possesses the jewel has come out of the house. Why, the Prophet said, 'Islam began a stranger'; he did not say, 'The oriental began a stranger.' So the Prophet, God bless him and give him peace, when he was defeated was the wronged party, and when he defeated his enemies he was still the wronged party. For in both cases he was in the right; and the wronged party is he who is in the right.

The Prophet's heart, God bless him and give him peace, ached for the prisoners. God most High, to comfort the Prophet, sent down a revelation saying: Say to them, 'In your present state of bondage and chains, if you resolve upon righteousness God will deliver you out of this, and will restore to you that which has gone, and many times as much, and will grant you forgiveness and benediction in the world to come—two treasures, one that has gone from you, and one the treasure of the world to come.'

The Parvāna asked: When the servant of God performs an action, does the grace and good arise from the action, or is it the gift of God?

The Master answered: It is the gift of God and the grace of God. But God out of His exceeding lovingkindness attributes to the servant both, declaring, 'Both are yours.'

No soul knows what comfort is laid up
for them secretly, as a recompense for that
they were doing.

The Parvāna said: Since God is of such lovingkindness, then every-one who seeks in truth shall find.

The Master answered: But without a guide this does not come to pass. So, when the Israelites were obedient to Moses, upon whom be peace, ways were opened up to them even through the sea; dust was brought up out of the sea and they passed over. But when they began to be disobedient, they remained so many years in the wilderness. The leader of a given time is bound to secure the welfare of those whom he perceives to be bound to him and strictly obedient. For instance, when a group of soldiers are strictly obedient in the service of their commander, he too expends his intellect upon their welfare and is bound to work to secure it. But when they are not obedient, how should he expend his intellect to look after their interests?

The intellect in the body of a man is like a commander. So long as the subject members of the body are obedient to it, all the body's affairs proceed well and perfectly; but when they are not obedient, all its affairs come to disorder. Do you not see how, when a man is drunk with taking wine, what disorders are effected by these hands and feet and this tongue, all subjects of his entity? Then on the following day, when he is sober again he cries, 'Alas, what have I done? Why did I strike? Why did I speak abusively?'

So things proceed in perfect order only when there is a leader in that village, and the villagers are obedient to him. The intellect takes thought for the welfare of these subjects in the time when they are at its command. Thus, the intellect thinks, 'I will go'; but it only goes when the foot is obedient to it, otherwise it does not conceive this thought.

Just as the intellect is commander in the midst of the body, so these different entities, who are humankind, together with their several intellects, knowledge, speculation, and learning, are in relation to the saint all unalloyed body, and he is the intellect in the midst of them. Now when these human kind, who are the body, are not obedient to that intellect their affairs all fall into confusion and ruefulness. Now when they are obedient, they must be obedient in such a fashion that whatever the saint does they are obedient, and do not have recourse to their own intellect. For it may well be that with their own intellect they do not understand his action; therefore they must obey him. Similarly when a child is apprenticed to a tailor he must obey his master; if he gives him a patch to sew he must sew that patch, if he gives him a hem he must sew that hem. If he wishes to learn his trade, he must surrender his own initiative completely and become entirely submissive to his master's orders.

We hope that God most High may bring upon us such a state, namely His providential care, which is superior to a hundred thousand strivings and strugglings.

The Night of Power is better than a thousand months.

This statement and that statement are one and the same: 'One tugging from God most High is better than the service of all men and jinns.' That is to say, when His providential care intervenes, it does the work of a hundred thousand strugglings and more. Struggling is fine and good and mightily useful, but what is it compared with God's providential care?

The Parvāna asked: Does God's providential care bestow struggling?

The Master answered: Why should it not? When providential care comes, struggling also comes. Jesus, upon whom be peace—what a struggle he made! He spoke whilst yet in the cradle.

He said, 'Lo, I am God's servant;
God has given me the Book.'

John the Baptist described him whilst yet in his mother's womb. Speech came without struggling to Muhammad the Messenger of God:

In whose breast God has expanded. . . .

First comes grace. When out of error wakefulness enters into him, that is the grace of God and the pure gift of the Lord. If this were not so, how then did it not befall those other friends who were his associates? Grace and requiting are like a spark of fire that leaps. First it is a gift; but when you add cotton waste and nurse that spark, making it

66

increase, then it is grace and requiting. First of all man is small and weak.

For man was created a weakling.

But when you have nursed that weakling fire it becomes a world and sets a universe aflame; that little fire becomes great and mighty.

Surely thou art upon a mighty morality.

I said: Our Master loves you very much.

The Master said: Neither my coming nor my speaking is commensurate with my love. I say whatever comes into me. If God wills, He makes these few words profitable and maintains them within your breast, bestowing mighty benefits. If God wills not, grant that a hundred thousand words are spoken, they will not lodge in the heart but will pass by and become forgotten. Similarly a spark of fire lights upon a burnt rag: if God wills, that one spark will take and become large; if He wills not, a hundred sparks will fall on that tinder and not remain, leaving no mark.

To God belong the hosts of the heavens.

These words are the host of God. By God's authority they open and seize fortresses. If He commands many thousands of horsemen to go and show their faces at such and such a fortress but not to capture it, so they will do; if He commands a single horseman to seize that fortress, that same single horseman will open its gates and capture it. He delegates a gnat against Nimrod, and it destroys him. 'Equal in the eyes of the gnostic are a dang and a dinar, a lion and a cat.' For if God most High bestows His blessing, one dang does the work of a thousand dinars and more; if He withholds His blessing from a thousand dinars, they do not the work of one dang. So too if He commissions the cat, it destroys the lion as the gnat destroyed Nimrod; if He commissions the Lion, all lions tremble before him or become his ass. Just so, certain dervishes ride on lions. Just so, the furnace became *coolness and safety* to Abraham, upon whom be peace, verdure and a rose-plot, since it was not God's authorisation that the fire should consume him. In short, when men realise that all things are of God, all things become one and the same in their eyes.

Of God I hope that you will hear these words too within your hearts, for that is profitable. If a thousand thieves come from without, they cannot open the door so long as they have no fellow-thief within to open from within. Speak a thousand words from without, yet so long as there is none to confirm them from within they are unprofitable. So too with a tree: as long as there is no freshness in its roots, though you pour a thousand torrents of water over it, it will nothing profit. First there must be a freshness in its roots for the water to succour it.

> What though a man a myriad lights descry,
> Except the eye be bright, those lights must die.

Though the whole world be ablaze with light, except there be light within the eye, that man will not behold that light. The root of the matter is that receptiveness which is within the soul.

The soul is one thing, and the spirit is another. Do you not see how in sleep the soul fares abroad? The spirit remains in the body, but the soul wanders and is transformed. When 'Alī said, 'He who knows his own self knows his Lord,' he was speaking of this soul.

The Master said: If we say that he was speaking of this soul, that is no small matter. If on the other hand we explain it as meaning that Soul, the listener will understand it as referring to this soul, since he does not know that Soul. For instance, you take a little mirror in your hand. The object shows clearly in the mirror: whether it shows large or small, it is still that object. Mere words cannot ensure understanding; words only reveal the inward impulse of the listener.

Outside this world of which we are speaking there is another world for us to seek. This world and its delights cater to the animality of man; these all feed his animality, whilst the root principle, man, goes into a decline. After all, they say, 'Man is a rational animal.' So man consists of two things. That which feeds his animality in this material world is these lusts and desires. But as for that which is his true essence, its food is knowledge and wisdom and the sight of God. The animality

68

in man flees away from God, whilst his humanity flees away from this
world.

One of you is an unbeliever,
and one of you a believer.

Two persons are warring within this one entity.

Who shall succeed? Whom Fortune makes her friend.

There is no doubt that this world is a world of winter. Why is the
name 'solid' given to inanimate things? Because they are all solidified.
These stones and mountains, and the garments worn by the entity, are
all solidified. If this world is not a world of winter why are they
solidified? The inner substance of this world is elementary; though
itself invisible, by its effects it can be known that it is wind and
bitter cold.

It is like the season of winter, when all things are solidified. What
manner of winter is it? Winter of the reason, not of the senses. When
that Divine zephyr comes along the mountains begin to melt, the world
turns to water; just as when the warmth of July comes along, all things
solidified begin to liquefy. On the resurrection day when that zephyr
blows, all things will melt away.

God most High makes these words our army round about you, to
be a barrier for you against the enemy and to be the means of overmastering the enemy. For there are enemies, enemies within and enemies without. Yet they are nothing: what thing should they be? Do
you not see how a thousand infidels are captive to one infidel who is
their king, and that infidel is captive to his thoughts? Hence we realise
that thoughts have their effect, since through one feeble and muddled
thought so many thousands of men and worlds are prisoners. Consider
then, where there are thoughts unbounded, what grandeur and splendour are theirs, and how they vanquish the enemy and what worlds
they subdue! When I see distinctly what myriads of forms unbounded,
what armies unending stretching through waste upon waste, all are
prisoners of one person, and that person prisoner to a contemptible
little thought! These who are all prisoners of one thought—where do
they stand, compared with thoughts mighty, infinite, weighty, holy,
sublime?

Hence we realise that thoughts have their effect. The forms all are followers and mere instruments; without thought they are immobilised and 'solid.' So he who regards the form is also 'solid'; he cannot penetrate the meaning. He is a child and immature, even though in form he be aged and a centenarian. 'We have returned from the lesser struggle to the greater struggle': that is to say, we were at war with forms, and had drawn up our ranks against 'formal' adversaries; now we draw up our ranks against the armies of thoughts, so that good thoughts may defeat bad thoughts and drive them out of the kingdom of the body. This then is indeed the greater struggle and the greater battle.

So thoughts have their effect, for they work without the body's mediation; just as the Active Intellect without any instrument keeps the heavens turning. Therefore the philosopher says that thoughts require no instrument.

> You are a substance, and the dual worlds
> Are your accidents:
> To seek the substance in the accident
> Makes little sense.

> The man who looks into the heart for knowledge
> Deserves your tears;
> The man who looks into the soul for reason
> Has earned your jeers.

As it is accident, one must not dwell upon accident. For this substance is like a musk-pod, and this material world and its delights are like the scent of the musk. This scent of the musk is but transient, for it is mere accident. He who has sought of this scent the musk itself and has not been content with only the scent, that man is good. But he who has been satisfied to possess the scent, that man is evil; for he has grasped after a thing that does not remain in his hand. For the scent is merely the attribute of the musk. So long as the musk is apparent in this world, its scent comes to the nostrils. When however it enters the veil and returns to the other world, all those who lived by its scent die. For the scent is attached to the musk, and departs whither the musk reveals itself.

Happy then is he who reaches the musk through the scent and becomes one with the musk. Thereafter for him remains no passing away; he has become eternal in the very essence of the musk and takes on the predicament of the musk. Thereafter he communicates its scent to the world, and the world is revived by him. Only the name of what he was survives in him: as with a horse or any other animal that has turned to salt in a salt-pan, only the name of horse remains to it. In effect and influence it is that ocean of salt. What harm does that name do to it? It will not bring it out of its saltiness. And if you give some other name to this salt-mine, it will not lose its saltiness.

So it behoves a man to eschew these pleasures and delights, which are the ray and reflection of God. He must not become content with this much; even though this much is of God's grace and the radiance of His beauty, yet it is not eternal. With reference to God it is eternal, with reference to man it is not eternal. It is like the rays of the sun which shine into houses; for all that they are the rays of the sun and are light, yet they are attached to the sun. When the sun sinks, the light no more remains. Hence it behoves us to become the Sun, so that the fear of separation may no more remain.

There is giving, and there is knowing. Some have gifts and bounties, but not knowledge; some have knowledge, but not gifts. But when both are present, that man is mightily prosperous. Such a one is truly in-comparable; yet for the purpose of example he may be compared. A man is going along the road, but he does not know whether this is the road or whether he is off the road. He goes on blindly, hoping that perchance a cock will crow or some other sign of habitation may appear. What is he compared with the man who knows the road and travels on, not needing sign or waymark? He has his set task. So knowing excels all else.

13

The Prophet, upon whom be peace, said: 'The night is long: do not shorten it by your sleeping. The day is bright: do not cloud it with your sins.'

The night is long for telling secrets and asking for one's needs without the distraction of other men, without the disturbance of friends and foes. Then is secured a privacy and a tranquillity; God draws down the veil, so that acts may be guarded and preserved from hypocrisy and done wholly for God. At night the hypocrite stands revealed from the sincere man; the hypocrite is exposed. At night all things are veiled, and by day they are exposed; but at night the hypocrite is exposed.

'As nobody sees,' he says, 'for whose sake should I do it?'

'Somebody sees,' they answer him. 'But you are not somebody, that you should see Somebody. 'That Somebody sees, in whose hand's clutch all men are. In the time of distress all call upon Him; in the time of toothache, earache, eyeache, in doubt and fear and insecurity. In secret all call upon Him, trusting that He will hear and will grant their request. Privily, privily they distribute alms, to ward off evil and restore from sickness, trusting that He will accept their gifts and alms. When He has restored them to health and peace of mind, that sure faith departs again and the phantom of anxiety returns.'

'O God,' they cry, 'what a state we were in, when in all sincerity we called upon Thee in that prison corner. For a hundred repetitions of *Say, He is God* unwearying Thou didst grant our requests. Now that we are outside the prison we are still as much in need as we were inside the prison, that Thou mayest bring us out of this prison of the world of darkness into the world of the prophets, which is the world of light. Why does not the same deliverance come without the prison and without the state of pain? A thousand phantoms descend, whether they do wonderful good or not, and the influence of those phantoms yields a thousand languors and wearinesses. Where is that sure faith which burns up all phantoms?'

God most High answers them, 'As I have said, the animal soul in you is your enemy and My enemy.

Take not My enemy and your enemy for friends.

Strive always against this enemy in prison; for when he is in prison and calamity and pain, then your deliverance appears and gathers strength. A thousand times you have proved that deliverance comes to you out of toothache and headache and fear. Why then are you chained to bodily comfort? Why are you ever occupied with tending the flesh?

Forget not the end of the thread: constantly deny your carnal soul its desires, till you have attained your eternal desire and find deliverance out of the prison of darkness.

> *But as for him who feared the Station of his Lord*
> *and forbade the soul its caprice,*
> *surely Paradise shall be the refuge.'*

14

Shaikh Ibrāhīm said: Whenever Saif-al-Dīn Farrukh beat anybody, he would immediately occupy himself with someone else until the beating was over. In this way and fashion no one's intercession could succeed.

The Master said: Whatever you see in this world corresponds exactly with what is in the other world; rather, all these things are samples of the other world. Whatever exists in this world has been brought here from that world.

> *Naught there is, but its treasuries are with Us*
> *and We send it not down*
> *but in a known measure.*

The bald man of Baalbek carries on his head trays and various drugs, a pinch from every heap—a pinch of pepper, a pinch of mastica. The heaps are infinite, but there is no room in his tray for more. Man is like the bald man of Baalbek, or a druggist's shop. He is loaded with pinches and pieces out of the treasuries of the attributes of God, all in boxes and trays, so that he may engage in this world in trade suitable to Him—a piece of hearing, a piece of speech, a piece of reason, a piece of generosity, a piece of knowledge.

Men there are who are hawkers of God; they go about hawking, and night and day they fill the trays. You empty or fritter away to make your living; by day you empty, and by night they fill again and give replenishment.

For instance, you see the brightness of the eye. In that world there are eyes and sights and regards of various kinds. A sample of those has been sent to you, for you to look about the world. Sight is not confined

73

to such dimensions, but a man cannot bear more than this. 'All these attributes are with Us unlimited; We send them to you in a known measure.'

So consider how many thousands of people, generation after generation, have come and filled themselves from this Sea, and become empty again. Consider what heaps those are. The longer a man stays upon that Sea, the colder his heart grows for the tray. You may suppose then that the world issues from that Mint, and returns to the Mint again.

Surely we belong to God, and
to Him we return.

Surely we: that is to say, all our parts have come from there and are samples of there, and again return there, small and great, and of all living creatures. But in this tray they soon become visible; without the tray they are not visible. For that world is a subtle world and comes not into sight; yet how wonderful it comes! Do you not see how the spring breeze becomes visible in the trees and grasses, the rose-beds and sweet herbs? Through the medium of these you gaze upon the beauty of spring. But when you look upon the spring breeze itself, you see nothing of these things. It is not because those spectacles and rose-beds are not in the breeze; after all, are these not its rays? Rather, within the spring breeze are waves of rose-beds and sweet herbs; but those waves are subtle and do not come into sight, only through some medium they are revealed out of their subtlety.

Likewise in man these qualities are hidden, and only become manifest through an inward or outward medium—one man through speech, another through discord, another through war and peace. You cannot see the attributes of man: examine yourself, and you will not find anything. So you suppose yourself empty of these attributes. Yet it is not the case that you have changed from what you were, only these things are hidden in you, like the water in the sea. The waters leave not the sea save through the medium of a cloud; they do not become visible except in a wave. The wave is a commotion visible from within you, without an external medium. But so long as the sea is still, you see nothing. Your body is on the shore of the sea, and your soul is of the sea. Do you not see how many fishes and snakes and birds and creatures of all kinds come forth and show themselves, and then return to the sea? Your attributes, such as anger and envy and lust and the rest, come forth from this sea.

So you may say that your attributes are subtle lovers of God. You cannot perceive them save through the medium of the tongue; when they become naked, because of their subtlety they come not into sight.

15

In man there is a passion, an agony, an itch, an importunity such that, though a hundred thousand worlds were his to own, yet he would not rest nor find repose. These creatures dabble successively in every trade and craft and office; they study astronomy and medicine and the rest, and take no repose; for they have not attained the object of their quest. Men call the beloved 'heart's ease' because the heart finds ease in the beloved. How then should it find ease and rest in any other?

All these pleasures and pursuits are as a ladder. Inasmuch as the steps of the ladder are not a place wherein to dwell and abide but are for passing on, happy is he who the quicker becomes vigilant and aware. Then the road becomes short for him, and he wastes not his life upon the steps of the ladder.

Someone asked the question: The Mongols seize property, and from time to time they give property to us. This is a strange situation. What is your ruling?

The Master answered: Whatever the Mongols seize has come as it were into the grasp and treasury of God. In the same way when you fill a jug or a barrel from the river and carry it away, that becomes your property so long as it is in the jug or barrel, and nobody has the right to interfere. Anyone who takes from the jug without permission is guilty of theft by violence. But once the water is poured back into the river, it passes out of your ownership and is lawful for all to take. So our property is unlawful to them, whereas their property is lawful to us.

'There is no monkhood in Islam: the congregation is a mercy.' The Prophet, God's blessings be upon him, laboured for solidarity, since the gathering of spirits has a great and momentous effect, whereas in singleness and isolation that is not achieved. That is the secret of why mosques were erected, so that the inhabitants of the parish might gather there and greater mercy and profit ensue. Houses are separate for the purpose of dispersion and the concealment of private relations: that is their use. Cathedral mosques were erected so that the whole city might be assembled there. The Kaaba was instituted in order that the greater part of mankind might gather there out of all cities and climes.

Someone said: When the Mongols first came to these parts they were naked and bare, they rode on bullocks and their weapons were of wood. Now they are sleek and well-filled, they have splendid Arab horses and carry fine arms.

The Master said: In that time when they were desperate and weak and had no strength, God helped them and answered their prayer. In this time when they are so powerful and mighty, God most High is destroying them at the hands of the feeblest of men, so that they may realise that it was through God's bounty and succour that they captured the world, and not by their own force and power. In the first place they were in a wilderness, far from men, without means, poor, naked and needy. By chance certain of them came as merchants into the territory of the Khvarizmshah and began to buy and sell, purchasing muslin to clothe their bodies. The Khvarizmshah prevented them, ordering that their merchants should be slain, and taking tribute from them; he did not allow their traders to go there. The Tartars went humbly before their king, saying, 'We are destroyed.' Their king asked them to give him ten days' grace, and entered a deep cave; there he fasted for ten days, humbling and abasing himself. A proclamation came from God most High: 'I have accepted your supplication. Come forth: wherever you go, you shall be victorious.' So it befell. When they came forth, by God's command they won the victory and captured the world.

Someone said: The Tartars also believe in the resurrection, and say that there will be a judgement.

The Master answered: They lie, desiring to associate themselves with the Muslims. 'We also know and believe,' they say. A camel was once asked, 'Where are you coming from?' It replied, 'From the baths.' The retort came, 'That is evident from your pads!' If they really believe in the resurrection, what evidence is there to prove it? The sins and wrongs and evils that they have committed are like snow and ice piled together heap on heap. When comes the sun of penitence and contrition, tidings of the other world and the fear of God, it will melt those snows of sinfulness as the sun in heaven melts the snow and ice. If some snow and ice should say, 'I have seen the sun, and the sun of summer has shone upon me,' and it still remained snow and ice, no intelligent man would believe it. It is not possible that the summer sun should come and leave the snow and ice intact.

Though God most High has promised that good and evil shall be rewarded at the resurrection, yet an ensample of that comes to pass every moment and at every instant. If happiness enters into a man's heart, that is his reward for making another happy; if he becomes sorrowful, it is because he has brought sorrow upon a fellow-man. These are presents from the other world and tokens of the day of recompense, so that by these little things men may come to understand those great matters, even as a handful of corn is offered as a token of the whole heap.

The Prophet, God's blessings be upon him, for all his majesty and greatness one night felt pain in his hand. It was revealed to him that that pain was the effect of the pain in the hand of 'Abbās. For he had taken 'Abbās captive and had bound his hands together with all the prisoners. Although that binding of his hands was done at God's order, yet it brought its recompense.

So you may realise that these gripes and depressions and dumps that come upon you are the effect of some injury and sin that you have committed. Though you do not remember in detail what and what you have done, yet from the recompense know that you have done many evil deeds. You do not know whether that evil resulted from negligence or ignorance, or because an irreligious companion made light of your sins so that you do not recognise them as sins. Consider the recompense, how much you are contracted and how much you are expanded: certainly contraction is the recompense of disobedience to God, and expansion is the recompense of obedience to Him. Why, the Prophet himself, God bless him and give him peace, because he turned a ring upon his finger was rebuked: 'We did not create you for idleness and play.'

What, did you think that We created you only for sport?

77

Estimate from this whether your day is passed in disobedience or obedience.

God occupied Moses, upon whom be peace, with the affairs of men. Though he was at God's command and altogether occupied with God, yet God occupied one side of him with men for the general good. Khaḍir He occupied with Himself wholly. Muhammad, God bless him and give him peace, He occupied at first wholly with Himself; thereafter He commanded him, 'Call the people, counsel them and reform them.' Muhammad, God's blessings be upon him, wept and lamented, saying, 'Ah, my Lord, what sin have I committed? Why drivest Thou me from Thy presence? I have no desire for men.' God most High said to him, 'Muhammad, do not sorrow. I will not abandon you only to be occupied with men. Even in the midst of that occupation you shall be with Me. When you are occupied with men, not one hair of the head of this hour you spend with Me, not one will be taken from you. In whatever matter you are engaged, you will be in very union with Me.'

Someone asked: The eternal decrees and that which God most High has predestined—do they change at all?

The Master answered: What God most High has decreed in eternity —that there shall be good for good and evil for evil—that decree will never change. For God most High is a wise God: how should He say, 'Do evil, that you may find good'? If a man sows wheat, shall he gather barley? Or if he sows barley, shall he gather wheat? That is impossible. All the saints and prophets have said that the recompense of good is good, and the recompense of evil evil.

And whoso has done an atom's weight of good shall see it,
and whoso has done an atom's weight of evil shall see it.

If you mean by the eternal decree what we have stated and expounded, that never changes: God forbid! But if you mean that the recompense of good and evil increases and so changes, that is to say, the more good you do the greater good you will receive, and likewise the more wrong you do the greater evil you will see, there certainly change enters in; but the original decree does not change.

Some quibbler said: But we see how sometimes a wicked man turns virtuous, and a virtuous man turns wicked.

78

The Master answered: Well, that wicked man did some good, or meditated some good, so that he became virtuous. So too the virtuous man who became wicked did some evil or meditated some evil so that he became wicked. Consider how it was with Iblis when he protested to God regarding Adam.

> Thou
> createdst me of fire, and him Thou
> createdst of clay.'

After having been supreme amongst the angels he was cursed to eternity, and banished from the Throne. So we say again that the recompense of good is good, and the recompense of evil evil.

Someone asked: A man has taken a vow to fast one day. If he breaks that vow, is there expiation?

The Master answered: According to the Shāfi'ī code expiation is required even in the case of a single statement, because Shāfi'ī holds that a vow is the same as an oath, and whoever breaks an oath is required to make expiation. According to Abū Ḥanīfa however a vow does not carry the meaning of an oath and so expiation is not required.

There are two kinds of vows: one absolute, and the other restricted. An absolute vow is when a man says, 'It is incumbent upon me to fast one day'; a restricted vow is, 'Such and such is incumbent upon me if so and so comes.'

The Master added: A certain man had lost an ass. For three days he fasted with the intention that he should find his ass. After three days he found his ass dead. He was distressed, and in his distress he lifted his face to heaven and said, 'If in lieu of these three days that I have observed fast I should not eat six days in Ramadan I would not be a man at all, you would make a profit out of me!'

Someone asked: What is the meaning of 'greetings' and 'prayers' and 'blessings' upon the Prophet?

The Master answered: It means that these acts of adoration and service and worship and attention do not come from us and we are not free to perform them. The truth is that 'blessings' and 'prayers' and 'greetings' belong to God; they are not ours, they are wholly His and belong to Him. In the same way in the season of spring people sow seeds, go out into the wilderness, and make journeys. All these

79

activities are the gift and bounty of spring; otherwise they would still be as they were, shut up in houses and caves. Hence this refreshment and enjoyment belong to spring, and spring is the dispenser of enjoyment.

Men regard the secondary causes, and do not distinguish between them and the actualities. But to the saints it has been revealed that secondary causes are no more than a veil, so that men do not see and recognise the Creator. Thus, someone speaks from behind a curtain. People suppose that it is the curtain speaking, not realising that the curtain has nothing to do with it, and is a veil. When the man emerges from the curtain it is made known that the curtain was a pretext. God's saints see beyond the causes the actualities as they are discharged and eventuate. Thus, a camel came forth from a mountain; Moses' staff became a serpent; out of the hard rock twelve fountains flowed. Muhammad, God's blessings be upon him, without any instrument, by a mere sign split the moon asunder. Adam, upon whom be peace, came into existence without mother and father; Jesus, without a father. For Abraham, upon whom be peace, out of the fiery furnace roses and a rose-bower sprang up; and so on and so on.

Seeing these things, they have realised that secondary causes are a pretext, the effective cause being other. Causes are only a veil, to occupy the common people. God promised Zachariah, upon whom be peace, 'I will give you a son.' Zachariah cried, 'I am an old man, and my wife is old. My instrument of lust has become feeble, and my wife has reached a state in which it is not possible for her to conceive a child. Lord, from such a woman how shall a son be born?'

> *'Lord,' said Zachariah,*
> *'how shall I have a son,*
> *seeing I am an old man*
> *and my wife is barren?'*

The answer came, 'Take heed, Zachariah! You have lost the clue. I have shown you a hundred thousand times that actualities are without causes. That you have forgotten, and you do not realise that causes are the pretext. I am able this very instant before your very eyes to produce out of you a hundred thousand sons, without wife and without pregnancy. Indeed if I make the sign, a whole people stand forth manifest in this world, completely formed, mature and possessing knowledge. Did I not cause you to be, without mother and father, in the world of spirits? Did you not receive graces and favours from Me aforetime, ere you came into this physical being at all? Why do you forget these things?'

The several states of the prophets and saints and of other men, good and evil, according to their ranks and substance, may be set forth in a parable. Slaves are brought out of heathenland into the realm of Muslimdom and are there sold. Some are brought at the age of five years, some at ten, some at fifteen years. Those who were brought as children, having been nurtured for many years amongst Muslims and now grown old, forget utterly that other country and no trace of it remains in their memory. Those brought a little older remember a little; those much older recollect much more.

Even so the spirits in the other world were in the Presence of God.

> *'Am I not your Lord?'*
> *They said, 'Yes.'*

Their food and sustenance was the speech of God, without letters and without sounds. When any one of these has been brought into this world as a child, when he hears that Speech he remembers nothing of his former state and sees himself a stranger to that Speech. That party of men are veiled from God, being wholly sunk in unbelief and error. Some remember a little bit, and ardour and yearning for the other side are quickened in them: they are the believers. Some, when they hear that Speech, their former state becomes manifest before their eyes even as it was so long ago; the veils are entirely removed and they are joined in that union; those are the prophets and the saints.

Now I will counsel my friends earnestly. When those brides of heavenly truth show their faces within you and the secrets are revealed, beware and beware that you tell not that to strangers, and describe it not to other men. Tell not to every man these words of mine that you hear. 'Impart not wisdom to those not meet for it, lest you do wisdom wrong; and withhold it not from those meet to receive it, lest you do them wrong.' If a fair and adorable one surrenders to you and is privily in your house, saying, 'Show me not to any man, for I belong to you,' never would it be proper and seemly for you to parade her in the bazaars and to call to every man, 'Come and see this beauty!' That would never be agreeable to the adorable one; she would turn to others, and be enraged against you.

God has made these words unlawful to them. Even so the dwellers in Hell lament to the dwellers in Paradise, saying, 'Well now, where is your generosity and your humanity? Out of those gifts and bounties which God most High has bestowed on you, if out of charity and common kindness you sprinkle and confer just a little upon us, what would that be?

> The earth has its share of the cup
> Of generous men when they sup.

We are burning and melting in this fire. Out of those fruits, or out of those limpid waters of Paradise if you sprinkle a drop or two upon our souls, what would that be?'

> *The inhabitants of the Fire shall*
> *call to the inhabitants of Paradise:*
> *'Pour on us water, or of that God*
> *has provided you!'*
> *They will say: 'God has forbidden them*
> *to the unbelievers.'*

The dwellers in Paradise give answer, saying, 'God has forbidden that to you. The seed of this bliss was in the abode of the world below. Since you did not sow and cultivate there, namely by faith and sincerity and good works, what should you gather here? Even if we confer upon you out of generosity, since God has forbidden that to you it will burn your throats and stick in your gullets. If you put it in your wallet, it will be torn and all will be spilled.'

A crowd of hypocrites and strangers came into the presence of Muhammad, God's blessings be upon him. They were expounding mysteries, and lauding the Prophet, God bless him and give him peace. The Prophet intimated to his Companions saying. 'Cover up your vessels.' He meant, 'Cover up and keep covered your bottles and cups and pots and pitchers and barrels, for there are creatures unclean and venomous; lest they fall into your bottles and unwittingly you drink water from those bottles and suffer injury.' He bade them, in this formal manner, 'Conceal wisdom from strangers, and in their presence stop your mouths and tongues, for they are mice and are not worthy of this wisdom and grace.'

The Master said: That Amir who has just left our company—though he did not understand in detail what we were saying, yet he realised in summary that we were calling him to God. I take as a sign of under-standing that supplication and wagging of the head and affection and passion. Well, the countryman who comes into the city hears the call to prayer; though he does not know in detail the meaning of the call to prayer, yet he understands its purport.

16

The Master said: Whoever is loved is beautiful, but this statement is not reversible; it does not necessarily follow that whoever is beautiful is loved. Beauty is a part of lovableness, and lovableness is the root principle. If a thing is loved it is of course a beautiful thing; a part of a thing cannot exist apart from its whole, and is inherent in that whole.

In Majnūn's time there were many girls more beautiful than Lailā, but they were not loved of Majnūn.

'There are girls more beautiful than Lailā,' they used to tell Majnūn. 'Let us bring some to you.'

'Well,' Majnūn would reply, 'I do not love Lailā after form. Lailā is not form. Lailā in my hand is like a cup; I drink wine out of that cup. So I am in love with the wine which I drink out of it. You have eyes only for the beaker, and are unaware of the wine. If I had a golden beaker studded with precious stones, and in the beaker there were vinegar or something else other than wine, of what use would that be to me? An old broken gourd in which there is wine is better in my eyes than such a goblet and a hundred like it.'

A man requires to be moved with passion and yearning for him to tell the wine apart from the beaker. So it is with the man who is hungry, not having eaten anything for ten days, and the other man who is full and has eaten five times a day. Both see a loaf of bread. The full man sees the form of the bread, whereas the hungry man sees the form of the living soul. For this bread is like the goblet, and the pleasure it imparts is as the wine in the goblet. That wine cannot be perceived save by the regard of appetite and yearning. Therefore acquire appetite and yearning, so that you may not be merely a viewer of form, but in all being and space you may see the Beloved.

These creatures are as cups, and these sciences and arts and branches of knowledge are inscriptions upon the cup. Do you not see that when the cup is broken those inscriptions no more remain? The wine therefore is the thing, which is in the cup of the physical moulds, and he who drinks the wine sees that

The abiding things, the deeds of righteousness . . .

The man who asks must first conceive two premisses. First, he must be certain that he is erring in what he says, and that something different is the case. Secondly he must reflect that over and above this, and better than this, there is a statement and a wisdom of which he knows nothing. Hence we realise the meaning of the saying, 'Asking is the half of knowing.'

Everyone has his face turned to somebody, and the ultimate object of all is God. In this hope all men expend their lives. But as between these two there must be one who discriminates and who knows, as between the two, which of them is hitting the mark; who is scarred with the blow of the polo-stick of the King, so that he declares and believes that there is One God.

A man is said to be absorbed when the water has absolute control of him and he has no control of the water. The man absorbed and the swimmer are both in the water; but the former is carried along and borne by the water, whereas the swimmer carries his own strength and moves at his own free will. So every movement made by the man absorbed, and every act and word that issues from him, all that proceeds from the water and not from him: he is present there as the pretext. In the same way when you hear words coming from a wall, you know that they do not proceed from the wall but that there is someone who has brought the wall into speech.

The saints are like that. They have died before physical death and have taken on the status of door and wall. Not so much as a hair's tip of separate existence has remained in them. In the hands of Omnipotence they are as a shield: the movement of the shield proceeds not from the shield. This is the meaning of the statement, 'I am the Truth': the shield says, 'I am not there at all, the movement proceeds from the Hand of God.' Regard such a shield as God, and do not use violence against God; for those who rain blows against such a shield have declared war against God and ranged themselves against God.

From the time of Adam down to the present day you hear what things have befallen such as have used violence against God—Pharaoh, Shaddad, Nimrod, the peoples of 'Ad and Lot and Thamud, and so on and so on. And that shield stands firm till the resurrection, age after age; now in the form of prophets, now in the form of saints; to the end that the godfearing may be distinguished from the ungodly, God's enemies from His friends.

Therefore every saint is God's proof against men, whose rank and station are determined by the degree of their attachment to him. If they act hostilely against him, they act hostilely against God; if they befriend him, they have made friendship with God. 'Whosoever sees him has seen Me; whosoever repairs to him has repaired to Me.'

God's servants are confidants of the sanctuary of God. Just as God most High has cut away from His servitors every vein of separate existence and lust, every root of perfidy, inevitably they have become masters of a whole world and intimate with the Divine mysteries, which *none but the purified shall touch.*

The Master said: If that man has turned his back on the tombs of the great saints, he has done so not out of disavowal and neglect: he has turned his face towards their souls. For these words which proceed from my mouth are their soul. It does no harm to turn the back on the body and the face towards the soul.

It is a habit with me, that I do not desire that any heart should be distressed through me. During the séance a great multitude thrust themselves upon me, and some of my friends fend them off. That is not pleasing to me, and I have said a hundred times, 'Say nothing to any man on my account; I am well content with that.' I am affectionate to such a degree that when these friends come to me, for fear that they may be wearied I speak poetry so that they may be occupied with that. Otherwise, what have I to do with poetry? By Allah, I care nothing for poetry, and there is nothing worse in my eyes than that. It has become incumbent upon me; as when a man plunges his hands into tripe and washes it out for the sake of a guest's appetite, because the guest's appetite is for tripe.

After all, a man considers what wares are needed in such and such a city and what wares its inhabitants want to buy; those wares he buys, and those he sells, even though the articles be somewhat inferior. I have studied many sciences and taken much pains, so that I may be able to offer fine and rare and precious things to the scholars and researchers, the clever ones and the deep thinkers who come to me. God most High Himself willed this. He gathered here all those sciences, and assembled here all those pains, so that I might be occupied with this work. What can I do? In my own country and amongst my own people there is no occupation more shameful than poetry. If I had remained in my own country, I would have lived in harmony with their temperament and would have practised what they desired, such as lecturing and composing books, preaching and admonishing, observing abstinence and doing all the outward acts.

The Amir Parvāna said to me, 'The root of the matter is acts.' I replied, 'Where are the people of action and the seekers of action, so that I may show them action? Now you seek after words, and have cocked your ears to hear something. If I do not speak, you become upset. Become a seeker of action, so that I may show you action! I am looking all over the world for action, so that I may show you action! I am looking all over the world for a man to whom I may show action. Since I find no purchaser of action but only of words, I occupy myself with words. What do you know of action, seeing that you are not a man of action? Action can only be known through action, science can only be understood through science; form through form, meaning through meaning. Since there is not one traveller upon this road and it is empty, how will they see if we are on the road and in action?'

After all, this action is not prayer and fasting. These are the forms of action; action is an inward meaning. After all, from the time of Adam to the time of Muhammad, God bless him and give him peace, prayer and fasting were not in the form we know, but action was. So this is the form of action; action is a meaning within a man. Similarly you say, 'The medicine acted'; but that is no form of action, it is its meaning. Again they say, 'That man is agent in such and such a city'; they see

86

nothing of mere form but call him agent in respect of the works which appertain to him.

Hence action is not what men have generally supposed. Men suppose that action is this outward show; but if a hypocrite performs that form of action it does not profit him, since the meaning of sincerity and faith is not in him.

The root principle of all things is speech and words. You have no true knowledge of speech and words, and consider them of little account. Speech is the fruit of the tree of action, for words are born of action. God most High created the world by a word.

His command, when He desires a thing, is to say to it
'Be,' and it is.

You may have faith in your heart, but unless you speak it in words it is nothing worth. Prayer too, which is an act, is not perfect unless you recite the Koran. When you say, 'In this present age words are of no account,' you negate this assertion also by means of words. If words are of no account, how is it that we hear you say that words are of no account? After all, you say that also by means of words.

Someone asked: When we do a good deed and perform a righteous act, if we entertain hopes and expectations of a good recompense from God, does that harm us?

The Master answered: By Allah, one must always entertain hope. Faith itself consists of fear and hope. Someone once asked me, 'Hope itself is goodly, so what is this fear?' I replied, 'Show me a fear that is without hope, or a hope without fear. Since the twain are never apart, how can you ask such a question?' For example, a man has sown wheat; he naturally hopes that wheat will come up, whilst at the same time he is afraid lest some impediment or blight may intervene. Hence it is realised that there is no such thing as hope without fear, nor can one ever conceive of fear without hope or hope without fear. Now if a man is hopeful and expectant of recompense and benefit, he will assuredly apply himself with greater diligence to that action. Expectation is a wing, and the stronger the wing the longer the flight. If on the other hand he is without hope he becomes slothful, and no more good and service proceeds from him. Similarly a sick man will drink a bitter medicine and will give up ten sweet pleasures, but if he has no hope of being restored to health how will he be able to endure this?

'Man is a rational animal.' Man is a compound of animal and speech; just as the animal is constant in him and inseparable from him, so too speech is constant in him. If he does not speak outwardly, yet he speaks inwardly; he is constantly speaking. He is like a torrent in which clay is mixed up; the pure water is his speech, whilst the clay is his animality; but the clay in him is accidental. Do you not see how those pieces of clay and material moulds have departed and rotted away, whilst their speech and narration and their sciences, bad and good, have remained?

The 'man of heart' is a plenum; when you have seen him, you have seen all. 'All game is in the belly of the wild ass.' All creatures in the world are parts of him, and he is the whole.

> All, good and evil, parts of the dervish be,
> And whoso is not so, no dervish is he.

Now when you have seen him who is the whole, assuredly you will have seen the whole world, and whomsoever you see after him is a mere repetition. Their speech is contained in the words of the whole; when you have heard their words, every word you may hear thereafter is a mere repetition.

> Whoso beholds him, in whatever place,
> Has seen all men and viewed the whole of space.

The poet says:

> Thyself a true transcription art
> Of the archetype Divine,
> Or else a glass, wherein the King's
> Own loveliness doth shine.
>
> Whatever then in all the world
> Without thyself doth lie,
> Whatso thou cravest, in thyself
> Seek, and declare, "Tis I!'

17

The Nā'ib said: Before this, the unbelievers used to worship and bow down to idols. We are doing the selfsame thing in the present time. We go and bow down and wait upon the Mongols, and yet we consider ourselves Muslims. We have so many other idols in our hearts too, such as greed, passion, temper, envy, and we are obedient to all of them. So we act in the very same way as the unbelievers both outwardly and inwardly; and we consider ourselves Muslims!

The Master answered: But here is something different, in that it enters your thoughts that this conduct is evil and utterly detestable. The eye of your heart has seen something incomparably great which shows up this behaviour as vile and hideous. Brackish water discloses its brackishness to one who has drunk sweet water, and 'things are made clear by their opposites.' So God implanted in your soul the light of faith which sees these things as hideous. Confronted by beauty, this appears hideous. Else, since other men are not so affected, they are perfectly happy in their existing state, saying, 'This is absolutely fine.' God most High will grant you your heart's desire. Where your ambition is, that will be yours. 'The bird flies with its wings, the believer flies with his ambition.'

There are three kinds of creatures. First there are the angels, who are pure intelligence. Worship and service and the remembrance of God are their nature and their food: that they eat and by that they live. Just so the fish in the water lives by the water; its mattress and pillow is the water. Angels are not under any burden of obligation. Inasmuch as the angel is divested and pure of lust, what favour does he confer if he does not gratify his lust or conceive and indulge carnal desire? Since he is pure of these things, he has not to struggle against them. If he obeys God's will, that is not accounted as obedience; for that is his nature, and he cannot be otherwise.

Secondly there are the beasts, who are pure lust, having no intelligence to prohibit them. They too are under no burden of obligation.

Lastly there remains poor man, who is a compound of intelligence and lust. He is half angel, half animal; half snake, half fish. The fish draws him towards the water, the snake draws him towards the earth.

He is forever in tumult and battle. 'He whose intelligence overcomes his lust is higher than the angels; he whose lust overcomes his intelligence is lower than the beasts.'

> The angel is saved by knowledge,
> The beast by brute ignorance;
> Midway between, and struggling—
> Such a predicament is man's!

Now some men have so faithfully followed their intelligence that they have become entirely angels and pure Light. They are the prophets and the saints. They have been delivered out of fear and hope:

> *No fear shall be on them, neither shall they sorrow.*

In some men lust has overcome their intelligence, so that they have taken on entirely the status of animals. Some again are still struggling. These last are the people who feel within them an agony and anguish, a sorrow and a repining; they are not satisfied with their own manner of life. These are the believers. The saints are waiting for them, to bring them unto their own station and to make them as themselves; the satans too are waiting for them, to draw them to the lowest of the low, even towards themselves.

> We desire this, others desire that end;
> Who shall succeed? Whom Fortune makes her friend.

> *When comes the help of God, and victory,*
> *and thou seest men entering God's religion in throngs,*
> *then proclaim the praise of thy Lord, and seek His forgiveness;*
> *for He turns again unto men.*

The exoteric commentators interpret the foregoing Sura as follows. Muhammad, may God bless him and give him peace, had the high ambition, 'I would make all the world Muslims and bring them into the path of God.' When he saw his death approaching he cried, 'Ah, did I not live to call men unto God?' God most High answered, 'Do not grieve. In that very hour when you pass away, provinces and cities which you would conquer by armies and by the sword I will convert to obedience and to the Faith, every one of them, without armies. The sign of that is, that at the end when you are dying you will see men entering in throngs and becoming Muslims. When this sign comes, know that the time for your departure has arrived. Then give praise, and seek forgiveness, for thither you shall come.'

The esoteric commentators, however, explain the text otherwise. According to them it means, that man supposes that he will drive away from himself reprehensible qualities by labour and striving. Having struggled very hard and expended all his powers and means, he falls into despair. Then God most High says to him: You thought that that would come to pass through your own power and action and labour. This is the law which I have laid down, namely, whatever you possess, expend it in My way. After that, My grace will supervene. Upon this infinite road I command you to journey, with the feeble hands and feet that you possess. I know well that with feet so feeble you will never accomplish this journey; indeed, in a hundred thousand years you will not be able to accomplish a single stage of this journey. But when you are going along this road, even as you collapse and fall and have no strength left to struggle farther, then God's loving providence will carry you on. Even so a child, so long as it is a suckling is carried in the arms, but when it is grown it is set free to walk. Now, in this hour when your powers no more remain—in that time when you possessed these powers and struggled hard, from time to time, between sleeping and waking, I showed you grace whereby you derived strength to seek Me and were filled with hope; so in this hour, when your own means fail, behold My graces and gifts and lovingkindnesses! For mer. are coming unto you in throngs such that you would not have witnessed so much as an atom of that after a hundred thousand strivings.

Then proclaim the praise of thy Lord, and seek His forgiveness.

Seek forgiveness for these thoughts and conceits. For you conceived that that task would be accomplished by your own hands and feet, and did not see it would be brought about by Me. Now that you have seen it is brought about by Me, seek forgiveness—

for He turns again unto men.

I do not love the Amir on account of worldly considerations, for his rank and learning and activity. Other men love him for that sake, not seeing the Amir's face, but his back. The Amir is like a mirror, and these attributes are like precious pearls and gold inlaid on the back of the mirror. Those who love gold and pearls look at the back of the mirror; but those who love the mirror do not look at the pearls and the gold. Their faces are always upon the mirror, and they love the mirror for itself as a mirror. Because they see in the mirror fair beauty, they grow not weary of the mirror. But he who has a hideous face full of blemishes sees in the mirror only ugliness; he quickly turns the mirror and looks for those precious stones. Yet what does it harm the face of the mirror, if its back is studded with a thousand kinds of engravings and precious stones?

So God compounded animality and humanity together so that both might be made manifest. 'Things are made clear by their opposites.' It is impossible to make anything known without its opposite. Now God most High possessed no opposite. He says, 'I was a hidden treasure, and I wanted to be known.' So he created this world, which is of darkness, in order that His Light might become manifest. So too He manifested the prophets and the saints, saying, 'Go forth with My Attributes unto My creation.' They are the theatre of the Light of God, so that friend may be disclosed from foe, brother from stranger told apart.

That Reality, *qua* Reality, has no opposite, only *qua* form: as Iblis in comparison with Adam, Pharaoh in comparison with Moses, Nimrod in comparison with Abraham, Abū Jahl in comparison with Muhammad, God bless him and give him peace, and so *ad infinitum.* So through the saints the opposite of God is disclosed; though in reality He has no opposite. Through the enmity and opposition they disclosed, their affairs prospered and acquired wider celebrity.

> *They desire to extinguish with their mouths the light*
> *of God; but God will perfect His light, though*
> *the unbelievers be averse.*

The poet says:

> The moon sheds light when all is dark;
> The dog's reaction is to bark.
> Is that the moon's fault? Tell me true:

'Tis the dog's nature so to do.
The moonlight fills all heaven with mirth,
The dog's a vapour belched by earth.

Many there are whom God most High chastises by means of plenty
and wealth and gold and rulership, and their souls flee away from that.
A dervish saw in Arabia a prince riding, on his brow the illumination
of the prophets and saints. He said, 'Glory be to Him who chastises
His servants by means of affluence!'

18

Ibn Muqrī recites the Koran correctly. Yes: he recites the form of the
Koran correctly, but he has no knowledge of its meaning. This is proved
by the fact that when its meaning is required, he refuses it. He recites
blindly. He is like a man who holds a sable in his hand; he is offered
another sable better than that, but he refuses it. So we realise that he
does not know what sable really is; someone has told him that this is
sable, and in blind compliance he has taken it into his hand. It is like
children playing with walnuts; offer them the nut itself, or the oil of
the walnut, and they will refuse it, saying, 'The walnut is the thing that
goes spinning along. This makes no noise, and it doesn't spin along.'
Yet God's treasuries are many, and God's sciences are many. If he
recites this Koran with knowledge, why does he reject the other Koran?

I expounded to a Koran-teacher: The Koran says,

> Say: 'If the sea were ink
> for the Words of my Lord,
> the sea would be spent before the Words of My Lord are spent.'

Now with fifty drams of ink one can transcribe the whole of this Koran.
This is a symbol for God's knowledge, all knowledge belonging to God,
not this only.

An apothecary puts a pinch of medicine in a piece of paper. You say,
'The whole of the apothecary's shop is in this paper.' That is foolishness. After all, in the time of Moses and Jesus and the other prophets
the Koran existed. God's speech existed, but it was not in Arabic.

I expounded the matter thus, but I saw that it made no impression upon the Koran-teacher; so I let him go.

It is related that in the time of the Prophet, God bless him and give him peace, any of the Companions who knew by heart one Sura or half a Sura was called a great man and pointed out—'He has a Sura by heart'—since they devoured the Koran. To devour a maund of bread or two maunds is certainly a great accomplishment. But people who put bread in their mouths without chewing it and spit it out again can 'devour' thousands of tons in that way. 'Many a Koran-reciter there is whom the Koran curses': this was therefore said of the man who is not apprised of the meaning of the Koran.

Yet it is good that this should be so. God has closed in heedlessness the eyes of certain people so that they may cultivate this present world. If certain men were not made oblivious of the other world, the world would not be populated at all. It is heedlessness that gives rise to cultivation and population. Consider the child, now: he grows up quite heedlessly and becomes tall, but when his reason reaches maturity he ceases to grow. So the cause and reason of cultivation is heedlessness, and the cause of desolation is heedfulness.

What I am saying is motivated by one of two things: either I speak out of envy, or I speak out of compassion. God forbid that it should be envy! It is stupid to envy one who is worthy of envy; what then of one who is not worthy? No; I speak out of great compassion and mercy, for I wish to draw my dear friend on to the true meaning.

It is related that a certain person on the way to the pilgrimage fell into the desert, and was overcome by a mighty thirst. Presently he espied afar off a small and tattered tent. He pushed on to that place, and seeing a young girl cried aloud, 'I am a guest! My goal is gained!'

So saying, he alighted and sat down and asked for water. They brought him water, the consuming of which was hotter than fire and more brackish than salt; as it went down, from lip to throat it burned every part. The man out of extreme compassion addressed himself to counselling the woman.

'I am under an obligation to you for the degree of relief I have found at your hands,' he said. 'Compassion has welled up within me. Give good heed to what I say to you. Behold, Baghdad is nearby, and Kufa and Wasit and the rest. If you are sorely afflicted, by squatting here

94

and there and by rolling along from place to place you can bring yourselves thither. For there are to be found plentiful sweet, cool water,
foods of various kinds, baths, luxuries, rich delights.' And he enumerated the pleasures of those cities.

A moment later a Bedouin came on the scene who was the woman's
husband. He had caught a few brace of desert rats, which he bade the
woman to cook. They gave some to the guest, who being in such
desperate straits partook of them. After that, in the middle of the
night, the guest slept outside the tent. The woman spoke to her husband.

'Didn't you hear all the stories our guest had to tell?'

And she repeated to her husband the guest's entire narrative.

'Don't listen to these things,' the Bedouin answered. 'There are
many envious people in the world. When they see some folk enjoying
ease and plenty they envy them, and want to set them wandering
and to deprive them of their fortune.'

So it is with these people. When anyone out of pure compassion
offers them a piece of advice, they impute it to envy. But if there are
roots in a man, in the end he will turn his face to the truth; if from the
day of the Primordial Covenant a drop has been sprinkled upon him,
in the end that drop will deliver him out of all confusion and misery.
Come then! How long will you be remote from us and estranged?
How long locked up in confusion and melancholy madness? Yet what
is a man to say to a people who have never heard anything the like of
it from anyone, neither from his own teacher?

> Since greatness never once his forebears graced,
> He cannot bear to hear the great ones praised.

Although it is not so attractive at first to face the truth, the farther
one proceeds the sweeter it appears; contrary to the outward form,
which appears attractive at first, but the longer you sit with it the
chillier you become. What is the form of the Koran, compared with its
meaning? Examine a man: what is his form, compared with his meaning?
If the meaning of that form of a man departs, not for a single moment
will he be let loose in the house.

Our Master Shams al-Dīn, God sanctify his spirit, once said: A
great caravan was making its way towards a certain place. They found

95

no sign of habitation, neither any water. Suddenly they came upon a well, but there was no bucket. So they took a kettle and some rope, and lowered this kettle into the well. They drew at the rope, but the kettle broke away. They sent down another, but it broke away too. After that they tied people from the caravan with a rope and sent them down into the well, but they did not come up again.

Now there was an intelligent man present. He said, 'I will go down.' They let him down, and he was nearly at the bottom of the well when a terrible black creature suddenly appeared.

'I will never escape,' the intelligent man remarked. 'But at least let me keep my wits about me and not lose my senses, so that I can see what is going to happen to me.'

'Don't make a long story of it,' the black creature said. 'You're my prisoner. You won't escape unless you give me the right answer. Nothing else will save you.'

'Ask on,' said the man.

'Where is the best place?' came the question.

'I am a prisoner, and helpless,' the man reflected. 'If I say Baghdad or some other place, it may be that I will have insulted his own home-town.' Then he spoke aloud, 'The best place to live in is where a man feels at home. If that is in the bowels of the earth, then that's the best place; if it's in a mousehole, then that's the best place.'

'Well said, well said!' cried the negro. 'You've escaped. You're a man in a million. Now I've let you go, and set free the others on account of your blessing. Henceforth I'll shed no more blood. I bestow on you all the men in the world for the love of you.'

Then he gave the people of the caravan water to satisfy their needs.

The purpose of this story is the inner meaning. One can tell the same meaning in another form, only the lovers of traditional forms accept this version. It is difficult to speak with them; if you speak these very same words in another parable they will not listen.

19

The Master said: Someone said to Tāj al-Dīn Qubā'ī, 'These doctors of divinity come amongst us and deprive the people of their religious beliefs.' He answered, 'It is not the case that they come amongst us and deprive us of our beliefs. Otherwise, God forbid that they should be of us. For instance, suppose you have put a golden collar on a dog; you do not call it a hunting dog by reason of that collar. The quality of being a hunting dog is something specific in the animal, whether it wear a collar of gold or of wool.'

A man does not become a scholar by virtue of robe and turban; scholarship is a virtue in his very essence, and whether that virtue be clothed in tunic or overcoat, it makes no difference. Thus, in the time of the Prophet, God bless him and give him peace, the hypocrites sought to waylay the Faith. So they used to put on the prayer-robe, in order to make those who imitated the ritual slack in the way of religion; for that they could not contrive until they made themselves out to be Muslims. Otherwise, if a Christian or a Jew impugned the Faith, how would people listen to him?

So woe to those that pray
and are heedless of their prayers,
to those who make display
and refuse charity.

This is merely words: you have that light, but you do not have humanity. Seek after humanity: that is the true purpose, the rest is mere longwindedness. When the words are elaborately decorated, the purport is forgotten.

A certain greengrocer was in love with a woman, and he sent messages by the lady's maid.

'I am like this, I am like that. I am in love, I am on fire. I find no peace. I am cruelly treated. I was like this yesterday. Last night such and such happened to me.' And he recited long, long stories.

The maid came into the lady's presence and addressed her as follows.

'The greengrocer sends you greetings and says, "Come, so that I may do this and that to you."'

'So coldly?' the lady asked.

'He spoke at great length,' answered the maid. 'But this was the purport.'

The purport is the root of the matter; the rest is merely a headache.

20

The Master said: Night and day you are at war, seeking to reform the character of women and to cleanse their impurity by yourself. It is better to cleanse yourself in them than to cleanse them in yourself. Reform yourself by means of them. Go to them, and accept whatever they may say, even though in your view their words are absurd. And eschew jealousy; though it is a manly attribute, yet through that good attribute evil attributes enter into you.

It was on account of this truth that the Prophet said, God bless him and give him peace, 'There is no monkhood in Islam.' The way of monks was solitude, dwelling in mountains and not taking women, giving up the world. God most High and Mighty indicated to the Prophet, God bless him and give him peace, a strait and hidden way. What is that way? To wed women, so that he might endure the tyranny of women and hear their absurdities, for them to ride roughshod over him, and so for him to refine his own character.

Surely thou art upon a mighty morality.

By enduring and putting up with the tyranny of women it is as though you rub off your own impurity on them. Your character becomes good through forbearance, their character becomes bad through domineering and aggression. When you have realised this, make yourself clean. Know that they are like a garment; in them you cleanse your own impurities and become clean yourself.

If you cannot succeed with yourself, deliberate with yourself in a rational way as follows. 'Let me pretend that we have never been married. She is a whore. Whenever lust overmasters me I resort to her.' Thus rid yourself of manly pride and envy and jealousy, until such time that beyond such deliberation you experience pleasure in struggling and enduring, and in their absurdities discover spiritual joy. After that, without suchlike deliberation you will desire to endure and struggle and to submit yourself to oppression, since you see definite advantage to yourself in that.

It is related that the Prophet, God bless him and give him peace, one night returned with his Companions from a raid. He bade them beat the drum saying, 'Tonight we will sleep at the gate of the city, and enter tomorrow.' They asked, 'Messenger of God, to what good purpose?' He said, 'It may be that you will see your wives cohabiting with strange men and you would be pained, and a commotion would arise.' One of the Companions did not hear; he entered and found his wife with a stranger.

The way of the Prophet now, God bless him and give him peace, was this. It is necessary to endure pain, ridding oneself of jealousy and manly pride, pain over extravagance and clothing one's wife, and a hundred thousand other pains beyond all bounds, that the Muhammadan world may come into being. The way of Jesus, upon whom be peace, was wrestling with solitude and not gratifying lust; the way of Muhammad, God bless him and give him peace, is to endure the oppression and agonies inflicted by men and women. If you cannot go by the Muhammadan way, at least go by the way of Jesus, that you may not remain altogether outside the pale.

If you have the serenity to endure a hundred buffets, seeing the fruits and harvest of that, or believing in your hidden heart, 'Since they have spoken and told of this, then such a thing is true; let me be patient until the time when that whereof they have told comes to me also'—after that you will see, since you have set your heart on this, saying, 'Though this hour I have no harvest of these sufferings, in the end I will reach the treasures,' you will reach the treasuries, aye, and more than you ever desired and hoped.

If these words have no effect upon you at this moment, after a while when you become more mature they will have a very great effect. That is the difference between a woman and a scholar. Whether you speak to a woman or do not speak, she remains still the same and will not abandon her ways; words have no effect on her, indeed she becomes worse.

For instance, take a loaf and put it under your arm, and deny it to other men, saying, 'I will not give this to anyone at all. Give it? Why, I won't even show it.' Though that loaf has been cast against the door and dogs even will not eat it because bread is so plentiful and cheap, yet the moment you begin to refuse it everybody is after it and set their hearts on it, pleading and protesting, 'Certainly we want to see that loaf which you refuse and keep hidden.' Especially if you keep that loaf in your sleeve for a year, insisting emphatically that you will neither give it away nor show it, their eagerness for the loaf passes all bounds; for 'Man is passionate for what he is denied.'

The more you order a woman, 'Keep yourself hidden,' the greater her itch to show herself; and people through her being hidden become more eager for that woman. So there you sit in the middle, augmenting eagerness on both sides; and you think yourself a reformer! Why, that is the very essence of corruption. If she has in her the natural quality not to want to do an evil deed, whether you prevent her or not she will proceed according to her good temperament and pure constitution. So be easy in mind, and be not troubled. If she is the opposite, still she will go her own way; preventing her in reality does nothing but increase her eagerness.

These fellows keep saying, 'We saw Shams al-Dīn Tabrīzī, Master, we really saw him.' Fool, where did you see him? A man who cannot see a camel on the roof of a house comes along and says, 'I saw the hole of a needle and threaded it.' That is a fine story they tell of the man who said, 'Two things make me laugh—a negro painting his nails black, and a blind man putting his head out of the window.' They are exactly like that. Blind inwardly, they put their heads out of the window of the physical body. What will they see? What does their approval or disapproval amount to? To the intelligent man both are one and the same; since they have seen neither to approve nor to disapprove, whichever they say is nonsense.

First it is necessary to acquire sight, then one must look. Moreover even when sight has been acquired, how can one see so long as they must not be seen? In this world there are so many saints who have achieved union; and other saints there are beyond these, the saints called the Veiled Ones of God. The former saints are ever pleading humbly, 'O Lord God, show unto us one of Thy Veiled Ones.' So long as they do not truly desire him, or so long as he must not be seen of them, however seeing their eyes may be they cannot see him. Now as for those tavern-haunting strumpets by whom none must be seen, of course they cannot reach them or see them. How can one see the Veiled Ones of God or know them without their will?

This is not an easy matter. The angels said:

While we proclaim Thy praise and call Thee Holy.

'We are full of love. We are spiritual beings. We are pure light. They, who are humans, are a gluttonous, blood-spilling handful who shed blood.' All this is in order that man may tremble for himself. For the spiritual angels, who had neither wealth nor rank nor any veil, pure light whose food was the Beauty of God, pure love whose eyes were keen and far-seeing, hovered between disavowal and confession, that man might tremble for himself: 'Woe, what am I? What do I know?' Likewise, that if some light shone upon his face and he felt a certain joy, he might give thanks a thousandfold to God, saying, 'How am I worthy of this?'

This time you will experience greater joy in the words of Shams al-Dīn. For the sail of the ship of man's being is belief. When there is a sail, the wind carries him to a mighty place; when there is no sail, all words are mere wind.

The lover-beloved relationship is very pleasant; everything between them is sheer informality. All these formalities are for the sake of others. This is prohibited to all other but love.

I would have given a great exposition of these words, but the hour is untimely, and one must labour very much and dig out rivers to reach the pool of the heart. The people are weary, or the speaker is weary and proffers an excuse. Else, that speaker who transports not the people out of weariness is not worth two pence.

One cannot call any lover proof of the beauty of the beloved, and one cannot establish in any lover's heart proof of the hatred of the beloved. Hence it is realised that in this matter proofs do not operate. Here one must be a seeker of love.

If in this verse I exaggerate the right of the lover, that is not true exaggeration. Moreover, I see that the disciple has expended all his own 'meaning' for the sake of the master's 'form':

> Thou whose form is fairer far
> Than a thousand meanings are.

For every disciple who comes to the master must first abandon his own 'meaning,' being in need of the master.

Bahā' al-Dīn asked the question: Surely he does not abandon his own 'meaning' for the sake of the master's 'form' but for the sake of the master's 'meaning'?

The Master answered: It is improper that this should be so. If this were so, then both would be masters. Now you must labour to acquire an inward light, that you may escape and be secure from this fire of confusions. When a man has acquired such an inward light, all mundane circumstances appertaining to this world such as rank, command, vizierate, shining upon his inward heart pass like a lightning-flash; just as with worldlings the circumstances of the unseen world, such as the fear of God, and yearning for the world of the saints, shine upon their hearts and pass like a lightning-flash. The people of God have become wholly God's and their faces are turned on God; they are preoccupied with and absorbed in God. Worldly passions, like the lust of an impotent man, show briefly but do not take root and pass away. The worldlings are the opposite of this regarding the affairs of the world to come.

21

The Master said: Sharīf Pāy-sūkhta says:

> He who dispenses of His grace,
> Indifferent to time and space,
> Himself the Spirit of the Whole
> Is independent of the soul.

> Whatever thing your ranging thought
> Within its compass may have brought,
> That thing adores, as only Lord,
> Him who needs not to be adored.

These words are very shameful; they are neither praise of the King nor self-praise. Mannikin, what joy pray does it give you that He should be supremely independent of you? This is not the language of friends, this is the language of enemies. The enemy indeed may say, 'I am indifferent to you and independent.' Now consider the loving and ardent Muslim who when in a state of ecstatic joy addresses that Beloved, that He is independent of him! He would be like a stoker sitting in the baths and saying, 'The Sultan is indifferent and independent of me, a

mere stoker, indeed he is indifferent to all stokers.' What joy would
such a miserable stoker feel in the thought that the king was indifferent
to him? No, the right words for the stoker to speak are the following:
'I was on the roof of the baths. The Sultan passed by. I hailed him. He
looked well at me and then passed me by, still looking at me.' Such
words might well give joy to that stoker. As for saying, 'The king is
indifferent to stokers'—what sort of praise for the king is that, and what
joy does it give the stoker?

> Whatever thing your ranging thought
> Within its compass may have brought—

Mannikin, what thing indeed will pass within the compass of your
thought, except that *men* are independent of your thought and fancy,
and if you relate to them your thoughts they are bored and run away?
What thought can there be of which God is not independent? The
Verse of Self-sufficiency was revealed with reference to the unbelievers;
God forbid that believers should be so addressed! His 'independence'
is indubitable, mannikin; but if you have a spiritual state that is worth
anything at all, He is not 'independent' of you, according to the degree
of your greatness.

Shaikh-i Maḥalla used to say, 'First see, then converse. Every one
sees the Sultan, but it is the favourite who enjoys converse with him.'
The Master said: This is askew and shameful and topsy-turvy. Moses,
upon whom be peace, enjoyed converse and afterwards sought to see.
Moses' station was the station of converse; the station of Muḥammad,
God bless him and give him peace, was the station of seeing. How
then can the Shaikh's statement be correct at all?

The Master said: Someone said in the presence of Shams al-Dīn
Tabrīzī, may God sanctify his soul, 'I have established the existence of
God by a categorical proof.' On the following morning our Master
Shams al-Dīn said, 'Last night the angels came down and blessed that
man, saying, "Praise be to God, he has established the existence of
our God! God give him long life! He did no injury to the right of
mortals!" '

Mannikin, God exists of a certainty; there is no need of a proof to
establish His existence. If you do anything at all, establish yourself in

some rank and station before Him; otherwise, He exists of a certainty without proof.

Nothing there is, that does not proclaim His praise.

Of this there is no doubt. The lawyers are clever men, a hundred per cent competent in their own speciality. But between them and the other world a wall has been built, to preserve their empire of *licet* and *non licet*. Did that wall not exist as a veil for them, no one would consult them and their work would be abolished.

This is like what our great Master said, God sanctify his great soul: 'The other world is like a sea, and this world is like foam. God most Great and Glorious desired to keep the foam in prosperous order. He therefore set certain people with their backs to the sea so as to keep the foam in order. If they were not occupied with that, men would destroy one another and the foam would inevitably fall into ruin. So a tent was pitched for the King, and He kept certain people occupied in constructing this tent. One says, "If I did not make the tent-rope how would the tent come out right?" Another says, "If I do not make the tent-pin where will they tie the rope?" Everybody knows that these are all servants of that King who will sit in the tent and gaze upon the Beloved. If the weaver gives up weaving and seeks to be a vizier, the whole world will remain naked and bare; so he was given a joy in that craft, so that he is content. Therefore that people was created to keep the world of foam in order, and the world was created for the maintenance of that Saint.'

Blessed is he for whose maintenance the world was created, not he for the maintenance of the world. God bestows on every man contentment and happiness in the work that is his, so that if his life should be a hundred thousand years he would still do the same work. Every day his love for that work becomes greater, and subtle skills are born to him in that craft, in which he takes infinite joy and pleasure.

Nothing there is, that does not proclaim His praise.

There is one praise for the rope-maker, another for the carpenter who makes the tent-poles, another for the maker of the tent-pins, another for the weaver who weaves the cloth for the tent, another for the saints who sit in the tent and contemplate in perfect delight.

Now these people who come to us, if we keep silent they are disgusted and hurt, whilst if we say something it must be appropriate to their attainment. We fret, and they go away and reproach us, saying, 'He is bored with us and runs away.' How should the fuel run away from the cook pot, unless the cook pot runs away? It cannot. So the running away of the fire and the fuel is not running away at all. The truth is, that when he sees that the vessel is weak he withdraws some distance from it; so in reality it is the pot that runs away in every case. Therefore our running away is their running away. We are a mirror: if there is a move in them to run away it appears in us; we run away on their account. A mirror is that in which people see themselves; if they see us as weary, that weariness is theirs. For weariness is an attribute of weakness. Here there is no room for weariness: what has weariness to do?

It happened to me in the baths that I showed exceeding submission to Shaikh Ṣalāḥ al-Dīn, and Shaikh Ṣalāḥ al-Dīn showed great submission to me. Confronted by that submission, I protested. The thought came into my mind, 'You are carrying submission beyond proper bounds. Submission is better by degrees; first you kiss the hand of the man, then his foot. Little by little you come to a point where it does not show any more, and he has become habituated. Of course he must not be incommoded, matching courtesy with courtesy, when you have habituated him gradually to that submission.'

You must behave in the same way with friends and enemies, doing things gradually. For instance with an enemy, first you offer him advice little by little; if he does not heed, you strike him; if he does not heed, you drive him away. God says in the Koran:

> *And those you fear may be rebellious*
> *admonish; banish them to their couches,*
> *and beat them.*

The work of the world goes on after this fashion. Do you not see the peace and friendliness of spring? In the beginning it shows warmth little by little, then it becomes greater. Look too at the trees, how little by little they advance; first a smile, then they show their trappings of leaves and fruit, like dervishes and Sufis offering everything, gambling away all that they possess.

A man dispatches every task in this world and the next, exaggerating at the beginning of his task. That task is not attainable by him, if his proper way is discipline. It has been said, if a man eats one maund of bread, he should diminish it daily by a dram's weight, gradually. In that way, before a year or two is past he will have brought down that maund to half a maund, reducing it in such a manner that the body does not notice it. So it is with worship, withdrawing into solitude, attending to the service of God, and prayer. If a man prays with his whole heart, when he enters upon the Way of God first for a while he will observe the five prescribed prayers; after that he will add to them *ad infinitum*.

22

The root of the matter is that Ibn Chāvish should guard against backbiting in regard to Shaikh Ṣalāḥ al-Dīn. Perchance that would profit him, and these shadows and this overcovering would be removed from him.

What does this Ibn Chāvish say regarding himself? Men have left their own country, their fathers and mothers, their households and kinsmen and families, and have journeyed from Hind to Sind, making boots of iron until they were cut to shreds, haply to encounter a man having the fragrance of the other world. How many men have died of this sorrow, not succeeding and not encountering such a man! As for you, you have encountered such a man here in your own house, and you turn your back on him. This is surely a great calamity and recklessness.

He used to counsel me regarding the Shaikh of Shaikhs Ṣalāḥ al-Ḥaqq wa'l-Dīn, God perpetuate his rule, that he was a great and mighty man, as was manifest in his face. 'The least thing, from the day I entered the service of our Master, was that I never heard him any day mentioning your name except as Our Master, Our Lord, Our Creator. I never heard him change this expression on a single day.' Is it not his evil ambitions that have now inhibited him? Today he says of Shaikh Ṣalāḥ al-Dīn that he is nothing.

What wrong has Shaikh Ṣalāḥ al-Dīn ever done him? It is only that, seeing him falling into the pit, he says to him, 'Do not fall into the pit.' This he says out of compassion for him above all other men; and he detests that compassion. For when you do something displeasing to Ṣalāḥ al-Dīn, you find yourself in the midst of his wrath; and when you are plunged in his wrath, how will you be cleared? But whenever you find yourself shrouded and blackened by the smoke of Hell, and he counsels you saying, 'Do not dwell in my wrath; move from the house of my wrath and anger into the house of my grace and my compassion; for if you do something pleasing to me, you will enter the house of my love and my grace'—then your heart is cleared of darkness and becomes full of light.

He counsels you for your own sake and for your own good; and you impute that compassion and counsel to some ulterior motive. What ulterior motive or enmity should a man like that have towards you? Is it not the case, that whenever you are excited by tasting forbidden drinks, or hashish, or by listening to music, or by some other means, in that hour you are pleased with your every enemy, forgiving him and longing to kiss his hands and feet? In that hour, unbeliever and believer are all alike in your eyes. Now Shaikh Ṣalāḥ al-Dīn is the very root of this spiritual joy; all the seas of joy are in him. How should he hate any man, or have designs against him? I take pity for God's servants. And even if it were not so, what designs should he have against such as locusts and frogs? How can he, who possesses such empire and grandeur, be compared with these miserable paupers?

Is it not the case, that they say that the Water of Life is to be found in darkness? That darkness is the body of the saints, in whom is found the Water of Life. The Water of Life can only be encountered in darkness. If you abhor this darkness and fight shy of it, how will the Water of Life ever come to you?

Is it not the case that if you seek to learn sodomy from sodomites, or harlotry from harlots, you cannot learn that unless you put up with a thousand disagreeable things, beatings, and thwarting of your desires? Only so can you attain what you desire, and learn that thing. How then, if you desire to procure eternal and everlasting life, which is the station of the prophets and the saints, and nothing disagreeable ever occurs to you, and you never give up anything, how shall that come to pass?

What the Shaikh prescribes for you is the same as what the Shaikhs of old prescribed, that you leave your wife and children, your wealth and position. Indeed, they used to prescribe for a disciple, 'Leave your wife, that we may take her'; and they put up with that. As for you, when he counsels you a simple thing, how is it that you do not put up with that?

> *Yet it may happen that you will hate a thing which is better for you.*

What do these people say? They are overcome by blindness and ignorance, not considering how a person, when he loves a youth or a woman, will fawn and grovel and sacrifice all his wealth, seeking somehow to trick her by expending his every effort, if only he may conciliate her, night and day not wearying of this, wearying of all else. Then is the love of the Shaikh and the love of God less than this?

As for him, at the least prescription and counsel and boldness he objects and deserts the Shaikh. Hence it is known that he is no lover or seeker. Were he a true lover and seeker, he would put up with many times what we have described. To his heart, dung would be honey and sugar.

23

The Master said: I must go to Tuqat, for that region is warm. Although the climate of Antalya is warm, there the majority of the people are Rumis and do not understand our language; though even amongst the Rumis there are people who do understand it. I was speaking one day amongst a group of people, and a party of non-Muslims was present. In the middle of my address they began to weep and to register emotion and ecstasy.

Someone asked: What do they understand and what do they know? Only one Muslim in a thousand understands this kind of talk. What did they understand, that they should weep?

The Master answered: It is not necessary that they should understand the inner spirit of these words. The root of the matter is the words themselves, and that they do understand. After all, every one acknowledges the Oneness of God, that He is the Creator and Provider, that He controls every thing, that to Him all things shall return, and that it is He who punishes and forgives. When anyone hears these words, which are a description and commemoration of God, a universal commotion and ecstatic passion supervenes, since out of these words comes the scent of their Beloved and their Quest.

Though the ways are various, the goal is one. Do you not see that there are many roads to the Kaaba? For some the road is from Rum, for some from Syria, for some from Persia, for some from China, for some by sea from India and Yemen. So if you consider the roads, the variety is great and the divergence infinite; but when you consider the goal, they are all of one accord and one. The hearts of all are at one upon the Kaaba. The hearts have one attachment, an ardour and a great love for the Kaaba, and in that there is no room for contrariety. That attachment is neither infidelity nor faith; that is to say, that attachment is not confounded with the various roads which we have mentioned. Once they have arrived there, that disputation and war and diversity touching the roads—this man saying to that man, 'You are false, you are an infidel,' and the other replying in kind—once they have arrived at the Kaaba, it is realised that that warfare was concerning the roads only, and that their goal was one.

For instance, if a bowl had a soul it would be the slave of the fashioner of the bowl and would make love to him. Now as for this bowl which hands have fashioned, some say it should be placed like this on the table; some say the inside of it needs to be washed, some say the outside of it needs to be washed; some say all of it; some say it needs not to be washed at all. The diversity of opinion is confined to these things; as to the fact that the bowl certainly had a creator and fashioner and did not come into existence of itself, on this all are agreed and none has a contrary view.

To resume: now all men in their inmost hearts love God and seek Him, pray to Him and in all things put their hope in Him recognising none but Him as omnipotent and ordering their affairs. Such an apperception is neither infidelity nor faith. Inwardly it has no name. But when the water of apperception flows out of the heart towards the mill-race of the tongue and becomes congealed, it acquires form and expression; there it is given the name of infidelity and faith, good and evil. It is the same with plants growing out of the earth. At first they have no form at all; but when they make their appearance in this world, in the beginning they all look fine and delicate and are white. As they set foot farther into this world they become thick and coarse, and acquire a different colour.

When believer and infidel sit together and say nothing by way of expression; they are one and the same. There is no sequestration of thoughts; the heart is a free world. For the thoughts are subtle things, and cannot be judged. 'We judge by outward profession, and God is in charge of men's secret hearts.' God most High uncovers the thoughts in you, not with a hundred thousand labours and efforts are you able to get rid of them. As for the saying that God has no need of any instrument, do you not see how He uncovers those ideas and thoughts in you without any instrument, without any pen, without any pigment?

Those thoughts are like birds of the air, and wild deer. Until you catch them and imprison them in a cage, it is not allowable by law to sell them. It is not in your power to sell a bird on the wing; for delivery is a condition of sale, and since it is not in your power, how can you deliver it?

Thoughts then, so long as they are in the heart, are without name and token; they cannot be judged either for unbelief or for Islam. Would any judge say, 'In your heart you agreed on this, or you sold thus,' or 'Come, take an oath that in your heart you did not think thus'? No judge would say that, because no one can judge the heart. Thoughts are birds of the air. Once, however, they have been expressed, then immediately they can be judged as belonging to unbelief or Islam, good or evil.

There is a world of bodies, a world of ideas, a world of fantasies, a world of suppositions. God most High is beyond all worlds, neither within them nor without them. Consider then how God controls these ideas, forming them without material means, without pen or instrument. As for this fancy or that idea, if you were to tear open the breast and search particle by particle you would never find that thought within it; not in the blood, not in the vein, not above, not below, not in any part whatever would you find it, being immaterial and not in time or space; neither would you find it without the breast.

Since His control over these ideas is so subtle as to be without trace, consider how subtle and without trace is He who is the Creator of all these! Just as these physical bodies are gross in relation to the inner ideas of the persons, so these subtle and insubstantial ideas in relation to the subtlety of God are gross bodies and forms.

> If out of the veil appeared
> The Holy Spirit, then
> As gross flesh would be reckoned
> The minds and souls of men.

God most High is not contained within this world of ideas, nor in any world whatsoever. For if He were contained within the world of ideas, it would necessarily follow that he who formed the ideas would comprehend God, so that God would then not be the Creator of the ideas. Thus it is realised that God is beyond all worlds.

> *God has indeed fulfilled the vision He*
> *vouchsafed to His Messenger truly:*
> *'You shall enter the Holy Mosque,*
> *if God wills.'*

All men say, 'We will enter the Kaaba.' Some men say, 'If God wills, we will enter.' Those who use the expression 'if God wills' are the true lovers of God. For the lover does not consider himself in charge of things and a free agent; he recognises that the Beloved is in charge. Hence he says, 'If the Beloved wills, I will enter.'

Now the literalists take the Holy Mosque to be that Kaaba to which people repair. Lovers, however, and the elect of God, take the Holy Mosque to mean union with God. So they say, 'If God wills, we will attain Him and be honoured with the sight of Him.' But for the beloved to say 'If God wills' is rare indeed. It is the tale of a stranger, and it requires a stranger to hear and to be able to hear the tale of a stranger. God has certain servants who are beloved and well-loved, and God most High seeks after them, discharging on their behalf all the duties of a lover. Just as the lover would say 'If God wills I will enter,' so God most High says on behalf of that stranger 'If God wills.'

If I were to occupy myself with expounding that subtlety, even the saints who have attained God would lose the thread of the discourse. How then is it possible to speak of such mysteries and mystic states to mortal men? 'The pen reached thus far, and then its point broke.'

One man does not see a camel on the top of a minaret; how then shall he see the thread of a hair in the mouth of the camel?

To resume the former exposition: those lovers who say, 'if God wills,' that is, 'The Beloved is in charge: if the Beloved wills, we will enter the Kaaba'—such men are absorbed in God. There is no room for other, and the remembrance of other is unlawful. What place is there for other? For until a man has effaced himself, God is not contained there. 'There is none dwelling in the house but God.'

The vision He vouchsafed to his Messenger: now this vision is the dreams of lovers and true men of God, and the interpretation of that vision is revealed in the other world. When you see in a dream that you are riding on a horse, you will gain your goal; yet what connexion has the horse with the goal? If you dream that you have been given coins of good currency, the meaning is that you will hear true and good words from a learned man; in what respect does a coin resemble a word? If you dream that you have been hanged on a gibbet, you will become the chief of a people; how does a gibbet resemble chieftainship and leadership? So it is that we have said that the affairs of the world are a dream. 'This world is as the dream of a sleeper': their interpretation in the other world will be quite otherwise, not resembling this. That will be interpreted by a Divine Interpreter, for to Him all things are revealed.

Similarly a gardener on entering the orchard looks at the trees. Without seeing the fruit on the branches, he judges this tree to be a date, that a fig, that a pomegranate, that a pear, that an apple. Since the true man of God knows the science of trees, there is no need to wait for the resurrection for him to see the interpretations, what has transpired and what was the issue of that dream. Such a man has seen aforetime what the issue will be, just as a gardener knows aforetime what fruit this branch will surely yield.

All things in this world, wealth, wife and raiment, are sought after for something other, they are not sought for themselves. Do you not see that even if you had a hundred thousand dirhams and were hungry and could not find any bread, you would not be able to eat and feed yourself on those dirhams? A wife is for the sake of children, and to satisfy the passion. Clothes are to ward off the cold. In like manner all things are concatenated with God most Glorious: He is sought and desired for His own sake, not for any other thing. For inasmuch as He is beyond all and better than all and nobler than all and subtler than all, how should He be desired for less than Himself? So 'unto Him is the final end'; when they have reached Him, they have reached their entire goal, beyond there is no transcending.

This human soul is a forum of doubts and difficulties. By no means can it be rid of doubts and difficulties except it be truly in love; then all its doubts and difficulties vanish. 'Your love for a thing renders you blind and deaf.' When Iblis would not bow down before Adam and opposed the Divine command, he said:

> *Thou createdst me of fire, and him Thou createdst of clay.*

'My essence is of fire, and his essence is of clay. How is it seemly for the higher to bow down before the lower?' When God cursed Iblis on account of this sin and opposition and contending with God and banished him, he said, 'Alas, O Lord! You made all things. This was your tempting me; now you are cursing me and banishing me.' When Adam sinned, God most High expelled him from Paradise. God most High said to Adam, 'O Adam, when I egged you on and urged you to commit that sin why did you not dispute with Me? After all, you had a perfect case. You did not say, "All things proceed from Thee and Thou madest all. Whatever Thou desirest in the world comes to pass, and whatever Thou desirest not will never come to pass." You had such a right and clear and valid case, why did you not argue it?' Adam answered, 'I knew that well, Lord. But I did not forget my manners in Thy presence, and Love did not suffer me to reprove.'

The Master said: This sacred law is a watering-place, a fountain-head. It may be likened to the court of a king, wherein are the king's edicts, to command and prohibit, government, equity, justice for nobles and commons. All the edicts of the king are infinite and innumerable, very good and very beneficial, and on them the stability of the world rests. But the status of dervishes and fakirs is one of conversation with the King, and of knowing the science of the Ruler. What is knowledge of the science of the edicts, compared with knowing the science of the Ruler and conversation with the King? There is a vast difference.

My companions and their various estates are as a school in which there are many scholars. The headmaster pays each scholar according to his qualification, giving to one ten, one twenty, one thirty. We too dispense our words according to each man's degree and qualification. 'Speak to men according to the degree of their intelligence.'

24

Every man puts up these sacred edifices with a particular intention: either to display his generosity, or for the sake of fame, or to gain a reward in heaven. God most High should be the true object in exalting the rank of the saints and honouring their tombs and graves. They themselves require not to be honoured, for they are honoured in themselves. If a lamp desires to be placed on high, it desires that for the sake of others, not for its own sake. What matters it to a lamp, whether it is below or above? It is still a lamp shedding light. But it desires that its light should reach others. The sun which is in the height of heaven—if it were below it would still be the same sun, only the world would remain in darkness. So the sun is on high not for its own sake but for that of others. It follows then that the saints are exalted above and indifferent to such things as 'above' and 'below' and the reverence of men.

You yourself, being vouchsafed a fragment of ecstasy and a flash of grace from the other world, in that moment are indifferent to 'above' and 'below' and mastery and leadership, and self too which is nearer to you than all; these things do not enter your mind. So how should the saints, who are the seam and mine and source of that light and ecstasy, be fettered by 'below' and 'above'? Their glorying is in God; and God is independent of 'below' and 'above.' This 'below' and 'above' belongs to us who have feet and heads.

The Prophet, God's blessings be upon him, said: 'Do not prefer me above Jonah son of Matthew, in that his ascension was in the belly of the whale while my ascension was in heaven upon the Throne.' He meant, 'Do not assign preferment to me over him, if you prefer me at all, for the reason that his ascension was in the belly of the whale while mine was above in heaven. For God most High is neither above nor below; His epiphany is the same, whether above or below and in the belly of the whale. He is exalted far above 'above' and 'below'; all things are one to Him.'

There are many persons who perform works having a different aim, whilst God's purpose is other. God most Glorious desired that the religion of Muhammad, God bless him and give him peace, should be high honoured and spread abroad and should abide for ever and ever. So consider how many commentaries have been made on the Koran, in how manifold volumes. The aim of the writers was to display their own virtuosity. Zamakhsharī filled his *Kashshāf* with so many minutiae of grammar and lexicography and rhetoric in order to display his own learning; but it was also in order that God's purpose might be attained, namely the exaltation of the religion of Muhammad. So all men too are doing God's work, though ignorant of God's aim. God has another purpose for them; He desires that the world should remain in being. They are occupied with their lusts; they gratify their lust with a woman for the sake of their own enjoyment, but the result is the birth of a child. They labour similarly for their own pleasure and enjoyment, and that too is a means of maintaining the order of the world. In reality therefore they are serving God, only they do not act with that intention.

In the same way they build mosques at such great expense upon doors and walls and roof, but all with a view to the kiblah. The kiblah is the true aim and object of honour, and its honouring is all the greater for all that that was not their aim.

This greatness of the saints is not a formal matter. By Allah, indeed they have an elevation and a greatness, but it is beyond space and time. The dirham is above the copper-piece: what is the meaning of 'above the copper-piece'? From the standpoint of form it is not above. Suppose for instance that you place a silver dirham on the roof, and a gold piece under; assuredly the gold will be superior in all circumstances. Gold is above silver, and ruby and pearl are above gold, whether the one or the other is 'below' or 'above.' Similarly the chaff is 'above' the sieve and the corn remains 'under' it: how should the chaff be 'above' the corn? Assuredly the corn is 'above' though physically it is below. So you speak of the superiority of the corn not from the standpoint of form; in the world of realities, inasmuch as that substance is inherent in it, it is 'above' in all circumstances.

25

A person entered. The Master said: He is beloved, and humble, this is due to his substance. Similarly if a branch is loaded with fruit, that fruit draws it down; whereas the branch which has no fruit raises its head on high, like the white poplar. When the fruit exceeds bounds, they put props under the branch so that it may not come down altogether.

The Prophet, God bless him and give him peace, was extremely humble. All the fruits of this world and the next were gathered upon him, so of course he was humbler than all men. He said, 'No man ever preceded the Messenger of God in making a greeting.' No man was able to precede the Prophet in offering greetings because the Prophet would outstrip him out of extreme humility and so would greet him first. Even supposing that he did not greet the other first, even so he was humble and preceded the other in speaking, for they learned the greeting from him and gave heed to him. All that men of former and latter times possess, they possess it all as a reflection of him, and are his shadow. Though a man's shadow may enter the house before him, in reality the man precedes, though in form the shadow precedes. Grant that the shadow precedes the man, yet it is a derivative of the man.

These characteristics are not a product of the present moment; these particles existed from that primeval time in the particles and parts of Adam—some bright, some half-bright, some dark. In this hour they become apparent, but this splendour and brightness is of aforetime; its particle in Adam was altogether purer and brighter and more humble.

Some men look at the beginning, and some men look at the end. These who look at the end are great and mighty men, for their gaze is fixed on the issue and the world beyond. But those who look at the beginning, they are the more elect. They say, 'What need is there for us to look at the end? If wheat is sown at the beginning, barley will not grow at the end, if barley is sown, wheat will not grow.' So their gaze is fixed on the beginning. There are other people still more elect who look neither at the beginning nor at the end, the beginning and the end do not enter their minds, they are absorbed in God. And there are yet other people who are absorbed in worldly things; they look neither at the beginning nor at the end, being exceeding heedless; these are the fodder of Hell.

So it is realised that Muhammad was the foundation. 'But for thee I would not have created the heavens.' Every thing that exists, honour and humility, authority and high degree, all are of his dispensation and his shadow, for all have become manifest from him. Even so, whatever this hand does it does in the shadow of the Mind, for the Mind's shadow is over it; though in truth the Mind has no shadow, yet it has a shadow without a shadow, just as 'meaning' has an entity without an entity. Were not the shadow of Mind over a man, all his members would become atrophied; the hand would not grasp in due manner, the foot could not go straight upon the road, the eye would not see anything, whatever the ear heard it would hear awry. So these members in the shadow of Mind perform all their various tasks duly, well and appropriately. In reality all those actions proceed from the Mind; the members are the instrument.

In like manner there is a great man, the caliph of his time. He is like the Universal Mind, and the minds of other men are as his members. Whatever they do is in his shadow. If anything crooked issues from them, that is because the Universal Mind has lifted its shadow from his head. So it is that when a man begins to go mad and engages in unseemly activities, everybody realises that reason has departed from his head and no more casts its shadow over him; he is far exiled from the shadow and shelter of Mind.

Mind is a congener of the angel. Though the angel has a definite form and feathers and wings while Mind has not, in reality they are one and the same, act the same and are one in nature. One must not regard the form when in reality they act the same. For instance, if you dissolve their form they will all be Mind; nothing outward would remain of feathers and wings. So we realise that they were all Mind, but embodied; they are called embodied intelligences. Similarly a bird may be fashioned of wax complete with feathers and wings, but for all that it is wax. Do you not see that when you melt it, the bird's feathers and wings and head and feet altogether become wax? Nothing whatsoever remains that can be separated out; all turns to wax. So we realise that it is wax, and the bird that was fashioned of wax is the same wax, embodied and having taken on a certain shape but wax nevertheless. Ice likewise is nothing but water; therefore when you melt it it all becomes water. But before it became ice and was still water, you could not take it into your hand and it would not enter the hand; once it was frozen however you could take it in your hand and put it in your skirt. So there is no greater difference than this; the ice is still water, and they are one and the same thing.

The situation of man is like this. They took the feathers of an angel, and tied them to the tail of an ass, that haply the ass in the ray and society of the angel might become an angel. For it is possible that he may become of the same complexion as the angel.

> Reason lent to Jesus pinions
> And to heaven he flew and higher;
> Had his ass had half a wing,
> He would not have hugged the mire.

So what cause for wonder would it be, if his ass should become a man? God is able to do all things. After all, the child when it is first born is worse than an ass; it puts its hand into filth and carries it to its mouth to lick; the mother beats it and prevents it. The ass at least has some sort of discrimination; when it urinates, it opens its legs so that the urine may not trickle on them. Yet the child, which is worse than an ass, God most High is able to make into a man; if He should make the ass a man, what would be so astounding in that? Before God, nothing is a cause for astonishment.

At the resurrection all the members of a man, scattered severally apart, hand and foot and the rest, will speak. The philosophers interpret this allegorically. They say: When the hand 'speaks,' perhaps some sign or token appears on the hand taking the place of speech, such as a scratch or an abscess. It is possible in this sense to say that the hand 'speaks'; it gives information, 'I ate something causing inflammation, so that my hand became like this.' Or the hand is wounded and has become black; men say that the hand 'speaks,' giving information that 'A knife struck me' or 'I rubbed myself against a black pot.' The 'speaking' of the hand and the other members is after this manner. So much for the philosophers. The Sunni theologians say: God forbid! No indeed! On the contrary, this sensible hand and foot will speak, just as the tongue speaks. On the day of resurrection a man will deny, saying, 'I did not steal.' His hand will say, 'Yes, you stole, I took' in plain language. That person will turn to his hand and foot, saying, 'You did not speak of old; how is it that you speak now?' It will say:

God gave us speech, as He gave everything speech.

'That Person gave me speech who gave everything speech. He gives speech to door and wall, stone and clod. That Creator who gives speech to everyone also gives me speech.' Your tongue causes you to speak; your tongue is a piece of flesh, the hand is a piece of flesh, speech is a piece of flesh. Is the tongue endowed with reason? From what you have seen in plenty, it does not appear impossible to you. Otherwise, the tongue is a pretext with God; when He commanded it to speak it spoke. Whatsoever He commands and decrees, that thing speaks.

Words come according to the attainment of a man. Our words are like water which a superintendent of water lets flow. What does the water know, into which plain the superintendent has let it flow, whether into a cucumber-bed, or an onion-bed, or a rose-bed? This I know: that when the water comes in abundance, there the lands are thirsty and extensive, whilst if it comes in small quantity I know that the land is small—a little orchard, or a tiny courtyard. 'He inculcates wisdom by the tongue of the preachers according to the aspirations of the listeners.' I am a cobbler: the leather is plentiful, but I cut and stitch according to the size of the foot.

> I am the shadow of a man,
> I am his measure;
> So much as his stature is,
> So much my treasure.

In the earth there is an animalcule which lives under the earth and is in darkness. It has no eyes or ears, because in the place where it dwells there is no need for eyes and ears. Since it has no need of eyes, why should it be given them? It is not that God has a scarcity of eyes and ears, or that He is miserly; but He gives in need. A thing given needlessly would turn into a burden. God's wisdom and grace and bounty remove burdens; how should He impose a burden on anyone? For instance, to give a tailor the tools of a carpenter, adze, saw, a file and the rest, and to say 'Take these'—that would prove a burden to him since he cannot work with them. So He gives a thing according to need, and that is all.

Just as those worms live in that darkness under the earth, so there are men who are content and satisfied to dwell in the darkness of this world, having no need of that world and yearning not for the Vision. Of what use to them would be the eye of clairvoyance and the ear of understanding? Their work in this world prospers with the sensible eye which they possess; since they have no design on the other side, why give them the clairvoyance which would be useless to them?

> Do not suppose no travellers
> Yet go upon the road,
> Men perfect in all attributes,
> The traceless men of God.
>
> Because you are not privy to
> The secrets of the skies,
> You fancy in your vain conceit
> None others gain that prize.

Now this world goes on by reason of heedlessness; if it were not for heedlessness, this world would not remain in being. Yearning for God, recollection of the world to come, intoxication, ecstasy—these are the architects of the other world. If all these should supervene, we would to a man depart to the other world and would not remain here. God most High desires that we should be here, so that there may be two worlds. So he has appointed two sheriffs, one heedlessness and the other heedfulness, that both houses may remain inhabited.

26

The Master said: If I appear to be remiss in gratitude and appreciation and offering thanks for the kindnesses and endeavour and support you show me both directly and indirectly, this is not out of arrogance or indifference, or because I do not know what it behoves the recipient of a favour to say and do by way of requital. But I was aware from the purity of your faith that you do those things sincerely for the sake of God; so I leave it to God to thank you Himself, since you have done these things for Him. If I were to concern myself with thanking you and doing you verbal honour and praising you, it would be as though some part of the reward which God is going to give you had already come to you, some part of your recompense had already been paid.

Humble attitudes, offering thanks and applause——these are worldly pleasures. When you have gone to worldly pains, such as the sacrifice of wealth and position, it is better that the recompense should come entirely from God. Therefore I do not offer thanks because the offering of thanks is a worldly matter.

No one can eat wealth. Wealth is sought after for other than itself. With wealth horses, servant-girls and slaves are purchased and appointments are sought, so that men praise and applaud them. So it is the world itself that is held in high esteem, and to it the praise and applause is directed.

Shaikh Nassāj of Bukhara was a great and spiritual man. The learned and great ones used to come to visit him, kneeling before him. The Shaikh was unlettered. They desired to hear from his tongue the expounding of the Koran and Traditions of the Prophet. He would say, 'I do not know Arabic. You translate the verse of the Koran or the Tradition, so that I may tell you its meaning.' They would translate the verse, and then he would begin to expound and verify it. He would say, 'The Prophet, God bless him and give him peace, was in such and such a situation when he uttered this verse. The circumstances were as follows.' Then he would explain in detail the level of that situation, the ways leading up to it, and how the Prophet ascended to it.

One day a descendant of 'Alī was praising in his presence a certain cadi, saying, 'There is no cadi like him anywhere in the world. He does not take bribes. He dispenses justice amongst men without partiality or favour, purely and sincerely for the sake of God.' Shaikh Nassāj replied, 'What you are saying, that he does not take bribes, is certainly a lie. You, a descendant of 'Alī, of the family of the Prophet, God bless him and give him peace, praise and applaud him on the grounds that he does not take bribes. Is this not a bribe? What bribe could be better than this, that you should give such an account of him to his face?'

Shaikh al-Islām Tirmidhī once said. 'The reason why Saiyid Burhān al-Dīn, God sanctify his great soul, expounds truths so well is because he studies the books and secret writings and treatises of the masters.' Someone remarked, 'Well, you also study them. How is it that you do not speak as he does?' Tirmidhī answered, 'He is a man of suffering and striving and godly works.' The man said, 'Why do you not speak of this and mention this? You only repeat what you have read. That is the root of the matter. We speak of that; you too speak of that!'

They were not concerned with the other world at all; they had fixed their hearts upon this world entirely. Some had come for the sake of eating bread, some to inspect the bread. They desire to learn these words and then to sell them. These words are like a beautiful bride; if a beautiful maiden is purchased to sell again, how can that maiden love her purchaser or fix her heart on him? Since the pleasure of that merchant is in selling, he is as good as impotent; he buys the girl to sell her, not having the manhood and virility to purchase her for himself.

If a fine Indian sword falls into the hands of a hermaphrodite, he takes it in order to sell it; if a Pehlevi bow falls into his hands, that is also in order to sell it since he has not the strength of arm to draw the bow. He desires that bow for the string's sake, and he has not the aptitude for the string. He is in love with the string. When the hermaphrodite sells that, he gives the price of it for rouge and indigo. What else shall he do? Marvellous! When he sells it, what shall he buy better than that?

These words are Syriac! Beware, do not say, 'I have understood.' The more you have understood and grasped them, the farther you will be from understanding them. The understanding of this is in not understanding. All your trouble and misfortune and disappointment arise from that understanding. That understanding is a fetter for you; you must escape from that understanding, to be anything at all.

You say, 'I filled the sheep-skin from the sea, and the sea could not be contained in my sheep-skin.' This is absurd. Yes, if you say, 'My sheep-skin was lost in the sea,' that is excellent; that is the root of the matter. Reason is excellent and desirable until it brings you to the door of the King. Once you have reached His door, divorce reason; for in that hour reason is a sheer loss to you, a highway robber. When you have reached the King, surrender yourself to Him; you have no use then for the how and the wherefore.

For instance, you have an uncut cloth which you want to have cut into a tunic or a cloak. Reason has brought you a tailor. Until that moment reason was fine, for it brought the cloth to the tailor. Now in this very moment reason must be divorced and you must abandon yourself wholly to the control of the tailor. In the same way, reason is fine for the sick man until it brings him to the physician; when it has brought him to the physician, after that reason is no use to him, and he must surrender himself to the physician.

Your companions hear your clandestine cries. It becomes evident who of them has something, who has a true substance in him and a responsive soul. Amongst a train of camels, the camel that is in rut becomes evident from his eyes, his manner of walking, his foam and other things.

> *Their mark is on their faces, the trace of prostration.*

Though it is the root of the tree that drinks, it becomes evident on the head of the tree, through the branches and leaves and fruit. The tree that does not drink and is withered, how shall it remain concealed? These loud shouts which they utter—the secret of this is that they understand many words from a single word, from a single letter realise all the overtones. It is like a man who has read the *Wasīṭ* and the *Muṭawwal* books; as soon as he hears a single word from the *Tanbīh*, inasmuch as he has read its commentary he understands from one problem all the root principles and problems. He offers observations on that single letter as much as to say, 'Underlying this I understand many things and see many things. That is because I have laboured much on that subject, turning night into day, and I have found the treasures.'

> *Did We not expand thy breast for thee?*

The expansion of the breast is infinite. Once that expansive commentary has been read, from a hint a man understands much. He who is still a beginner understands of that word only the meaning of that one word; what inner knowledge and ecstasy should be his? Words come according to the capacity of the hearer. If a man does not draw out, the wisdom also does not come out. According as he draws and sucks, so the wisdom descends. Else he says, 'Amazing! Why do the words not come?' The answer comes, 'Amazing! Why do you not draw?' He who gives you not the power to listen gives neither to the speaker the impulse to speak.

In the time of the Prophet, God bless him and give him peace, a certain unbeliever had as a slave a Muslim, a man of true substance. One morning his master ordered him, 'Fetch basins. I am going to the baths.' On the way they went the Prophet, God bless him and give him peace, was praying in the mosque with his Companions. The slave said, 'Master, for God's good sake take this bowl for a moment, so that I may make a couple of genuflections, then I will attend you.' Entering the mosque, he prayed. The Prophet, God bless him and give him peace, came out, and his Companions also came out. The slave remained alone in the mosque. His master waited for him till mid-morning, then he shouted, 'Come out, slave!' The slave answered, 'They won't let me go, as the work has got beyond bounds.' The master put his head inside the mosque to see who it was that would not let the slave go. But for a shoe and a shadow he saw nobody; nobody stirred. He said, 'Well, who is it that won't let you come out?' The slave replied, 'The same One who will not suffer you to come in, the very same One whom you do not see.'

Man is always in love with the thing which he has never seen nor heard nor understood; night and day he seeks after it. I am the slave of him whom I do not see, who is weary and runs away from what he has understood and seen. It is for this reason that the philosophers deny ocular vision, saying: If you see, it is possible that you will become satiated and weary, and this is not feasible. The Sunni theologians say: It is in the moment when He appears single-coloured. For in every instant He appears in a hundred colours.

Every day He is upon some labour.

If He should reveal Himself a hundred thousand times, not one will resemble another. You also this very moment see God; every instant in His works and acts you see Him multicoloured. Not one act of His resembles another act. In time of gladness is one epiphany, in time of weeping is another epiphany, in time of fear another, in time of hope another. Since the acts of God, and the epiphany of His acts and works, are infinitely various, not one being like another, therefore the epiphany of His Essence is likewise infinitely various as is the epiphany of His acts: judge of that by this analogy.

You yourself too, being a part of the Divine omnipotence, every moment take on a different form and are not constant in any one.

There are certain servants of God who proceed from the Koran to God. Others more elect come from God, find the Koran here, and know that God has sent it down.

It is We who have sent down the Remembrance,
and We watch over it.

The commentators say that this refers to the Koran. This too is good; but it can also mean, 'We have placed in you a substance, a seeking, a yearning. We watch over that, not letting it go to waste but bringing it to a definite place.'

Once say 'God', then stand firm under all calamities that rain upon you. A certain man came to Muhammad, God bless him and give him peace, and said to him, 'Truly I love you.' The Prophet said, 'Take heed what you say.' The man repeated, 'Truly I love you.' The Prophet said, 'Take heed what you say.' The man said, 'Truly I love you.' The Prophet said, 'Now stand firm, for with my own hand I am going to slay you, woe upon you!'

In the time of Muhammad, God bless him and give him peace, a certain man said, 'I do not want this religion. By Allah, take back this religion, for I do not want it. Ever since I entered your religion I have not had peace for a single day. Wealth has gone, wife has gone, child has vanished, respect has vanished, strength has vanished, lust has vanished.' The Prophet answered, 'God forbid! Wherever our religion has gone, it comes not back without uprooting a man and sweeping cleaning his house.'

None but the purified shall touch it.

For it is as one beloved. So long as there remains in you a single trace of self-love, He will not show His face to you and you will not be worthy of union with Him, neither will He give you access to Him. You must become wholly indifferent to yourself and the world, become the enemy of yourself, so that the Friend may show His face. So our religion, in whatsoever heart it lodges, withdraws not its hand from that heart until it brings that heart to God and dissevers it from all that is unlawful.

The Prophet, God bless him and give him peace, said to that man, 'For this reason you have not peace and do sorrow, because sorrowing is an evacuation of those first joys'. So long as that thing remains in your stomach, they do not give you anything to eat. At the time of evacuation a man eats nothing; when he has finished evacuating, then he eats food. You too be patient, and grieve; grieving is an evacuation. After the evacuation joy supervenes, a joy which has no sorrow, a rose without a thorn, a wine without crop-sickness.

Why, in this world night and day you seek quiet and rest. That cannot be attained in this world; yet not for one instant you give up seeking. Such comfort even as you find in this world is like a lightning-flash which passes and endures not. And then, which lightning is it? Lightning there is full of hail, full of rain, full of snow, full of suffering. For instance, a man has set out for Antalya. He goes towards Caesarea hoping to reach Antalya, and does not abandon his efforts for all that it is impossible for him by this route to reach Antalya. But the man who goes by the Antalyan road, though he is lame and feeble, yet will reach his goal, since that is the end of the road.

Inasmuch as no task in this world can be accomplished without suffering, neither likewise any task aimed at the next world, at all events devote this suffering with the next world in view, so that it may not be wasted! 'You say, O Muhammad, take away religion from me, for I cannot find rest. How should our religion let any man go, before it brings him to the goal?'

Men tell how a certain teacher out of indigence wore in the winter season a single garment of cotton. By chance the torrent had brought down a bear out of the mountains, carrying it along with its head hidden in the water. The children, seeing its back, cried, 'Teacher, look! A fur coat has fallen into the water, and you are cold. Take it!'

The teacher in the extremity of his need and coldness jumped in to catch the fur coat. The bear quickly plunged its claws into him. The teacher was thus caught by the bear in the water.

'Teacher,' the boys shouted, 'either fetch the fur coat, or if you cannot, let it go, and you come out!'

'I am letting the fur coat go,' answered the teacher. 'But the fur coat isn't letting me go. What am I to do?'

How should God's ardour let you go? Here is cause for thanks, that we are not in our own hands, we are in God's hands. Even so a child when it is small knows naught but milk and its mother. God most High by no means left the child there; He led it on to eat bread and to play, and in like manner drew it on from there till He brought it to the stage of reason. So too in this worldly state, which is infancy compared with the other world and another kind of breast—God does not leave you there, but brings you thither, so that you may realise that this was infancy and nothing at all. 'I am amazed at a people who are dragged to Paradise in chains and fetters. *Take him, and fetter him, and then roast him*—in Paradise, then roast him in union, then roast him in Beauty, then roast him in Perfection.'

Fishermen do not drag out a fish all at once. When the hook has entered its throat they draw it a little, so that it may lose blood and become weak and feeble; they let it loose again, then again draw it in, until it becomes altogether weak. When the hook of Love falls into a man's throat, God most High draws him gradually so that those bad faculties and blood which are in him may go out of him little by little. *God grasps, and outspreads.*

'There is no God but God': that is the faith of the common folk. The faith of the elect is this: 'There is no He but He.' So, a man sees in a dream that he has become king, and is seated on the throne, servants and chamberlains and princes standing around him. He says, 'I must be the king, and there is no king other than I.' This he says in his sleep; when he awakens and sees nobody in the house but himself, then he says, 'I am, and there is nobody other than I.' For this a wakeful eye is necessary; a slumbrous eye cannot see this, for this is not its function.

Every sect denies every other sect. These people say, 'We are true and revelation belongs to us, and they are false.' Those people say exactly the same. So the two and seventy creeds deny one another, then say with one accord that all are without revelation. So all are in accord on there being no revelation to any of the others, and agree also that out of the lot of them only one has revelation. There is therefore a need for a believer having discrimination and sagacity to know which one that is. 'The believer is sagacious, discriminating, understanding, intelligent.' Faith is that same discrimination and perception.

Someone interjected: Those who do not know are many, and those who know are few. If we are to occupy ourselves with distinguishing between those who do not know and have no true substance and those who do possess that substance, it will be a long business.

The Master answered: Though it is true that those who do not know are many, when you know a few you have known them all. In the same way when you have known a single handful of corn, you know all the corn-stacks in the world. If you have tasted a piece of sugar, though halwa is made in a hundred different varieties, from the sugar you have tasted you know that sugar is in the halwa, since you have known the sugar. If a man who has eaten sugar from a sugar-cane (*shākh*) does not recognise sugar, maybe he has two horns (*shākh*)!

If these words appear repetitious to you, that is because you have not understood the first lesson, so it was necessary for me to say this every day. There was once a teacher, and a boy attended him for three months but did not go beyond 'A has nothing.' The boy's father came and said, 'I don't fail to pay your fees. If there has been any failure, tell me and I will pay more.' The teacher answered, 'The failure was not on your part, but the child doesn't go beyond this point.' He summoned the boy and said, 'Say, A has nothing.' The boy said, 'Has nothing'; he could not say 'A.' The master said, 'You see what the situation is. As he has not passed beyond this point and has not yet learned this, how can I give him a new lesson?' The father said, 'Praise belongs to God, the Lord of all being!'

We do not say 'Praise belongs to God, the Lord of all being' because there is a shortage of bread and blessing. Bread and blessing are without limit; but there is no more appetite, and the guests are sated. That is why 'Praise belongs to God' is said. This bread and this blessing do not resemble mundane bread and blessing, since even without appetite you can force yourself to eat mundane bread and blessing as much as you desire. Since it is inanimate, it follows you wherever you drag it; it has no spirit, to withhold itself from the unworthy. Very different is this Divine blessing, which is wisdom. It is a living blessing. So long as you have an appetite and exhibit utter desire, it comes towards you and becomes your food. But when appetite and inclination fail you cannot eat it and consume it by force. It hides its face in the veil and does not show you its face.

The Master was telling stories of the miracles of the saints. He said: It is not so wonderful or miraculous for a man to go from here to the Kaaba in a day or a moment. Such a miracle happens also to the simoom: in one day and in one moment the simoon travels wherever it wishes. What is a true miracle is this: that God should bring you from a lowly estate to a high estate, that you should travel from there to here, from ignorance to reason, from the inanimate to life. Just as at first you were earth and you were mineral, He brought you to the vegetable world; then you journeyed from the vegetable world to the world of clotted sperm and foetus, from the clotted sperm and the foetus to the animal world, from the animal world to the world of man.

These are the true miracles. God most High brought near to you such a journey. In these stations and ways that you came it never entered your thoughts and imagination that you would come, by which road you came, and how you came and were brought; yet you see most definitely that you have come. Even so you will be brought to a hundred other various worlds. Do not doubt it, and if you are told stories of that, believe them.

A bowl of poison was brought as a present to 'Umar, God be pleased with him.

'Of what use is this?' he asked.

'Its purpose,' they told him, 'is this, that when it is not thought in the public interest to kill a man openly, he is given a little of this and then he dies secretly. If it is an enemy who cannot be slain with the sword, with a little of this he may be killed clandestinely.'

'You have brought me a very good thing,' he said. 'Give it to me to drink; for within me is a mighty enemy whom the sword cannot reach. I have no greater enemy in the world than he.'

'There is no need for you to drink it all up in one gulp,' they told him. 'Just a dram is sufficient. This is sufficient for a hundred thousand persons.'

'He too, my enemy, is not one person,' said 'Umar. 'He is an enemy a thousand men strong, and has overthrown a hundred thousand.'

Thereupon he seized the cup and quaffed it all at one draught. At once the assembled multitude all became Muslims, crying, 'Your religion is true!'

'You have all become Muslims,' commented 'Umar, 'and this infidel has not yet become a Muslim.'

What 'Umar intended thereby was faith. This was not the faith of the common people. He had that faith, and more; indeed, he had the faith of the veracious. He was referring to the faith of the prophets and the elect and absolute certainty. That was what he hoped for.

The report of a lion spread abroad through all parts of the world. A certain man, marvelling at the rumour, made for that thicket from a far distance in order to see the lion. For a year he endured the rigours of the road and travelled from stage to stage. When he arrived at the thicket and espied the lion from afar, he stood still and could not advance closer.

'Why,' they said to him, 'you have set forth on such a long road out of love for this lion. This lion has a special quality: anyone who approaches him boldly, and lovingly rubs his hand upon him, is unharmed by the lion, but if anyone is afraid and timorous the lion is enraged against him. Some indeed he attacks, saying, "What is this bad opinion you have of me?" For such a creature you have trudged on for a year. Now you have reached near to the lion why do you stand still? Advance one step more!'

Not one had the courage to advance a further step. All said, 'The steps we took hitherto were all easy. We cannot take one step here.'

What 'Umar meant by that 'faith' was that step, to take one step in the presence of the lion towards the lion. That step is a great and rare matter, the concern only of the elect and intimate of God. This is the true step; the rest are mere footprints. That faith comes only to prophets, who have washed their hands of their own life.

A friend is a delightful thing. For a friend derives strength and life and increase even from the phantom of his friend. How marvellous! Lailā's phantom used to give strength to Majnūn and became his food. Since the phantom of a profane beloved has such strength and influence as to impart strength to his friend, why should you marvel that the phantom of the true Friend imparts strength to him in presence and absence alike? What place is this for a phantom? That is the very soul of all realities; that is not called phantom.

The world subsists on a phantom. You call this world real, because it can be seen and felt, whilst you call phantom those verities whereof this world is but an offshoot. The facts are the reverse. This world is the phantom world, for that Verity produces a hundred such worlds, and they rot and corrupt and become naught, and it produces again a new world and a better. That grows not old, being exempt from newness and oldness. Its offshoots are qualified by newness and oldness, but He who produces these is exempt from both attributes and transcends both.

An architect planned a house in his mind, forming the notion that its breadth would be so much, its length so much, its floor so much, its courtyard so much. People do not call that a 'fancy' since this concrete reality is born from the 'fancy' and is an offshoot thereof. But if some-one who is not an architect conceives such a notion and idea in his mind, then people certainly call that a 'fancy.' In common parlance men say of one who is not a builder and has not studied building, 'You are fanciful!'

27

It is better not to question the fakir, for that is as much as to urge and oblige him to invent a lie. For when a materialist questions him, he has to reply. He cannot answer him truthfully, since he is not worthy of or receptive to such an answer, and his mouth and lips are not suitable to take such a morsel. So the fakir must answer him appro-priately to his capacity and ruling star, namely by inventing a lie so as to get rid of him, and though everything that the fakir says is true and cannot be a lie, yet in comparison with his former answer and statement and truth that is a lie; except that to the listener it is relatively right, and more than right.

A certain dervish had a disciple who used to beg for him. One day out of the yield of his begging he brought some food to his master. The dervish ate the food. That night he experienced nocturnal emission.

'From whom did you bring that food?' he asked the disciple.

'A lovely girl gave it to me,' the disciple answered.

'By Allah,' rejoined the dervish, 'it is twenty years since I had a nocturnal emission. This was the effect of her morsel.'

This shows that the dervish must be cautious and not eat the morsel of everyone. For the dervish is delicate; things have their effect on him and become visible, just as a little blackness shows on a clean white gown; as for a black gown which has become black with grime for many years and has lost all whiteness, if a thousand kinds of filth and grease should trickle on it it would not appear on it to the people. This being so, the dervish must not eat the morsel of sinners and those who live on iniquity, and of materialists. For the morsel of such a man has an effect on the dervish, and corrupt thoughts manifest under the influence of that strange morsel—so that the dervish had nocturnal emission through consuming the food of that girl.

28

The litanies of the questers and travellers is that they shall be occupied with labour and devotion, and have apportioned their time so that every labour is assigned to its particular time. It is as though they have an overseer who draws them to that specific labour by rule of habit. For example, when such a man rises in the morning, that hour is more apt for worship since the soul is quieter and clearer; every person then does and performs the kind of service which is suitable to him and comes within the scope of his noble soul.

We are the rangers,
we are they that give glory.

There are a hundred thousand ranks. The purer a man becomes, the higher up he is promoted; the lesser is assigned to a lower rank, for 'Postpone them even as God has postponed them.'

This story is inevitably a long one. Whoever abbreviates this story abbreviates his own life and soul, but for God's preservation. As for the litanies of those who have attained union, I speak within the limits of comprehension—it is so, that in the morning the holy spirits and the pure angels, and those men *whom none knows but God* (whose names are hidden from men out of exceeding jealousy), come to visit them.

> *And thou seest men entering God's religion in throngs—*
> *and the angels shall enter unto them*
> *from every gate.*

You are seated beside them, and do not see, neither do you hear their speech and greetings and laughter. Yet what is so marvellous in this? When a man is sick and nigh unto death, he sees phantoms of which one sitting beside him has no knowledge, neither hears what they say. Those realities are a thousand times subtler than these phantoms; the latter the average man does not see or hear until he is sick, whilst those realities he will not see before his death and demise. Such visitants, knowing the refined states of the saints and their majesty, and knowing that from earliest morn so many angels and pure spirits have come to wait upon the shaikh, hesitate infinitely; for they must not intervene in the midst of such orisons, lest the shaikh be disturbed.

Even so the slaves are present every morning at the door of the king's palace. It is their use that each should have a fixed station, a fixed service, a fixed devotion. Some serve from afar, and the king looks not upon them nor pays heed to them. But the slaves of the king see that a certain one has been in attendance; when the king has departed, his use is that the servants should attend on him from every part, for servitude is no more. 'Take on the characteristics of God' has been realised: 'I am for him hearing and sight' has been realised.

This is an extremely majestic station, ineffable indeed; the majesty of it cannot be comprehended by spelling out m a j e s t y. Even if a little of its majesty should penetrate, neither the letter m itself would abide, nor pronunciation of the letter m, nor hand, nor aspiration. The whole city is devastated by the hosts of Light.

> *Kings, when they enter a city, disorder it.*

A camel enters a little house; the house is devastated, but in that ruin there are a thousand treasures.

> Only in ruins may a treasure be found;
> In thriving cities a hound is still a hound.

If I have expounded at such length the station of the travellers, how shall I expound the states of those who have attained? The latter has no end; the former has an end. The end of travellers is attainment; what should be the end of those who have attained to union, union to which there cannot be any separation? No ripe grape becomes again an unripe grape; no mature fruit ever again becomes raw.

> I hold it unlawful to speak
> Of these things to men;
> But when Thy name is mentioned,
> Many words I say then.

By Allah, I will not make it long, I make it short.

> Blood I consume, and Thou deemest
> That blood is wine;
> Thou deemest Thou gavest, but takest
> This soul of mine.

Whoever cuts this story short, it is as though he has abandoned the right road and is taking the road to the life-destroying wilderness, saying, 'Such and such a tree is near at hand.'

29

The Christian al-Jarrāḥ said: A number of the companions of Shaikh Ṣadr al-Dīn drank with me, and they said to me, 'Jesus is God, as you assert. We confess that to be the truth; but we conceal and deny it, intending thereby to preserve the Community.'

The Master said: The enemy of God has lied! God forbid! These are the words of one drunken with the wine of Satan the misguider, the humiliated, the humiliating, driven from the Presence of God. How could it be that a frail body, fleeing from the Jews' plotting from place to place, whose form was less than two cubits, should be the preserver of the seven heavens, the thickness of each of which is a distance of five hundred years and the thickness of each heaven to the next a distance of five hundred years, and every earth five hundred years, and from each earth to the next five hundred years? And under the Throne a sea whose depth is likewise, that sea the possession of God, reaching up to His ankles, aye, and many times the like of it? How could your reason acknowledge that the disposer and controller of all these is the feeblest of forms? Moreover, before Jesus is He who was the Creator of the heavens and the earth—glory be to Him, above what the wrong-doers assert!

The Christian said: Dust went to dust, and pure spirit to pure spirit.

The Master said: If the spirit of Jesus was God, whither departed his spirit? The spirit departs only to its Origin and Creator. If he was himself the Origin and Creator, whither should he depart?

The Christian said: So we found it stated, and we took it as our religion.

I said: If you find and inherit of the leavings of your father false gold, black and corrupt, you will not change it for gold of sound assay, free of alloy and adulteration. No; you take that gold, saying, 'We found it so.' Or you inherited from your father a paralysed hand; and you found a physic and a physician to mend that paralysed hand. You do not accept, saying, 'I found my hand so, paralysed, and I desire not to change it.' Or you found saline water on a farm wherein your father died and you were brought up, then you were directed to another farm whose water is sweet, whose herbs are wholesome, whose people are healthy; you do not desire to move to that other farm and drink the sweet water, that would rid you of all diseases and ailments. No; you say, 'We found that farm with its saline water bequeathing ailments, and we hold on to what we found.' God forbid! That is not the action or the words of an intelligent man possessed of sound senses. God gave you an intelligence of your own other than your father's intelligence, a sight of your own other than your father's sight, a discrimination of your own. Why do you nullify your sight and your intelligence, following an intelligence which will destroy you and not guide you?

Yūtāsh—his father was a cobbler. Yet when he attained the Sultan's presence and learned the manner of kings and how to be Master of the Sword and the Sultan conferred on him the highest rank, never did he say, 'I found my father a cobbler, so I do not want this post; on the contrary, give me, O Sultan, a shop in the market that I may practise cobbling.' Indeed even a dog, for all its baseness, once it has learned to hunt and become a hunter for the Sultan, forgets what it found its sire and dam doing, skulking in rubbish-heaps and wastelands and craving for carrion. On the contrary, it follows the Sultan's horses and follows after the game. So it is with the hawk: when the Sultan has trained it, it never says, 'We inherited from our fathers desolate haunts in the mountains and the devouring of dead things, so we will not heed the Sultan's drum, neither his game.'

If the intellect of the beast holds fast to what it has found better than what it inherited from its parents, it is monstrous and horrible that a man, superior to all the inhabitants of the earth in reason and discrimination, should be less than a beast. We take refuge with God from that!

Certainly it is right that he should say that the Lord of Jesus, upon whom be peace, honoured Jesus and brought him nigh to Him, so that whoever serves him has served the Lord, whoever obeys him has obeyed the Lord. But inasmuch as God has sent a prophet superior to Jesus, manifesting by his hand all that He manifested by Jesus' hand and more, it behoves him to follow that Prophet, for God's sake, not for the sake of the Prophet himself.

Only God is served for His own sake. Only God is loved; other than God is loved for the sake of God most High. Unto your Lord is the end—that is, the end that you should love a thing for other than that thing, seek it for other than it, until in the end you come to God and love Him for Himself.

> To clothe the Kaaba is a vain caprice:
> *My House* sufficient Kaaba-trapping is.

' To apply eye-black to the eyes is not the same as blackness of the eyes.' Just as worn-out and ragged clothes conceal the elegance of wealth and grandeur, so excellent clothes and fine raiment conceal the mark and beauty and perfection of fakirs. When the fakir's clothes are in shreds and patches, then his heart is opened.

30

There is a head which is adorned by a golden cap; and there is a head, the beauty of whose curls is concealed by a golden cap and a jewelled crown. For the curls of the lovely ones attract love; love is the throne-room of the hearts; the golden crown is an inanimate thing, whereof the wearer is the heart's beloved. We sought everywhere Solomon's ring, peace be upon him; we found it in poverty. In this beauteous one likewise took we our repose, and she was pleased with nothing so much as with this.

Well, I am a whoremonger; since I was little, this has been my trade. I know that this removes hindrances, this consumes veils; this is the root of all acts of obedience, the rest are mere branches. If you do not cut the throat of a sheep, of what use is it to blow on its trotter? Fasting leads to annihilation, where is the last of all pleasures.

And God is with the patient.

Whatever shop is in the bazaar, or any potion, or merchandise, or trade, the end of the thread of each one of these is the need of the human soul, and that end of the thread is hidden; until the need for those things arises, the end of the thread does not stir or become visible. Similarly with every religion, every faith, every grace, every miracle, all the states of the prophets—the end of the thread of every one of these is in the human spirit; until the need arises, that end of the thread does not stir or become visible.

Everything
We have numbered in a clear register.

The Master said: Is the agent of good and evil one thing or two things? The answer, from the point of view that in the time of hesitation they are in dispute one with the other, is categorically two; for one person cannot be opposed to himself. From the point of view that evil is inseparable from good—for good is the abandonment of evil, and the abandonment of evil is impossible without evil: that good is the abandonment of evil is proved by the fact that, were it not for the incitement of evil, there would be no abandonment of good—from this point of view they are not two. The Magians said that Yazdan is the creator of good things and Ahriman is the creator of evil and hateful things. To this we reply that desirable things are not apart from hateful things. The desirable cannot exist without the hateful, since the desirable is the cessation of the hateful, and the cessation of the hateful without the hateful is impossible. Joy is the cessation of sorrow; the cessation of sorrow without sorrow is impossible. So they are one and indivisible.

I said: Until a thing passes away, its use does not become manifest. So, until the letters of a word pass away into speech, their use does not reach the listener. Whoever says evil of the gnostic in reality says good of the gnostic; for the gnostic shies away from that quality, blame for which might settle on him. The gnostic is the enemy of that quality; hence, he who speaks evil of that quality speaks evil of the enemy of the gnostic and praises the gnostic; for the gnostic shies away from such a blameworthy thing, and he who shies away from the blameworthy is himself praiseworthy. 'Things become clear through their opposites.' Hence the gnostic knows that the critic is not really his enemy and his dispraiser.

I am as a smiling garden set about by a wall, and on that wall are all kinds of filth and thorns. The passer-by does not see the garden; he sees that wall and its uncleanness, and speaks evil of it. Why then should the garden be angry with him? Except that his evil speaking is to his own detriment; for he must put up with the wall in order to reach the garden. So by finding fault with the wall he remains far from the garden; hence he has worked his own destruction. Therefore the Prophet, God's blessings be upon him, said, 'I laugh as I slay.' That is, 'I have no enemy'—that he should be angry in chastising him. He kills the unbeliever in one way, so that the unbeliever may not kill himself in a hundred manners. So of course he laughs as he slays.

31

The policeman is always in search of thieves to capture them, and the thieves are running away from him. It happens rarely indeed that a thief should be in search of a policeman, and want to capture the policeman and get him into his hands.

God most High said to Bā Yazīd, 'What do you desire, Bā Yazīd?' He answered, 'I desire not to desire.'

Now mortal man can be in one of two states: either he desires, or he does not desire. To be wholly without desire—that is not a human attribute for then a man has become empty of himself, and wholly ceased to be; for had he continued to be, that human attribute would have remained in him, to desire and not to desire. But God most High desired to perfect Bā Yazīd and to make him a complete shaikh, so that thereafter a state should supervene in him wherein there was no room for duality and separation, and complete union and unity should prevail.

For all pains arise out of the fact that you desire something, and that is not attainable. When you no more desire, the pain no more remains.

Men are divided into various classes, and have different ranks on this Way. Some labour and strive to the end that what they desire in their hearts and thoughts they should not bring into action. That is within the scope of men. But that within the heart no itch of desire and thought should enter—that is not within the scope of man; only God's drawing can take that out of him.

Say: 'The truth has come, and falsehood has vanished away.'

'Enter, O believer, for thy light has extinguished My fire.' When the faith of the believer is perfect and true, he does what God does, whether it be himself or God drawing.

When it is stated that after Muhammad and the other prophets, upon whom be peace, revelation is not sent down upon any others, the fact is that it is sent down, only it is not called revelation. This is what the Prophet meant when he said, 'The believer sees with the Light of God.' When a man sees with God's Light he descries all things, the first and the last, the absent and the present; for how can anything be hidden from God's Light? If anything is hidden, then that is not God's Light. So the true meaning is revelation, even though they do not call it revelation.

When 'Uthmān, God be pleased with him, became caliph he went into the pulpit. The people waited to see what he would say. He kept silent and said nothing; he looked steadily at the people, and caused a state of ecstasy to descend upon the people so that they had no power to go out, and knew not where one another were sitting. Not by a hundred preachings and sermons and predications would have such an excellent state been brought about in them; precious lessons were imparted to them and secrets were revealed, that could not have been communicated by so much labour and preaching. To the end of the assembly he continued to look at them thus, saying not one word. When he desired to descend from the pulpit, he said, 'It is better for you to have a working Imam than a speaking Imam.'

What he said was the truth. If the purpose of speaking is to communicate instruction delicately and to effect a change of character, that had been accomplished without words many times better than might have been achieved by words. So what 'Uthmān said was perfectly correct. To resume: with reference to his description of himself as a 'working' Imam, during the time he was in the pulpit he did no external 'work' such as might have been visible; he did not pray, he did not go on the pilgrimage, he did not give in alms, he did not commemorate God, he did not even pronounce the caliph's address. We therefore realise that 'work' and 'action' are not confined to this form only; rather, these forms of work are merely the form of that true 'work' which is of the soul.

The Prophet, God bless him and give him peace, said: 'My Companions are as stars. Whomsoever of them you follow, you will be guided aright.' When a man looks at a star and finds his way by it, the star does not speak any word to that man; yet by merely looking at the star the man knows the road from roadlessness and reaches his goal. In the same way it is possible that by merely looking at God's saints they exercise control over you; without words, without questioning, without speech the purpose is achieved and you are brought to the goal of union.

> So let who will regard me: my regard
> Warns him who deems desire an easy thing.

In God's world there is nothing more difficult than enduring the ridiculous. Suppose for instance that you have read a certain book, corrected, emended, and fully vocalised it. Then someone sitting beside you reads that book all wrongly. Can you endure that? No, it is impossible. If however you have not read the book, it makes no difference to you whether the other man reads it wrongly or reads it right, you cannot distinguish wrong from right. So enduring the ridiculous is a great discipline.

The saints do not shirk discipline. The first discipline in their quest has been to slay the self and to eschew all desires and lusts. That is the 'greater struggle.' When they achieved and arrived and abode in the station of security, wrong and right became revealed to them. They know and see right from wrong. Still they are engaged in a great discipline; for these mortals do all things wrongly, and they see this and endure it. For if they do not so, and speak out and declare those mortals to be wrong, not one person will stay before them or give them the Muslim salute. But God most High has bestowed on them a great and mighty power and capacity to endure out of a hundred wrongnesses they mention one, so that it will not come difficult to the man. His other wrongnesses they conceal; indeed they praise him, saying, 'That wrong of yours is right,' so that by degrees they may expel from him these wrongnesses, one by one.

So, a teacher is teaching a child how to write. When he comes to writing a whole line, the child writes a line and shows it to the teacher. In the teacher's eyes that is all wrong and bad. The teacher speaks to the child kindly and cajolingly: 'That is all very good, and you have written well. Bravo, bravo! Only this letter you have written badly, this is how it ought to be. That letter too you have written badly.' The teacher calls bad a few letters out of that line, and shows the child how they ought to be written; the rest he praises, so that the child may not lose heart. The child's weakness gathers strength from that approval, and so gradually he is taught and assisted on his way.

God most High willing, we are hopeful that God most High will grant the Amir realisation of his designs and of all that he has in his heart. Those good fortunes too which he has not in his heart, knowing not what thing that is so as to desire it—we hope that those too will be realised; so that when he sees that, and those gifts of God come to him, he will be ashamed of these former wishes and desires. 'Such a thing lay before me. With the existence of such a fortune and such a grace, good gracious, how did I desire those things?' So he will feel ashamed.

That is called a 'gift' which does not enter the imagination of a man and does not pass by that way at all. For whatever passes into a man's imagination is the measure of his ambition and the measure of his capacity. But God's gift is the measure of God's capacity. Therefore that is a 'gift' which is worthy of God, not worthy of man's imagination and ambition. 'What eye has not seen, neither ear heard, neither has it entered into the heart of a man': what you expect of My bounty, that the eyes have seen and the ears have heard the like of it, and the like of it has been conceived in the hearts. But My bounty transcends all that.

32

The attribute of certainty is the perfect shaikh; good and true thoughts are his disciples according to their different degrees—first thought, then prevailing thought, then most prevailing thought, and so forth. Every thought as it expands becomes nearer to certainty and farther from doubt. 'If the faith of Abū Bakr were weighed': all thoughts suck milk at the breast of certainty, and increase. That milk-sucking and increase is a sign of the acquiring of an augmentation of thought through theory and practice, until each thought becomes certainty and all pass away entirely into certainty. For when they become certainty, thought no longer remains.

This shaikh and his disciples manifested in the physical world are forms of that shaikh of certainty. His disciples are a proof that those forms become changed age after age and generation after generation; whilst that shaikh of certainty and his sons, which are right thoughts, abide constant in the world, unchanging through the succession of ages and generations.

Again, erroneous, erring, doubting thoughts are the rejected of the shaikh of certainty. Every day they become farther away from him and more debased; for every day they increase in the acquisition of that which increases the evil thought.

In their hearts is a sickness,
and God has increased their sickness.

The masters eat dates, and the prisoners eat thorns. God most High says:

What, do they not consider how the camel was created?

Save him who repents, and believes, and
does a righteous deed.

Those, God will
change their evil deeds into good deeds.

142

Every acquisition such a man has made in corrupting thought now becomes a power in reforming thought. Thus, a cunning thief repented and became a policeman. All the trickeries of thieving which he practised now became a power for beneficence and justice. He is superior to all other policemen who were not thieves to begin with; for the policeman who has committed acts of theft knows the ways of thieves; the habits of thieves are not hidden from him. If such a man becomes a shaikh, he will be perfect, the Elder of the world and the Mahdi of the age.

33

They said, 'Keep away from us and approach us not':
How shall I keep away, seeing you are my need?

It must of course be realised that everyone, wherever he is, is inseparably alongside of his own need. Every living creature is alongside of his own need and constantly attached to it. 'His need is closer to him than his father and mother and cleaves to him.' That need is his fetter, drawing him in this direction and that just like a nose-ring or toggle. Now it is absurd that anyone should make a fetter for himself; for he is seeking to escape from his fetters, and it is absurd that one who seeks to escape should seek the fetter. So it necessarily follows that someone else has made the fetter for him. For instance, he seeks after health; so he would not have made himself sick, for it would be absurd for him to be both a seeker after sickness and a seeker after his own health.

If a man is alongside of his own need, he will also be alongside of the one who gives him that need; if he is constantly attached to his own toggle, he will be constantly attached to the one who draws the toggle. Except that his eyes are fixed on the toggle, so that he is without might and strength; if his eyes were fixed on him who draws the toggle, he would escape from the toggle, the toggle now being the one who draws his toggle. For he was toggled so that he should not proceed towards the toggle-drawer without the toggle. His eyes are not fixed upon Him who draws the toggle, so of course

We shall brand him upon the muzzle.

143

' We shall fix a toggle upon his nose and draw him against his will, since without a toggle he does not come towards Us.'

They say, 'When a man is past eighty, shall he play?'
I said, 'Shall he play before he is eighty, pray?'

God most High bestows of His grace upon elders a youthful passion whereof youths have no knowledge. For youthful passion brings a freshness and causes a man to leap and laugh and gives him the desire to play, because he sees the world as new and has not grown weary of the world. When such an elder sees the world as new, he is given a desire to play, and he bounds, and his skin and flesh augment.

Great is the glory of age, if the while grey hairs
Appear, the steed of playfulness runs amok.

So the glory of old age is greater than the glory of God! For it is in the spring that the glory of God appears, and in autumn old age prevails over that, not abandoning its autumnal nature. So the frailty of spring is the bounty of God; for with every shedding of teeth the smile of God's spring diminishes, and with every white hair the freshness of God's bounty is lost; with every weeping of autumnal rain the garden of Realities is despoiled. God is exalted above what the evildoers say!

34

I saw him in the form of a wild animal, upon him the skin of a fox. I made to seize him, and he was on a small balcony, looking down the stairs. He raised his hands, leaping about like this and that. Then I saw Jalāl al-Tibrīzī with him in the form of a stoat. He shied away, and I seized him, while he was making to bite me. I put his head under my foot and squeezed it hard, until all its contents came out. I looked at the fineness of his skin and said, 'This deserves to be filled with gold and precious stones, pearls and rubies, and things even more excellent than that.' Then I said, 'I have taken what I wanted. Shy away, shy one, where you will, and leap in whatever direction you see fit!'

He leaped about because he feared to be mastered; and in being mastered his true happiness resided. Doubtless he was **formed of** meteor fragments and the like, and his heart was drenched, and he desired to apprehend everything. He set out upon that road which he struggled hard to keep to and took refuge in, but that he could not do. For the gnostic is in such a case that he is not to be snared with those nets, nor is this game apt to be captured with these nets. If he is sound and straight, the gnostic is completely free to determine who shall capture him; no one can capture him except with his free consent.

You sat in your covert, watching for that prey, whilst that prey beheld you and your hidyhole and your cunning, a free agent. The ways by which he may pass are not restricted; he passes not by your covert, he only passes by ways which he has himself laid down.

And God's earth is wide.
And they comprehend not anything of His knowledge
save such as He wills.

Moreover when those subtleties fell upon your tongue and comprehension, they were subtleties no more; on the contrary, they were corrupted because of connexion with you. So everything, be it corrupt or sound, when it falls in the mouth and comprehension of the gnostic remains no more as it was but becomes something other, wrapt up and swathed in graces and miracles. Do you not see how the rod was wrapt up in the hand of Moses and did not remain as it was in the quiddity of a rod? So too with the Moaning Pillar and the Stick in the hand of the Prophet, and prayer in the mouth of Moses, and iron in David's hand, and the mountains with him—they did not remain in their quiddity but became something other, different from what they were. So too with subtleties and invocations, when they fall into the hand of the creature of darkness and brute body they remain not as they were.

> The Kaaba is a tavern at your prayers,
> So long as it is yours, your essence shares.

The unbeliever eats in seven stomachs; and that ass chosen by the ignorant houseboy eats in seventy stomachs. Even if he had eaten in one stomach, he would have been an eater in seventy stomachs; for everything that is of the hateful is hateful, just as everything that is of the beloved is beloved. If the houseboy had been here, I would have gone into him and counselled him and not left him until he drove him out and put him far away. For he is a corrupter of his faith, his heart, his spirit and his reason. Would that he had induced him to corrupt practices other than this, such as drinking wine and singing girls; for that would have been put right when treated by a man of Divine grace. But he filled the house with prayer rugs—would that he were rolled up in them and burned, so that the houseboy might escape from him and his mischief! For he corrupts his faith in the man of Divine grace and backbites him in his presence, while he holds his tongue and destroys himself. He has snared him with rosaries and litanies and prayer carpets.

Perchance one day God will open the eyes of the houseboy, and he will see what ruined him and drove him far from the compassion of the man of Divine grace. Then he will strike his neck with his own hand, saying, 'You destroyed me, so that there were gathered upon me my heavy loads of sin and my evil acts, even as they saw in their revelations the foulness of my deeds and my corrupt and sinful beliefs, gathered together behind my back in the corner of the house. I myself was concealing them from the man of Divine grace and putting them behind my back, whilst he was looking down on what I was hiding from him and saying, "What are you hiding? By Him in whose hand my soul rests, if I had summoned those foul forms they would have come forward unto me one by one and visibly, uncovering themselves and telling of their true state and of what was concealed in them." ' May God save all those who are wronged from the like of these highwaymen, who bar from the path of God by way of 'devotion'!

Kings play with the polo-stick in the maidan, to show the inhabitants of the city who cannot be present at the battle and the fighting a representation of the sallying forth of the champions and the cutting off of the enemies' heads, and their rolling about just as the balls roll in the maidan, their frontal charge and attack and retreat. This play in the maidan is as the astrolabe for the serious business in the fighting. In like manner, with the people of God prayer and spiritual concerts are a manner of showing the spectators how in secret they accord with God's commandments and forbiddings special to them. The singer in the concert is as the Imam at the ritual prayer. The people follow his lead. If he sings slowly, they dance slowly; if he sings briskly, they dance briskly—a representation of how in their inner hearts they follow the summons of commandment and forbidding.

35

I am amazed how these who have the Koran by heart understand nothing of the spiritual states of the gnostics. As the Koran states,

And obey thou not every mean swearer,

(The slanderer is precisely the man who says, 'Do not listen to So-and-so, whatever he may say, for he is just like that with you.')

backbiter, going about with slander,
hinderer of good.

The Koran is indeed a marvellous magician and a jealous, so contriving that he recites clearly into the ear of the adversary in such wise that he understands, but is no whit wiser and has no inkling of the delight thereof, or he snatches it away himself.

God has set a seal—

How wonderfully gracious He is! He sets a seal on him, who listens and does not understand, argues and does not understand. God is gracious, and His wrath is gracious, and His lock is gracious, but not like His lock is His unlocking, for the grace of that is indescribable. If I break myself into pieces, that will be through the infinite grace and will of His unlocking and incomparable opening.

Beware, do not suppose that I am sick and dying. That is by way of a veil. My slayer will be this grace of His, and His incomparableness. That dagger or sword which flashes forth is in order to repel the eyes of strangers, so that no ill-omened, profane, defiled eyes may perceive this slaying.

36

Form came as a branch of Love; for without Love this form would have no worth. A branch is that which cannot exist without the root.

Therefore God is not called a form; since form is the branch, He cannot be called the branch.

One said: Love too cannot take form and be compacted without form. Hence it is the branch of form.

We say: Why cannot Love take form without form? On the contrary, Love is the artificer of form. A hundred thousand forms are raised up by Love, pictured alike and realised. Though the picture does not exist without the painter, neither the painter without the picture, yet the painting is the branch and the painter is the root. It is like the moving of the finger with the moving of the ring.

So long as there exists no love for a house, no architect makes the form and conception of the house. In like manner one year corn is at the price of gold, another year it is at the price of dust. The form of the corn is the same; therefore the worth and value of the form of the corn came through love. Again, that science which you pursue with such love—in your eyes it is valuable, but in times when no one pursues any science no one learns and professes that science.

They say that Love is after all the want and need for a certain thing; hence the need is the root, and the thing needed is the branch. I say: After all, these words which you speak you speak out of need. After all, these words came into existence out of your need. When you had the inclination for these words, these words were born. Therefore the need was prior, and these words were born from it. Therefore the need existed without the words. Therefore love and need are not a branch of the words.

One said: After all, the object of that need was these words, so how can the object be the branch?

I said: The object is always the branch. For the object of the root of the tree is the branch of the tree.

37

The Master said: The allegation which they made against this girl is a lie and will not go farther. But something settled in the imagination of this company. The human imagination and heart are like a vestibule

—first they enter the vestibule, then they go into the house. This whole world is like one house: everything that comes into the interior of it, which is the portico, must necessarily appear and become visible in the house. For instance, this house in which we are seated—the form of it became visible in the heart of the architect, then this house came into being. So we said that this whole world is one house. Imagination and cogitation and thought are the vestibule of this house. Whatever you saw appearing in the vestibule, be sure that it becomes visible in the house. And all these things, good alike and evil, which appear in the world, all first appeared in the vestibule, then here.

When God most High wishes to produce in this world all manner of rare and wonderful things, orchards, gardens, meadows, sciences, compositions of various kinds, He first implants the desire and demand for them in the inward hearts, so that thence they may become visible. Similarly every thing which you see in this world, be sure that it exists in that world. For instance, whatever you see in the dew, be sure that it will be in the ocean, for this dew is of that ocean. In the same way this creation of heaven and earth, Throne and Footstool, and the other marvels—God implanted the demand for that in the spirits of the ancients, and so of course the world became visible accordingly.

People who say that the world is eternal—how should their words be listened to? Some say it is created in time: they are the saints and the prophets, who are more ancient than the world. God most High implanted the demand for the creation of the world in their spirits, and then the world appeared. So they know for a fact, and report on their own high authority, that the world is created in time. For instance, we who have dwelt in this house, our age is sixty or seventy. We have seen that this house did not exist; it is now a number of years since this house has existed. If living creatures are born in this house out of the doors and walls of this house, such as scorpions and mice and snakes and other mean creatures which live in this house, they were born and saw the house already constructed. If they should say, 'This house is eternal,' that would be no proof for us, since we ourselves have seen that this house is created in time. Just like those living things which have sprung out of the doors and walls of this house and neither know anything nor see anything apart from this house, so there are mortal creatures who have sprung out of this house of the world. They have no true essence within them; they have grown out of this place, and likewise they go down into this world. If they say that the world is eternal, that will be no proof against the prophets and saints, who existed millions of years before the world: why speak of years and numbers of years, when they are infinite and innumerable? They have seen the creation of the world in time, just as you have seen the creation in time of this house.

After that, the philosophaster says to the theologian, 'How do you know that the world was created in time?' You donkey, how do you know that the world is eternal? After all, your statement that the world is eternal simply means that it is not created in time, and that is testimony based upon a negative. Yet testimony based upon a positive is easier than testimony based upon a negative. For the meaning of testimony based upon a negative is this: this man has not done such and such a deed. Information regarding this is difficult. The person making such a statement must have been closely attached to the other from the beginning to the end of his life, night and day, sleeping and waking, for him to be able to say he never did this deed at all. Even so it may not be true: it is possible that the man making the statement has once been overtaken by sleep; or the other person may have gone to the privy, where the first man could not keep close to him. For this reason testimony based upon a negative is not admissible, since it goes beyond the bounds of possibility. But testimony based upon the positive is both possible and easy. A man simply says, 'I was with him for a moment, and he said this and did that.' Undoubtedly such testimony is acceptable, because it is within the bounds of human possibility. So now, you dog, it is easier to testify to creation in time, than for you to testify to the eternity of the world. For the upshot of your testimony is this, that the world is not created in time; therefore you will have given testimony based upon a negative. Now inasmuch as neither can be actually proved, and you have not yourselves seen that the world is created in time or eternal, you say to him, 'How do you know that it is created in time?' And he rejoins, 'You wittol, how do you know that it is eternal? After all, your claim is the more difficult and the more unlikely.'

38

The Prophet, God bless him and give him peace, was seated with his Companions. The unbelievers began to cavil with him. He said, 'Well, you are all agreed that there is one person in the world who is the recipient of revelation. Revelation descends on him; it does not descend upon every one. That person has certain marks and signs, in his actions and in his words, in his mien and in every part of him the token and mark may be seen. Since you have seen those tokens, turn your faces towards him and hold firmly to him, that he may be your protector.'

They were all confounded by his argument and were left with nothing more to say. They put their hands to the sword and continued to come and vex and molest and insult his Companions. The Prophet, God bless him and give him peace, said, 'Be patient, so that they may not say that they have prevailed over us. They desire by force to make the religion manifest. God will make manifest this religion.'

For some time the Companions prayed secretly and pronounced in secret the name of Muhammad, God bless him and give him peace. Then after a while the revelation came: 'You too unsheathe the sword and make war!'

Muhammad, upon whom be peace, is called 'unlettered'; not because he was incapable of writing and learning. He was called 'unlettered' because with him writing and learning and wisdom were innate, not acquired. He who inscribes characters on the face of the moon, is such a man unable to write? And what is there in all the world that he does not know, seeing that all men learn from him? What thing, pray, should appertain to the partial Intellect that the Universal intellect does not possess? The partial intellect is not capable of inventing anything of its own accord which it has not seen.

The fact that men compose books and set up new skills and buildings is no new composition. They have seen the likeness of that, and merely make additions to it. Those who invent something new on their own account, they are the Universal Intellect. The partial intellect is capable of learning, and is in need of teaching; the Universal Intellect is the teacher, and is not in need. So, when you investigate all trades, the root and origin of them was revelation; men have learned them from the prophets, and they are the Universal Intellect. There is the story of the raven: when Cain slew Abel and did not know what to do, the raven slew a raven and dug the earth and buried that raven and scattered dust on its head. Cain learned from the raven how to make a grave and how to bury. So it is with all the professions. Every one who possesses a partial intellect is in need of teaching, and the Universal Intellect is the founder of every thing. It is the prophets and saints who have effected union between partial intellect and Universal Intellect so that they have become one.

For instance, the hand and foot, the eye and ear and all the human senses are capable of learning from the heart and the intellect. The foot learns from the intellect how to walk, the hand learns from the heart and the intellect how to grasp, the eye and ear learn how to see and hear. If the heart and intellect did not exist, would these senses function or be able to operate?

Just as this body in comparison with the intellect and the heart is coarse and gross whilst they are subtle, and the gross subsists through the subtle; if it has any subtlety and freshness, it derives it from the subtle, and without the subtle it is useless and foul and gross and unseemly; so the partial intellect in comparison with the Universal Intellect is a tool, learning from it and deriving instruction from it, coarse and gross in comparison with the Universal Intellect.

Someone said: Remember us in your intention. Intention is the root of the matter. If there be no words, let there be no words; words are the branch.

The Master said: Well, this intention existed in the world of spirits before the world of bodies. So we were brought into the world of bodies without a good purpose! This is surely absurd; therefore words have their function and are full of utility. If you plant in the earth only the kernel of an apricot stone, nothing will grow; if you plant it along with its husk, then it will grow. From this we realise that the form also has a function. Prayer too is an inward matter. 'There is no prayer without the heart being present.' But it is necessary for you to bring the prayer into form, by making outward genuflection and prostration; then you derive benefit and attain your desire.

And they continue at their prayers.

This refers to the prayer of the spirit. The prayer of form is temporary and will not be continual. For the Spirit of the world is an infinite ocean; the body is the shore, finite and limited dry land. So continual prayer belongs only to the spirit. So the spirit also has its genuflection and prostration, but that genuflection and prostration must be manifested in form. For there is a union between meaning and form; until the two come together, they are of no benefit.

When you say that form is the branch of meaning, that form is the subject and the heart the monarch, after all these are only relative terms. When you say that this is a branch of that, until the branch exists how does the term 'root' become applicable to the other? So it became root out of this branch; if the branch had not existed, it would not even have had a name. When you speak of woman, there must necessarily be man; when you speak of Master, there must be one mastered; when you speak of Ruler, there must be one ruled.

39

Ḥusām al-Dīn Arzanjānī before entering the service and society of the dervishes was a great disputer. Wherever he went and seated himself, he engaged vigorously in disputation and controversy. He used to do it well and spoke excellently; but when he took up the company of dervishes his heart turned completely against that.

> It takes another love
> The end of one to prove.

'Whoever desires to sit with God most High, let him sit with the people of Sufism.' These intellectual sciences are a game and a waste of life, compared with the spiritual experiences of dervishes.

The present life is naught but a sport.

When a man has reached the age of discretion and is intelligent and completely formed, he no longer plays; or if he does, he keeps it secret out of exceeding shame so that no one may see him. This intellectual science and discussion and worldly whims are as the wind, and man is dust; when the wind tangles with the dust, wherever it reaches it makes the eyes sore, and nothing but conturbation and protestation accrues from its existence. But although man is dust, with every word he hears he weeps, and his tears are as running water.

> *Thou seest their eyes*
> *overflowing with tears.*

Now when instead of wind, water descends upon the dust, undoubtedly the exact opposite comes to pass. When dust gets water, fruit and grass and fragrant herbs and violets and roses grow.

This way of poverty is a way in which you attain all your desires. Whatsoever thing you have longed for will certainly come to you on this way, whether it be the shattering of armies, victory over the enemy, capturing kingdoms, reducing people to subjection, excelling your contemporaries, elegance of speech, eloquence, and all that is like to this. When you have chosen the way of poverty, all these things come to you. No man has ever travelled on this way and had cause to complain; contrary to other ways, for whoever has travelled on such a way and toiled, out of a hundred thousand only one objective has been gained, and that too not in such a manner that his heart should be happy and find repose. For every such way has its subsidiary means and paths to the attainment of that objective, and the objective cannot be attained save by way of those subsidiary means. That way is a distant way, and full of pitfalls and obstacles; it may be that those subsidiary means will fall short of the objective.

When however you have entered the world of poverty and practised it, God most High bestows upon you kingdoms and worlds that you never imagined; and you become quite ashamed of what you longed for and desired at first. 'Ah!' you cry. 'With such a thing in existence, how could I seek after such a mean thing?' But God most High says, 'If only you had risen above such a thing, not desiring it and disdaining it, all would have been well. But at the time when it entered into your thoughts, you eschewed it for My sake. My goodness is infinite, so of course I make that thing attainable to you too.'

So it happened with the Prophet, God bless him and give him peace. Before he attained his goal and became famous, observing the elegant speech and eloquence of the Arabs he always wished that he too might be endowed with the like elegance and eloquence. When the unseen world became revealed to him and he became drunk with God, his heart turned completely against that desire and longing. God most High declared, 'I have given thee that elegance and eloquence which thou soughtest.' The Prophet answered, 'Lord, of what use are they to me? I am indifferent to them and do not desire them.' God most High replied, 'Do not grieve. That too shall come to pass, and yet thy indifference shall still obtain and it will harm thee nothing.' God most High bestowed on him such speech that all the world, from his time down to the present day, have composed and still compose so many volumes expounding it, and still men fall short of comprehending it entirely. God most High also declared, 'Thy Companions out of weakness and fear for their lives and because of the envious, used to pronounce thy name secretly into the ear. I will publish thy greatness abroad to such a point that men will shout it aloud in sweet intonations five times daily on the high minarets in all regions of the world, so that it will be famous in the east and the west.'

So every man who has gambled himself upon this way, to him all objectives whether religious or mundane have become attainable, and none has ever had cause to complain of this way.

Our words are all the true coin, and the words of other men are but imitation. This imitation is a branch of the true coin. The true coin is like the foot of a man, and the imitation is as a wooden mould in the shape of a human foot; that wooden foot has been filched from the original foot and shaped to its measure. If no foot had existed in the world, whence would they have known of this imitation? Some speech therefore is true coin, and some imitation. They resemble each other, and there is need of a discriminator to recognise the true coin from the imitation. That discrimination is faith, and unbelief is lack of discrimination.

Do you not see how in the time of Pharaoh, when Moses' rod became a serpent and the rods and ropes of the magicians also became serpents, he who lacked discrimination saw all to be of the same kind and made no distinction between them; but he who possessed discrimination understood the magic from the true, and through discrimination became a believer? Hence we realise that faith is discrimination.

After all, the root of our jurisprudence is Divine revelation. But when it became mingled with the thoughts and senses and application of mortal men, that original grace vanished. In this moment, in what respect does it resemble the delicacy of the revelation?

Consider likewise this water which flows in Turut towards the city. There, where its fountainhead is, see how pure and fine it is! But when it enters the city and passes through the gardens and various quarters and the houses of the inhabitants, so many people wash their hands and faces and feet and other parts in it, and their clothes and carpets, and the urine of all the quarters and dung of horses and mules are poured into it and mixed up with it. Look at it when it passes out of the other side of the city! Though it is still the same water, turning the dust to clay, slaking the thirsty, making the plain verdant, yet it requires a discriminator to discover that the water has not retained its former clarity and that disagreeable things have been mingled with it. 'The believer is sagacious, discriminating, understanding, intelligent.'

The elder is not intelligent if he is preoccupied with playing; though he be a hundred years old, he is still raw and a child. A child, if he is not preoccupied with playing, is in reality an elder. Here age is of no consideration. *Water unstaling*—that is what is required. Water unstaling is that which cleanses all the impurities of the world, and they leave no trace in it. It remains limpid and clear as it was, not dwindling away in the stomach and not becoming adulterated and fetid. That is the Water of Life.

'A man shouted out when at prayer and wept. Is his prayer void or not?'

The answer to this question differs according to the circumstances. If he wept because he was shown another world beyond sensible things, that after all is called 'water of the eyes'; when he has seen a thing which is a congener and perfecter of prayer, that is the object of prayer and his prayer is in order and even more perfect. If on the other hand he wept on account of worldly things, or out of wrath because an enemy prevailed over him, or envy of another man because he possessed such abundance whilst he himself possessed none, then his prayer is docked and defective and void.

So we realise that faith is discrimination, distinguishing between truth and falsehood, true coin and imitation. Whoever is without discrimination remains deprived. These words which we speak are enjoyed by every man of discrimination, but are wasted on him who is without discrimination.

Two intelligent and well qualified townsmen out of compassion go and give testimony for the benefit of a countryman. But the countryman out of ignorance says something at variance with those two, so that their testimony yields no results and their labours are wasted. In this sense they say that the countryman has his testimony with him, but being overcome by a state of drunkenness and intoxicated he does not consider whether there is any discriminator present worthy and deserving of these words, so that he pours them out at random. In like manner a woman whose breasts are very full and painful will collect the dogs of the quarter and pour out her milk upon them.

Now these words have fallen into the hands of one without discrimination. It is as though you have given a precious pearl into the hand of a child who does not know its value. When he goes farther on, an apple is placed in his hand and the pearl is taken from him since he has no discrimination. So discrimination is a great possession.

Abū Yazīd when a child was taken by his father to school to learn jurisprudence. When he brought him before the schoolmaster he said, 'This is the jurisprudence of God.' They said, 'This is the jurisprudence of Abū Ḥanīfa.' He said, 'I want the jurisprudence of God.' When he brought him before the grammar-teacher he said, 'This is the grammar of God.' The teacher said, 'This is the grammar of Sībawaihi.' Abū Yazīd said, 'I do not want it.' So he spoke wherever his father took him. His father could do nothing with him, and let him be. Later he came to Baghdad upon this quest, and as soon as he saw Junaid he shouted, 'This is the jurisprudence of God!'

How can it happen that a lamb should not recognise its own mother on whose milk it has been suckled? That is born of reason and discrimination. So let the form go.

There was a certain shaikh who used to leave his disciples standing with their hands folded in service. They said to him, 'Shaikh, why do you not let this class sit down? This is not the practice of dervishes, this is the custom of princes and kings.' He replied, 'No. Be silent. I desire that they should respect this way, so that they may derive full benefit. Though respect lies within the heart, yet "the outward is the frontispiece of the inward." What is the meaning of "frontispiece"? The meaning of the frontispiece is that by it men may know for whom and to whom the letter is written. From the frontispiece of a book people may know what chapters and sections it contains. From outward respect, bowing the head and standing on the feet, it may be realised what respect they have inwardly, and in what manner they respect God. If they do not show respect outwardly, it becomes known that inwardly they are impudent and do not respect the men of God.'

40

Jauhar the Sultan's servant asked: During his lifetime a man is five times made to repeat the Muslim credo. He does not understand the words and does not memorise them correctly. After death what questions will he be asked, seeing that after death he forgets even the questions which he has learned?

I answered: If he forgets what he has learned, then of course he becomes *tabula rasa* and suitable for questions which have not been learned. You now this minute—from that minute to the present moment you are listening to me. Some part of what I say you accept, because you have heard the like of it before and accepted it; some you half accept; regarding some you hesitate. No one hears this rejection and acceptance and inward disputation on your part, for there is no instrument. Though you are listening, no sound comes to your ear from within you. If you search inwardly, you will find no speaker. This coming of yours to visit me is itself a question without throat and tongue, namely, 'Show me a way, and make clearer that which you have shown.' My sitting with you, whether silent or speaking, is an answer to your hidden questions. When you go back from here to wait upon the king, that is a question addressed to the king and an answer. Every day the king questions his servants without tongue: 'How do you stand? How do you eat? How do you look?' If anyone has a wry look within him, his answer inevitably comes awry and he cannot manage to give a straight answer. In the same way a man who stammers, however much he wishes to speak straight, is unable to do so. A goldsmith who rubs gold against the stone is questioning the gold, and the gold answers, 'This is I. I am pure,' or, 'I am alloyed.'

158

The crucible tells you itself, when you have been strained,
That you are gold, or mere copper with gold stained.

Hunger is a questioning of nature: 'There is a crack in the body's house. Give a brick. Give clay.' Eating is an answer: 'Take.' Not eating is also an answer: 'Now there is no need. That brick is not dry yet; it is not suitable to tap that brick.' The physician comes and takes the pulse. That is a question; the throbbing of the vein is the answer. Examination of the urine is an unostentatious question and answer. To cast a seed into the ground is a question: 'I want such and such fruit.' The growing of the tree is an answer without ostentation of tongue. Because the answer is wordless, the question must be wordless. Though the seed decays, the tree does not grow: that too is a question and an answer. 'Do you know not that the refusing of an answer is itself an answer?'

A king read a letter thrice, and did not write an answer. The subject wrote a complaint, saying, 'Thrice now I have petitioned your majesty. Let your majesty at least say whether my petition is accepted or rejected.' The king wrote on the back of the letter, 'Do you not know that the refusing of an answer is itself an answer, and that the answer to a fool is silence?'

The tree's not growing is a refusal to answer, therefore it is an answer. Every motion that a man makes is a question; whatever occurs to him, be it sorrow or joy, is an answer. If he hears a pleasant answer, he must show his thanks. Thanks is expressed by repeating the same kind of question to the one which received this answer. If he hears an unpleasant answer, he quickly asks God's forgiveness and does not repeat that kind of question.

> *If only, when Our might came upon them, they*
> *had been humble! But their hearts were hard.*

That is to say, they did not understand that the answer corresponds with their question.

> *And Satan decked out fair to them*
> *what they were doing.*

That is to say, they saw the answer to their question and said, 'This ugly answer is not appropriate to this question.' They did not realise that the smoke came from the fuel, not the fire: the drier the fuel, the less the smoke. You have entrusted a garden to a gardener: if a disagreeable odour is emitted there, suspect the gardener and not the garden.

A man said, 'Why did you kill your mother?' The other answered, 'I saw a thing that was not seemly.' The first man said, 'You ought to have killed the stranger.' The second man said, 'Then every day I would be killing someone.'

Now therefore, whatever happens to you, school your own soul, for then you will not have to fight with someone every day. If they say, *Everything is from God*, we reply: Then of necessity to reproach one's own self, and to let the world go, is also from God.

That is like the story of the man who shook down apricots from a tree and ate them. The owner of the orchard demanded of him, saying, 'Are you not afraid of God?' The man said, 'Why should I fear? The tree belongs to God, and I am God's servant. God's servant ate God's property!' The owner said, 'Wait and see what answer I shall give you. Fetch a rope, and tie him to this tree and beat him, till the answer is made clear!' The man said, 'Are you not afraid of God?' The owner answered, 'Why should I be afraid? You are God's servant, and this is God's stick. I am beating God's servant with God's stick!'

The moral is, that the world is like a mountain; whatever you say, whether it be good or evil, you hear the same from the mountain. If you conceive the idea, 'I spoke prettily and the mountain gave an ugly answer,' this would be impossible. When the nightingale sings in the mountain, does there return from the mountain the voice of a raven or the voice of a man or the voice of a donkey? Know for certain then that you have spoken like a donkey!

> Speak pleasantly, when by the mountain you pass;
> Why do you bray at the mountain like an ass?

> The azure sky sends back the note
> Of sweetness issued by your throat.

41

We are like a bowl on the surface of the water. The movement of the bowl on the surface of the water is controlled not by the bowl but by the water.

Someone said: This statement is of general application. But some people know that they are on the surface of the water, whereas some do not know.

The Master said: If the statement were of general application, then the particular specification that 'The heart of the believer is between two fingers of the All-Merciful' would not be correct. God also said:

The All-Merciful has taught the Koran.

It cannot be said that this is a general statement. God taught all sciences so what is this particularisation of the Koran? Similarly:

Who created the heavens and the earth.

What is this particularisation of the heavens and the earth, since He created all things in general? Undoubtedly all bowls travel on the surface of the water of Omnipotence and the Divine Will. But it is unmannerly to relate to It a despicable thing, such as 'O Creator of dung and farting and wind-breaking'; one only says, 'O Creator of the heavens' and 'O Creator of the minds.' So this particularisation has its significance; though the statement is general, yet the particularisation of a thing is an indication of the choiceness of that thing.

The upshot is, that the bowl travels on the surface of the water. The water carries one bowl in such a manner that every bowl gazes upon that bowl. The water carries another bowl in such a manner that every bowl runs away from that bowl instinctively and is ashamed of it. The water inspires them to run away and implants in them the power to run away, so that they say, 'O God, take us farther away from it'; whilst in the former case they say, 'O God, bring us nearer to it.'

The person who regards the situation as general says, 'From the standpoint of subjection, both kinds of bowl are equally subject to the water.' In reply one may say, 'If you only saw the grace and beauty and pretty sauntering of this bowl on the water, you would not have had such care for that general attribute.' In the same way a beloved person is a co-partner with all dungs and every manner of filth from the standpoint of existing. But it would never occur to the lover to say, 'My beloved is a co-partner with all manner of filth in the general description that both are bodies contained in a certain space and comprised in the six directions, created in time and subject to decay' and the rest of

161

the general descriptions. He would never apply these terms to the beloved; and anyone who described the beloved in this general manner he would take as an enemy and deem his particular devil.

Since therefore you find it in you to regard that general attribute, not being worthy to look upon our particular beauty, it is not proper to dispute with you; for our disputations are commingled with beauty, and it is wrong to disclose beauty to those who are not worthy of it. 'Impart not wisdom to those not meet for it, lest you do wisdom wrong; and withhold it not from those meet to receive it, lest you do them wrong.'

This is the science of speculation, it is not the science of disputation. Roses and fruit-blossoms do not bloom in the autumn, for that would be disputation; that is, it would be confronting and competing with the opponent autumn. It is not in the nature of the rose to confront autumn. If the regard of the sun has done its work, the rose comes out in an equable and just atmosphere; otherwise, it draws in its head and retires within its stem. The autumn says to it, 'If you are not a barren branch, confront me, if you are a man!' The rose says, 'In your presence I am a barren branch and a coward. Say whatever you will!'

> O monarch of all truthful men,
> How think you me a hypocrite?
> With living men I am alive,
> And with the dead as dead I sit.

You, who are Bahā' al-Dīn—if some old crone without any teeth, her face all wrinkles like the back of a lizard, should come and say, 'If you are a man and a true youth, behold, I have come before you! Behold, horse and the fair one! Behold, the field! Show manliness, if you are a man,'—you would say, 'God be my refuge! I am no man. What they have told you is all lies. If you are the mate, unmanliness is most comely!' A scorpion comes and raises its sting against your member, saying, 'I have heard that you are a man who laughs and is gay. Laugh, so that I may hear you laugh.' In such a case one would say, 'Now that you have come, I have no laugh and no gay temperament. What they have told you is lies. All my inclinations to laugh are preoccupied with the hope that you may go away and be far from me!'

Someone said: You sighed, and the ecstasy departed. Do not sigh, so that the ecstasy may not depart.

The Master answered: Sometimes it happens that ecstasy departs if you do not sigh, according to the various circumstances. If that had not been so, God would not have said

Abraham was a man who sighed, a clement man.

Nor would it have been right to display any act of obedience to God; for all display is ecstasy.

What you say, you say in order that ecstasy may ensue. So, if someone induces ecstasy, you attend that person in order that ecstasy may ensue. That is like shouting to a sleeper, 'Arise! It is day. The caravan is off.' Others say, 'Don't shout. He is in ecstasy. His ecstasy will start away.' The man says, 'That ecstasy is destruction, this ecstasy is deliverance from destruction.' They say, 'Don't make a confusion, for this shouting hinders thought.' The man says, 'This shouting will make the sleeper think. Otherwise what thinking will he do, whilst he is here asleep? When he has awakened, then he will start to think.'

So shouting is of two kinds. If the shouter is above the other in knowledge, his shouting will cause an increase of thought. For since his awakener is a man of knowledge and of wakefulness, when he awakens the other out of the slumber of heedlessness he informs him of his own world and draws him thither. So his thought ascends, since he has been called out of a high estate. When on the contrary the awakener is below the other in intellect, when he awakens him his gaze drops. Since his awakener is lower down, inevitably his gaze drops downwards and his thought goes to the lower world.

42

Those persons who have made or are in the course of making their studies think that if they constantly attend here they will forget and abandon all that they have learned. On the contrary, when they come here their sciences all acquire a soul. For all sciences are like images; when they acquire a soul, it is as though a lifeless body has received a soul.

163

All knowledge has its origin beyond, transferring from the world without letters and sounds into the world of letters and sounds. In yonder world, speaking is without letters and sounds.

And unto Moses God spoke directly.

God most High spoke with Moses, upon whom be peace. Well, He spoke not with letters and sounds, with throat and tongue. Letters require a throat and lips in order to be audible; God most High is exalted far above lips and mouth and throat. So prophets in the world without letters and sounds converse with God in a manner that the imaginations of these partial intelligences cannot attain or understand. But the prophets come down from the world without letters into the world of letters, and become children for the sake of these children; for 'I was sent as a teacher.' Now though this mass of people who have remained all the time in letters and sounds do not reach the spiritual states of the prophet, yet they derive strength from him, and wax and grow, and find comfort in him. Similarly the infant, though not knowing and not recognising his mother in detail, yet finds comfort in her and derives strength from her. So too the fruit finds comfort on the branch and becomes sweet and ripe, though knowing nothing of the tree. So with regard to that great saint and his letters and sounds, though the mass of men do not know him and do not attain to him, yet they derive strength from him and are nourished.

It is fixed in every soul that beyond reason and letter and sound there is something, a macrocosm. Do you not see how all men have a hankering after the demented and go to visit them? They say, 'It may be that this is in fact that, and true. Such a thing exists; but they have mistaken the place. That thing is not contained within the reason.' But not everything that is not contained in the reason exists. 'Every nut is round, but not every round thing is a nut' is a sign of that.

We say: Though such a man has a state which cannot be expressed in words and writing, yet from him reason and spirit derive strength and are nourished. This is not found in these demented ones around whom they circle; those who visit them are not transformed out of their own state and do not find repose in such a man. Even though they may think that they have found repose, that is not what we call repose. Thus, a child parted from his mother finds comfort for a moment in another; that is not what we call comfort, for the child has made a mistake.

Physicians say that whatever is agreeable to the temperament and is hankered after by it gives strength to a man and purifies his blood. This is true however only so long as a man is without disease. For instance, chalk is agreeable to the chalk-eater, but we do not say that it is good for his temperament, though he finds it agreeable. The bilious man finds sour things agreeable and sugar disagreeable. But that is no criterion of what is truly agreeable, because such a taste rests upon a distemper. The truly agreeable is what is agreeable to a man in the first place, before he falls sick. For instance, a man has his hand cut or broken and hung in a sling, so that it becomes all crooked. The surgeon makes it straight and sets it in its original place. That is not agreeable to the man, and indeed it pains him, just as much as its being crooked is agreeable to him. The surgeon says, 'First of all it was agreeable to you that your hand was straight, and you found comfort in that. When they made it crooked you felt pain and suffered. Though now its being crooked is agreeable to you, this agreeableness is false and is of no account.'

Similarly the spirits in the world of holiness found agreeable the commemoration of God and absorption in God, like the angels. If they fall sick and distempered through connexion with the body, and chalk-eating becomes agreeable to them, the prophet and the saint, who are physicians, say, 'This is not truly agreeable to you. This agreeableness is a lie. Something other is agreeable to you which you have forgotten. What is agreeable to your original and sound temperament is that which was in the first place agreeable to you. This sickness is now agreeable to you; you think this is agreeable, and do not believe the truth.'

A gnostic was seated before a grammarian. The grammarian said, 'A word must be one of three things: either it is a noun, a verb, or a particle.' The gnostic tore his robe and cried, 'Alas! Twenty years of my life and striving and seeking have gone to the winds. For I laboured greatly in the hope that there was another word outside of this. Now you have destroyed my hope.' Though the gnostic had in fact attained that word which was his purpose, he spoke thus in order to arouse the grammarian.

It is related that Ḥasan and Ḥusain, God be well pleased with them, once in the state of childhood saw a person who was making his ablutions all wrong and contrary to the law. They desired to teach him to make ablution in a better way. So they came to him and said, 'This tells me that you make your ablutions wrong. We will both make our ablutions before you, then you can see which of the two kinds of ablution accords with the law.' And they both made ablution before him. He said, 'Children, your ablution is very lawful and right and good. My ablution, wretch that I am, was wrong.'

The greater the number of guests become, the larger they make the house; the more the furnishings, and the more food prepared. Do you not see that since the stature of a little child is small, his thoughts too, which are as it were guests, are appropriate to the house of his body? He knows nothing apart from milk and his nurse. When he grows older the guests, his thoughts, also increase, and his house of reason and perception and discrimination becomes enlarged. When the guests of passionate love arrive they are too much for the house and demolish the house, and he builds anew. The King's veils and the King's out-riders and troops and attendants cannot be contained in his house. Those veils are not appropriate to this door; to accommodate those infinite attendants an infinite station is required. When the King's veils are hung, they provide all brightnesses and remove all coverings, so that the secret things become manifest—contrary to the veils of this present world, which augment the covering. These veils are the opposite of those veils.

> I suffer wrongs which I'll not specify
> That men may nothing know of my excuse
> Or my reproach; even as the candle weeps
> And no man knows whether the tears it sheds
> Are of its close companionship with fire
> Or for its being parted from the sweet.

Someone said: These verses were spoken by Qāḍī Abū Manṣūr Haravī.

The Master said: Qāḍī Manṣūr speaks obscurely and is hesitant and variable. But Manṣūr could not contain himself and spoke out bluntly.

The whole world is the prisoner of destiny, and destiny is the prisoner of the beauty; the beauty reveals and does not conceal.

Someone said: Recite a page of the Qāḍī's words.

The Master recited, and after that he said: God has certain servants who whenever they see a woman in a chaddur command, 'Raise the veil, so that we may see your face, what manner of person and thing you are. For when you pass by veiled and we do not see, disquietude will ensue, as to how this person was and what she was. I am not the sort of person to be tempted by you and enslaved by you if I see your face. It is a long time now that God has made me innocent and indifferent to you. I am quite secure that if I see you, you will not disturb me and tempt me. It is when I do not see you that I am disturbed, wondering what sort of a person it was.' These men are very different from that other party, the men of carnal passion. If they see the faces of the beautiful, they are captivated by them and become disturbed. So it is better in their case for them not to show their faces, so as not to tempt them. In regard to the spiritualists it is better to show their faces, so that they may be delivered out of temptation.

Someone said: In Khvarizm nobody is a lover, because in Khvarizm there are many beautiful women. No sooner do they see a beauty and fix their hearts on her than they see another still better than she, so that she no longer appeals to them.

The Master said: If there are no lovers for the beauties of Khvarizm, yet Khvarizm must have its lovers, seeing that there are countless beauties in that land. That Khvarizm is poverty, wherein are countless mystical beauties and spiritual forms. Each one you alight upon and are fixed on, another shows its face so that you forget the former one, and so *ad infinitum*. So let us be lovers of true poverty, wherein such beauties are to be found.

43

Saif al-Bukhārī went to Egypt. Every one likes a mirror, and is in love with the mirror of his attributes and attainments, while not knowing the true nature of his face. He supposes the veil to be a face, and the mirror of the veil to be the mirror of his face. As for you, uncover your face, so that you may find me to be the mirror of your face, and that you may know for sure that I am a mirror.

A man said: I know for a fact that the prophets and saints are all victims of a false presumption. There is nothing in it but mere pretence.

The Master said: Do you say this at random, or do you see and then speak? If it is the case that you see and then speak, vision is certainly proven as existing; indeed, it is the most precious and noblest thing in existence. The proof of the message of the prophets is merely their claim to vision; and that you have acknowledged. Moreover vision manifests only through an object of vision. Vision is a transitive; for vision to take place there must be an object and a subject of vision. The object of vision is the thing sought, and the viewer is the seeker; or the other way round. Your very denial establishes the existence of a seeker and a thing sought, and vision. The God-man relationship is a case where negation necessarily proves the positive.

They say, 'That crowd are disciples of that dimwit, and venerate him.' I say: That 'dimwit' of a shaikh is not inferior to a stone and an idol. Those who worship stones venerate and magnify them, and to them direct their hopes and longings, their petitions and needs and tears. The stone neither knows nor feels anything of this. Yet God most High has made stones and idols to be a means to this devotion in them, of which the stones and idols are entirely unaware.

A lawyer was once beating a boy. 'Why are you beating him?' he was asked. 'What crime has he committed?'

'You don't know this whoreson,' he answered. 'He spoils everything.'

'What does he do? What sin is he guilty of?' someone demanded.

'He runs away at the moment of emission,' the lawyer replied. 'That is, at the time of friction his phantom runs away, and my emission is nullified.'

There is no doubt that the lawyer was in love with the boy's phantom, and the boy was quite unaware of the fact. In the same way these disciples are in love with the phantom of this foolish shaikh, and he was oblivious of their 'banishment' and 'union' and all the phases of their love-life.

168

If misguided and misdirected love for a phantom produces ecstasy, yet it is nothing like the mutual love enjoyed with a real beloved who is aware and wide awake to the lover's condition. Similarly the man who embraces in the dark a pillar, thinking it to be a beloved, weeping and complaining, cannot be compared, in regard to the pleasure he enjoys, with one who is embracing his living and conscious friend.

44

Everybody on setting out and journeying to a certain place does so with a rational idea in mind: 'If I go there I shall be able to secure many advantages and attend to many affairs, my business will be set in order, my friends will be delighted, I shall defeat my enemies.' Such is the idea he has in mind; but his true objective is something other. He has made so many plans and thought out so many ideas, and not one has turned out according to his desire; for all that he continues to rely upon his own planning and choice.

> Ignoring Fate, man plots his little plan;
> God's Will consorts not with the plots of man.

This is illustrated by the experience of a man who sees in a dream that he has chanced into a strange city where he has no acquaintances; there is no one who knows him and he knows nobody. He becomes bewildered, vexed and sorrowful, regretting and saying to himself, 'Why did I come to this city where I have neither friend nor acquaintance, no one to shake me by the hand and press me on the lip?' On awaking he sees neither city nor people, and realises that all his anguish and sorrow and regret were to no purpose. So he repents of that state he found himself in, realising that it was quite wasted. Next time he falls asleep he sees himself by chance in exactly such a city again, and begins to feel the same sorrow and anguish and regret. He repents of coming to such a city and does not think or remember, 'When I was awake I repented of fretting so and realised that my grief was quite wasted, that it was a dream and to no purpose.'

That is exactly how things are. Men have seen a hundred thousand times their intentions and plans coming to nothing; nothing has proceeded in accordance with their desires. But God most High appoints oblivion to take charge of them so that they forget all that has happened, and once more follow their own ideas and wills. *God stands between a man and his heart.*

Ibrāhīm son of Adham, upon whom be God's mercy, at the time when he was a king had gone out hunting. He galloped in the track of a deer, until he became entirely separated from his soldiers and chanced far away. His horse was covered with sweat and weary, but still he galloped on. When he had passed beyond bounds in that wilderness, the deer suddenly began to speak. Turning back its face, it said, 'You were not created for this. This being was not fashioned out of not-being so that you might hunt me. Even supposing you catch me, what will be the result of that?'

When Ibrāhīm heard these words he cried aloud, and flung himself from the horse. There was no one in that desert apart from a shepherd. Ibrāhīm entreated him, saying, 'Take from me my royal robes encrusted with jewels, my arms and my horse, and give me your gown of coarse cloth, and tell no one, neither hint to any man what has passed with me.' He put on that rough gown and set out on his way. Now consider what his design was, and what his true objective proved to be! He desired to catch the deer; God most High caught him by means of the deer. So realise that in this world things happen as He wills, that His is the design and that the purpose is subject to Him.

Before becoming a Muslim, 'Umar, God be well pleased with him, entered his sister's house. His sister was chanting from the Koran in a loud voice

TA HA: We have not sent down . . .

When she saw her brother she hid the Koran, and became silent. 'Umar bared his sword saying, 'Surely tell me what you were reading and why you hid it, or this very instant I will chop off your head without quarter with the sword!' His sister feared greatly. Knowing his temper when angry and his fearfulness, in terror for her life she confessed, 'I was reading from these words which God most High revealed in this time to Muhammad, God bless him and give him peace.'

'Read on, so that I may hear,' said 'Umar. And she recited the whole of the Sura of *Taha*. 'Umar became furiously angry, his rage being such that he said, 'If I kill you this instant, that will be a killing of the defenceless. First I will go and cut off his head, then I will attend to you.'

In the extremity of his anger, holding a naked sword 'Umar set off for the Prophet's mosque. The chieftains of Quraish, seeing him on the way, exclaimed, 'Ha, 'Umar is after Muhammad. Assuredly if anything is to be done, it will be done in this way.' For 'Umar was a mighty and powerful and manly man; any army he marched against he surely vanquished, exposing their decapitated heads; so much so, that the Prophet declared always, God bless him and give him peace, 'God, succour my religion by means of 'Umar or Abū Jahl.' For those two were famous in his time for strength and manliness and heroism. Afterwards, when 'Umar became a Muslim, he always used to weep and say, 'O Messenger of God, woe for me if you had given Abū Jahl precedence over me and said, "God, succour my religion by means of Abū Jahl or 'Umar." What then would have happened to me! I would have continued in error.'

In short, he was on the way, with naked sword, making for the Prophet's mosque. Meanwhile Gabriel, upon whom be peace, revealed to Muhammad, God bless him and give him peace, 'Lo, Messenger of God, 'Umar is coming to convert to Islam. Take him to your bosom.' Just as 'Umar entered the door of the mosque, he saw as clear as clear that an arrow of light flew from Muhammad, upon whom be peace, and pierced his heart. He uttered a loud cry and fell down insensible. Love and passionate attachment manifested in his soul, and he would that he might dissolve into Muhammad in the extremity of his affection, and become effaced. He said, 'Now, Prophet of God, offer me the faith and speak that blessed word, that I may hear.' Having become a Muslim, he said, 'Now, in thanksgiving for having come against you with a naked sword and in expiation therefor, henceforward I will give quarter to no man whom I hear speaking improperly of you. With this sword I will strike his head apart from his body.'

Coming out of the mosque, he suddenly encountered his father. His father said, 'You have changed religion.' Immediately he struck off his head, and walked on holding in his hand the bloodstained sword. The chieftains of Quraish, seeing the bloodstained sword, said, 'Well, you promised that you would bring his head. Where is his head?' Said

171

'Umar, 'Here it is!' One of them said, 'You fetched his head from here?'
He answered, 'No. This is not that head. This is of the other
side.'

Now see what 'Umar proposed, and what God most High designed
thereby. So you may realise that all affairs turn out as He desires.

> Omar, the Prophet for to slay,
> Comes sword in hand upon the way;
> He falls into God's trap, and through
> Good fortune finds the vision true.

So if they say to you also, 'What have you brought?' Say, 'We have
brought the head.' If they say, 'We had seen this head,' say, 'No, this
is not that head, this is another head.' The true head is that in which is
a secret; otherwise, a thousand heads are not worth a penny.

They chanted the following verse.

> *And when We appointed the House to be*
> *a place of visitation for the people,*
> *and a sanctuary,*
> *and: 'Take to yourselves Abraham's station*
> *for a place of prayer.'*

Abraham said, 'O God, since Thou hast honoured me with the robe
of Thy approval and hast chosen me, vouchsafe this distinction to my
seed also.' God most High declared:

> *'My covenant shall not reach*
> *the evildoers.'*

That is to say, 'Those who are evildoers, they are not worthy of My
robe of honour and distinction.' When Abraham realised that God most
High extends not His loving care to the evildoers and the insolent, he
made a bargain. He said, 'O God, those who believe and are not evildoers—give them a portion of Thy provision and withhold it not from
them.' God most High declared, 'My provision is common to all men,
and all men shall have a share of it. All creatures enjoy their portion of
the benefits of this guesthouse. But the robe of My approval and acceptance and the honour of ennoblement and distinction are the special
portion of the elect and the chosen ones.'

The literalists say that what is intended by this 'House' is the Kaaba. For all who take refuge in the Kaaba find security from all mischief; there it is forbidden to hunt for game, there malice may not be done to any man. God most High singled out that House for Himself. That is all perfectly true and excellent; but that is the literal interpretation of the Koran. The spiritualists for their part say that the 'House' is the inward part of a man; that is to say, 'God, free my inward part of temptation and carnal occupations and cleanse it of passions and corrupt and idle thoughts, so that no fear may remain in it and security may ensue, so that it may become wholly the locus of Thy revelation, and no demon or devil or temptation may find a way into it.' Just as God most High has appointed meteors to watch over heaven, so as to prevent the accursed Satans from listening to the secrets of the angels, that none may become apprised of their secrets and that they may be far from all mischief. So this means, 'O God, do Thou likewise appoint the guardian of Thy loving care to watch over our inward part, to drive away from us the temptation of the Satans and the tricks of the carnal soul and desire.' Such is the statement of the esotericists and the spiritualists.

Every man stirs from his own place. The Koran is a double-sided brocade. Some enjoy one side, and some the other. Both are true, inasmuch as God most High desires that both peoples should derive benefit from it. In the same way a woman has a husband and a suckling child; each enjoys her in a different way. The child's pleasure is in her breast and her milk; the husband's pleasure is in intercourse with her. Some men are infants of the Way; they take pleasure in the literal meaning of the Koran, and drink that milk. But those who have reached years of full discretion have another enjoyment and a different understanding of the inner meanings of the Koran.

Abraham's station and place of prayer is a certain spot in the environments of the Kaaba where the literalists say two inclinations of prayer must be performed. This is excellent indeed, by Allah. But according to the spiritualists Abraham's station means you should cast yourself into the fire for God's sake, and bring yourself to this station by toiling and labouring in God's way, or nigh this station. A man has then sacrificed himself for the sake of God; that is to say, his self is no more of moment in his sight and he has ceased to tremble for himself. To perform two inclinations of prayer at Abraham's station is excellent:

but let it be such a prayer that the standing is performed in this world, and the bowing in the other world.

The meaning of the Kaaba is the heart of the prophets and the saints, which is the locus of God's revelation. The physical Kaaba is a branch of that. If it were not for the heart, of what use would the Kaaba be? The prophets and the saints have wholly forsaken their own desire, and are following the desire of God. So whatever He commands, that they do. To whomsoever God denies His loving care, be it even father or mother, to them they are indifferent; indeed in their eyes such a one is an enemy.

> Into thy hands we have given the reins of our heart;
> Whate'er thou declarest cooked, we declare it is burnt!

All that I say is a comparison, it is not a likeness. Comparison is one thing, and likeness is another. God most High has likened His Light to a lamp for the sake of comparison; the saints are likened to the glass of that lamp, also for the sake of comparison. God's Light is not contained in phenomenal being and space; how then should it be contained in a glass and a lamp? How should the orients of the Lights of Almighty God be contained in the heart? Yet when you seek after it, you find it in the heart; not as being a receptacle wherein that Light resides, but that you find that Light radiating from that place. In the same way you discover your image in the mirror; yet your image is not in the mirror, only when you look in the mirror you see yourself.

When things appear unintelligible and are enunciated by means of a comparison, then they become intelligible; and when they become intelligible, they become sensible. Thus, you may say that when a man closes his eyes he sees wonderful things and observes sensible forms and shapes; when he opens his eyes he sees nothing. No man considers this intelligible or believes in it; but when you state the comparison then it becomes realised. How is this? It is like a man who sees in a dream a hundred thousand things, of which it is not possible that in his waking state he should see a single one. Or it is like an architect who conceives inwardly a picture of a house, complete with breadth and length and shape: this does not appear intelligible to anyone. But when he draws the plan of the house on paper, then it becomes visible; and being given definite form it becomes intelligible in every detail to

174

anyone looking at it. Being intelligible, the architect then proceeds to build the house according to that design, and the house becomes sensible.

Thus it is realised that all unintelligibles become intelligible and sensible through use of a comparison. So it is that they say that in the other world books will fly, some into the right hand and some into the left. There too are the angels, the Throne, Hell and Heaven, the Balance, the Reckoning, and the Book: none of these can be realised save through the propounding of a comparison. Though in the present world there is no likeness to any of these things, yet through comparison they become certified. The comparison of those things in this world is the following. By night all men sleep, cobbler alike and king, judge and tailor, and all the rest. From all of them their thoughts take wing, and no thought remains to any one of them. Then at dawn it is as though the blast of Israfil's trumpet brings to life the atoms of their bodies; the thoughts of each one of them, like the books in the next world, fly headlong towards each man without any mistake being made—the tailor's thoughts to the tailor, the lawyer's thoughts to the lawyer, the blacksmith's thoughts to the blacksmith, the oppressor's thoughts to the oppressor, the thoughts of the just to the just. Does any man sleep through the night as a tailor and by day rise as a cobbler? No; for that was his work and preoccupation before, and he becomes occupied with that again. From this you may realise that the like obtains in the other world too, and that this is not absurd; in this world it actually happens.

So if a man, by employing this comparison, reaches the end of the thread, he contemplates and sniffs out in this world all the circumstances which prevail in the other world; all are uncovered to him, so that he comes to realise that all things are comprised in God's omnipotence. Many are the bones you can see mouldering in the grave, yet enjoying a sweet repose and a drunken sleep, fully aware of that enjoyment and intoxication. These are no idle words, for men say, 'May the dust lie sweet on him!' If the dust had no awareness of sweetness, how would men say such a thing?

> I pray that moon-faced idol
>   May live a hundred years,
> My faithful heart a quiver
>   For the shafts of her tears.

In the dust of her door my heart
So happy, happy died,
Praying, 'Lord, may her dust
Forever happy abide!'

The comparison of this is actual in the world of sensible phenomena. Thus, two persons are sleeping on one mattress. One sees himself in the midst of a banquet, a rose-garden, Paradise; the other sees himself in the midst of snakes, the guardians of Hell, scorpions. If you investigate as between the two, you will see neither the one nor the other. Why then should it be thought so surprising that the parts of some men even in the tomb experience pleasure and repose and intoxication, whilst some are in pain and torment and agony, yet you can see neither this nor that? Hence it is realised that the unintelligible becomes intelligible through the use of a comparison.

Comparison does not resemble likeness. Thus, the gnostic gives the name 'spring' to relaxation and happiness and expansion, and calls contraction and sorrow 'autumn': what formal resemblance is there between happiness and the spring, sorrow and the autumn? Yet this is a comparison without which the intellect cannot conceive and grasp that meaning. So it is that God most High declares:

Not equal are the blind and the seeing man,
the shadows and the light,
the shade and the torrid heat.

God here has related faith to light and unbelief to shadows, or He has related faith to a delightful shade and unbelief to a burning and merciless sun boiling the brain. Yet what resemblance is there between the brightness and subtlety of faith and the light of this world of ours, or between the sordidness and gloom of unbelief and the darkness of our world?

If any man falls asleep during the time when we are speaking, that slumber is not out of heedlessness but security. Thus, a caravan is travelling along a difficult and dangerous road in a dark night; they drive on in fear, lest harm should befall them from the enemy. As soon as the voice of a dog or a cock reaches their ears and they have come to the village they are carefree, and stretch out their legs and sleep sweetly. On the road, where there was no sound or murmur, they could not sleep for fear; in the village, where security obtains, for all the barking of dogs and crowing of cocks they are carefree and happy and fall asleep.

Our words too come from habitation and security; they are the sayings of prophets and saints. When the spirits hear the words of their familiar friends they feel secure and are delivered from fear; for from these words is wafted to them the scent of hope and felicity. In like manner a man travelling along on a dark night in a caravan in the extremity of his fear thinks every moment that thieves have mingled with the caravan. He desires to hear the words of his fellow travellers, and to recognise them by their words. When he hears their words he feels secure. 'Say: O Muhammad, recite!' Because your essence is subtle, the glances do not attain you; when you speak, they discover that you are the familiar friend of their spirits and feel secure, and are at peace. So speak!

The leanness of my body suffices to witness I am a man.
Who, but for my addressing you, would be invisible to you.

A certain creature inhabiting cornfields on account of its extreme smallness is invisible; but when it makes a sound, then people see it by means of the sound. That is, men are utterly immersed in the cornfield of this world, and your essence, because it is extremely subtle, is invisible. So speak, that they may recognise you.

When you wish to go to a certain place, first your heart goes and sees and informs itself of the conditions prevailing there; then your heart returns and draws your body along. Now all these other men are as bodies in relation to the saints and the prophets, who are the heart of this world. First they journeyed to the other world, coming out of their human attributes, the flesh and the skin. They surveyed the depths and heights of that world and this and traversed all the stages, so that it became known to them how one must proceed on that way. Then they came back and summoned mankind, saying, 'Come to that original world! For this world is a ruin and a perishing abode, and we have discovered a delightful place, of which we tell you.'

Hence it is realised that the heart in all circumstances is attached to the heart's beloved, and has no need to traverse the stages, no need to fear highwaymen, no need of the mule's packsaddle. It is the wretched body which is fettered to these things.

> I said to my heart, 'How is it,
> My heart, that in foolishness
> You are barred from the service
> Of Him whose name you bless?'

> My heart replied, 'You do wrong
> To misread me in this way,
> I am constant in His service,
> You are the one astray.'

Wherever you are and in whatever circumstances you find yourself, strive always to be a lover, and a passionate lover at that. Once love has become your property you will be a lover always, in the grave, at the resurrection, and in Paradise for ever and ever. When you have sown wheat, wheat will assuredly grow, wheat will be in the stook, wheat will be in the oven.

Majnūn desired to write a letter to Lailā. He took a pen in his hand and wrote these verses.

> Your name is upon my tongue,
> Your image is in my sight,
> Your memory is in my heart:
> Whither then shall I write?

Your image dwells in my sight, your name is never off my tongue, your memory occupies the depths of my soul, so whither am I to write a letter, seeing that you go about in all these places? The pen broke, and the page was torn.

Many a man there is whose heart is full of these words, only he cannot express them in terms of speech though he is a lover in quest and longing for this. This is not surprising, and this is no impediment to love; on the contrary, the root of the matter is the heart, and yearning and passion and love. Even so a child is in love with milk and from it derives succour and strength; yet the child cannot describe or define milk or give expression to it, saying, 'What pleasure I find in drinking milk and how weak and anguished I become through not drinking it,' for all that his soul is desirous and ardent for milk. The grown man on the other hand, though he describe milk in a thousand ways, yet finds no pleasure and takes no delight in milk.

45

What is the name of that youth? Saif al-Dīn ('Sword of the Faith').

The Master said: One cannot see a sword when it is in a scabbard. That man is truly the Sword of the Faith who fights for the faith and whose endeavours are wholly in God's cause, who reveals rectitude from error and distinguishes truth from falsehood. But first he fights with himself and improves his own character: 'Begin with yourself.' Likewise he directs all his moral counsels to himself, saying, 'After all, you are also a man. You have hands and feet, ears and understanding, eyes and a mouth. The prophets and saints too, who attained felicity and reached their goal—they also were men and like me had reason and a tongue, hands and feet. Why then were they vouchsafed the way? Why was the door opened to them, and not to me?' Such a man boxes his own ears and night and day fights with himself, saying, 'What did you do, and what motion proceeded from you, that you are not accepted?' So he continues, until he becomes the Sword of God and the Tongue of Truth.

For example, ten persons desire to enter a house. Nine find the way, and one remains outside and is not given the way. Certainly this person reflects inwardly and laments, saying, 'Why now, what did I do that they did not let me in? What lack of manners was I guilty of?' That man must attribute the fault to himself and recognise himself as remiss and lacking in manners. He should not say, 'This is what God does with me; what can I do? Such is His will; had He willed, He would have vouchsafed the way.' Such words are tantamount to abusing God and drawing the sword against God; in that sense he would be a Sword Against God, not the Sword of God.

God most High is far too exalted to have kith and kin. *He has not begotten, and has not been begotten.* No man has ever found the way to Him save through servanthood. *God is the All-sufficient; you are the needy ones.* It is not feasible for you to say of the person who has found the way to God, 'He was more God's kin, more His familiar, more connected with Him than I.' So nearness to God is not to be attained save through servanthood. He is the Giver Absolute; He filled the skirt of the sea with pearls, He clothed the thorn in the raiment of the rose, He bestowed life and spirit upon a handful of dust, all out of pure disinterest and without any precedent. All the parts of the world have their share from Him.

When a person hears that in a certain city there lives a generous man who bestows mighty gifts and favours, he will naturally go there in the hope of enjoying his share of that man's bounty. Since therefore God's bountifulness is so renowned and all the world is aware of His graciousness, why do you not beg of Him and hope to receive from Him a robe of honour and a rich gift? You sit in indolence saying, 'If He wills, He will give to me'; and so you importune Him not at all. The dog, which is not endowed with reason and comprehension, when it is hungry and has no bread comes up to you and wags its tail as if to say, 'Give me bread, I have no bread and you have bread.' That much discrimination it possesses. After all, you are not less than a dog, which is not content to sleep in the ashes and say, 'If he wills, he will give me bread of himself,' but entreats and wags its tail. So do you wag your tail, and desire and beg of God; for in the presence of such a Giver, to beg is mightily required. If you have no good fortune, ask for good fortune from One who is not niggardly, One who possesses great wealth.

God is mightily nigh unto you. Every thought and idea that you conceive, thereto God is closely attached, for it is He who gives being to that idea and thought and presents them to you. Only He is so exceeding near that you cannot see Him. What is so strange in that? In every act you perform your reason is with you and initiates that action; yet you cannot see your reason. Though you see its effect, yet you cannot see its essence. For instance a man went to the baths and became hot. Wherever he may be as he goes round the baths, the fire is with him and he feels hot through the effect of the heat of the fire; yet he does not see the fire itself. When he comes out of the baths and sees the fire actually, and knows that people become hot through fire, he realises that the heat of the baths also came from the fire. The human being is also a huge bath, having within itself the heat of reason and spirit and soul. But when you depart from the bath and proceed to the other world, then you see actually the essence of the reason and behold the essence of the soul and the spirit. You realise then that this cleverness was determined by the heat of the reason, those fallacies and pretences were derived from the soul, and life itself was the effect of the spirit. So you see precisely the essence of all three; but so long as you are in the bath you cannot see the fire sensibly, except through its effect. Take similarly the case of a man who has never seen running water. He is flung into water with his eyes bandaged. Something wet and soft strikes against his body, but he does not know what it is. When his eyes are unbandaged then he knows precisely that that was water. In the first place he knew it by its effect, now he sees its actual essence.

Therefore beg of God, and demand what you need of Him, for your petition will not be in vain.

Call upon Me and I will answer you.

We were in Samarqand, and the Khvarizmshah had laid siege to Samarqand and deployed his army to the attack. In that quarter dwelt an exceedingly beautiful girl, so lovely that there was none the match of her in all the city. I heard her saying, 'O God, how canst Thou hold it allowable to deliver me into the hands of evildoers? Well I know that Thou wilt never permit that, and on Thee I rely.' When the city was sacked and all its inhabitants were taken into captivity, the maidservants of the woman were also taken into captivity. But she suffered no hurt; for all her extreme beauty, no man so much as cast eyes on her. From this you may realise that whosoever has once committed himself to God has become secure from all harm and remained in safety, and that the petition of no man in His presence was ever in vain.

A certain dervish had taught his son, that whatever he asked for, his father would say, 'Ask it of God.' When he wept, and asked that thing of God, then that thing would be brought to him. The years passed thus. Then one day the child chanced to be alone in the house, and presently he hankered for some pottage. In the accustomed way he said, 'I want some pottage.' Suddenly a bowl of pottage materialised out of the unseen world, and the child ate to repletion. When his father and mother returned they said, 'Don't you want anything?' The child answered, 'I just asked for pottage and ate.' His father said, 'Praise be to

God, that you have got so far and your confidence and reliance upon God has grown so strong!'

When the mother of Mary bore Mary, she vowed to God to dedicate her to the House of God and not to do anything for her; she left her in a corner of the Temple. Zachariah demanded to look after the child. Every one requested to do the same. A dispute sprang up between them. Now in that time it was the custom that each party to a dispute should throw a stick into water; the one whose stick floated was deemed to prevail. It so happened that Zachariah's lot was the right one. They said, 'He has the right.' So every day Zachariah brought food to the child, and always found the very match of it in the corner of the mosque. He said, 'Mary, after all I am in charge of you. Whence do you get this?' Mary said, 'Whenever I feel the need of food, whatever I request God most High sends to me. His bounty and compassion are infinite; whosoever relies on Him, his trust is not in vain.' Zachariah said, 'O God, since Thou allowest every man's need, I also have a desire. Do Thou grant it me, and give me a son who shall be Thy friend, who without my prompting shall consort with Thee and be occupied with obedience to Thee.' God most High brought John into being, after his father was bent and feeble, and his mother too, who had not borne any child whilst she was young, being now of great age again had her course and became pregnant.

From this you may realise that all these things are but an occasion for the display of God's omnipotence; that all things are of Him, and that His decree is absolute in all things. The believer is he who knows that behind this wall there is Someone who is apprised of all our circumstances, one by one, and who sees us though we see Him not; of this the believer is certain. Contrary is the case of him who says, 'No, this is all a tale,' and does not believe. The day will come when God will box his ears; then he will be sorry, and will say, 'Alas, I spoke evil and erred. Indeed, all was He; and I denied Him.'

For instance, you know that I am behind the wall, and you are playing the rebeck. Undoubtedly you attend and do not stop, for you are a rebeck player. Prayer is not ordained so that all the day you should be standing and bowing and prostrating; its purpose is, that it is necessary that that spiritual state which possesses you visibly when you are at prayer should be with you always. Whether sleeping or waking, whether writing or reading, in all circumstances you should not be free from God's hand, so that *They continue at their prayers* will apply also to you.

So that speaking and keeping silent, that sleeping and eating, that being enraged and forgiving—all those attributes are the turning of a water-mill which revolves. Undoubtedly this revolving of the mill is by means of the water, because it has made trial of itself also without any water. So if the water-mill considers that turning to proceed from itself, that is the very acme of foolishness and ignorance.

Now this revolving takes place within a narrow space, for such are the circumstances of this material world. Cry unto God, saying, 'O God, grant to me, instead of my present journey and revolving, another revolving which shall be spiritual; seeing that all needs are fulfilled by Thee, and Thy bounty and compassion are universal over all creatures.' So represent your needs constantly, and never be without the remembrance of Him. For the remembrance of Him is strength and feathers and wings to the bird of the spirit. If that purpose is wholly realised, that is *Light upon Light*. By the remembrance of God, little by little the inward heart becomes illumined and your detachment from the world is realised. For instance, just as a bird desires to fly into heaven, though it does not reach the heaven, yet every moment it rises farther from the earth and outsoars the other birds. Or for instance, some musk is in a box, and the lid of the box is narrow; you insert your hand into the box but cannot extract the musk, yet for all that your hand becomes perfumed, and your nostrils are gratified. So too is the remembrance of God: though you do not attain the Essence of God, yet the remembrance of Almighty God leaves its mark on you, and great benefits are procured from the recollection of Him.

46

Shaikh Ibrāhīm is a noble dervish; when we see him, we are reminded of our beloved friends. Our Master Shams al-Dīn, who was greatly favoured by God, used always to say to the dervishes 'Our Shaikh Ibrāhīm,' relating him to himself.

Divine favour is one thing, and personal effort is something other.

The prophets did not attain the degree of prophethood through personal effort; they found that felicity through Divine favour. But it is the way of the prophets, that whoso attains that station lives a life of personal effort and virtue; that moreover is for the sake of the common people, that they may put reliance on them and their words. For the gaze of ordinary men does not penetrate into the inward heart. They see only externals; and when the common folk follow after the external, through the mediumship and blessing of the external they find the way to the internal.

After all, Pharaoh too made a great personal effort in the way of bounty and charity and the dissemination of good; but since the Divine favour was not present, inevitably his obedience and personal effort and beneficence had no lustre and all his generous actions remained hidden. Similarly a military commander in charge of a fortress is kind and generous to the people in that fortress. His object is to throw off allegiance to the king and to become a rebel. Inevitably his beneficence is without all worth and lustre.

Nevertheless one cannot entirely deny God's favour to Pharaoh. It may be that God most High favoured him secretly, causing him to be rejected for a good purpose. For a king is both vengeful and gracious; he both bestows robes of honour and consigns to prison. The spiritualists do not deny God's favour to Pharaoh altogether. The literalists however consider him to be a man wholly rejected; and that is beneficial, for the proper maintenance of external proprieties.

The king puts a man on the gallows, and he is hung up in a high place in the presence of the assembled people. He could also suspend him indoors, hidden from the people, by a low nail; but it is necessary that the people should see and take warning, and that the execution of the king's decree and the carrying out of his order should be visible. After all, not every gallows consists of wood. High rank and worldly fortune are also a gallows, and a mighty high one. When God most High desires to chastise a man, he bestows on him high rank in the world and a great kingdom, as in the cases of Pharaoh and Nimrod and the like. All those eminent positions are as a gallows on which God most High puts them, so that all the people may gaze upon it.

For God most High declares, 'I was a hidden treasure, and I desired to be known': that is to say, 'I created all the world, and the object of all that was to reveal Myself, now gracious, now vengeful.' God is not the kind of king for whom one herald is sufficient. If every atom in the world should become a herald, they would be yet incapable of proclaiming His qualities adequately.

So all men day and night are forever revealing God; except that some are aware and know that they are revealing Him, whilst some are unaware. Whichever the case may be, the revelation of God is certain. It is like when a prince orders a man to be beaten and taught a lesson. The victim shouts and screams; yet both are manifesting the prince's authority. Though the man being punished shouts with the pain, everyone realises that both beater and beaten are under the prince's authority; through both of them the prince's authority is clearly revealed. The man who acknowledges God is revealing God continually; the man who denies God is also revealing God. For it is unimaginable to establish a thing without denial; moreover it would be wholly without pleasure and relish. Thus, a controversialist proposes a motion at a meeting; if there is no one to oppose him and to say 'I do not agree' what does his affirmation amount to, and what savour is there in his point? For affirmation is pleasant only in the face of negation. In the same way this world too is a meeting for the declaration of God. Without a proposer and an opposer the meeting would lack all lustre. Both serve to declare God.

The brothers attended on the Commandant. The Commandant flew into a rage against them, saying, 'What are you all doing here?' They answered, 'We do not jabber and crowd together in order to annoy anyone. We do this to help one another to carry our burdens patiently and to assist one another.' In the same way people gather together at a wake; their object is not to drive Death away, but to console the bereaved party and to make him forget his grief.

'The believers are as it were a single soul.' The dervishes are in the situation of a single body; if one of the members feels pain, all the other parts are distressed. The eye gives up its seeing, the ear its hearing, the tongue its speaking; all assemble in that one place. The condition of true friendship is to sacrifice oneself for one's friend, to plunge oneself into tumult for the friend's sake. For all are directed towards one and the same thing; all are drowned in one and the same sea. That is the effect of faith, and the condition of Islam. What is the load which they carry with their bodies compared with the load which they carry with their souls?

They said, 'There is no harm; surely unto our Lord we are turning.'

When the believer sacrifices himself to God, why should he give a thought to distress and danger, to hand and foot? Since he is travelling to God, what need has he of hands and feet? God gave you hands and feet that you might travel from Him to these parts; but when you are travelling to Him who fashions feet and hands, if you lose control of your hands and stumble on your feet, and like Pharaoh's sorcerers go without hands and feet, what cause for grief is that?

> Poison is right good to sup
> When the fair one fills the cup;
> Bitter words are sweet to hear
> When the speaker is most dear.
>
> Full of savour is my love,
> Salt of wit, as I can prove;
> Very pleasant is its smart
> Rubbed into my wounded heart.

And God knows best.

47

God most High wills both good and evil, but only approves the good. For He said, 'I was a hidden treasure, and I desired to be known.' God most High undoubtedly wills to command and to prohibit. Commandment is only valid when the person commanded is by nature averse to what he is commanded to do. One does not say, 'Hungry one, eat sweetness and sugar': if these words are said, that is called not a commandment but a benefaction. Prohibition too does not rightly apply in the case of a thing which the man dislikes on his own account. One does not say, 'Don't eat the stone, don't eat the thorn': if these words were said, that would not be called a prohibition.

For commandment to do good and prohibition against evil rightly to apply one cannot dispense with a soul desiring evil. To will the existence of such a soul is to will evil. But God does not approve of evil, otherwise He would not have commanded the good. This is parallel to the case of a man who desires to teach: he desires that the pupil should be ignorant, for one cannot teach except when the pupil is ignorant. To desire a thing is to desire the prerequisites of that thing. But the teacher does not approve of the pupil's ignorance, otherwise he would not teach him. Again, the doctor desires that people should be ill, since he desires to practise his medicine; and he cannot display his medical skill unless people are ill. But he does not approve of people being ill, otherwise he would not attend them and treat them. Similarly the baker desires that people should be hungry, so that he may ply his trade and earn his living; but he does not approve of their being hungry, otherwise he would not sell bread.

For the same reason commanders and cavalry desire that their king should have an opponent and an enemy; otherwise their manly virtue and their love for the king would not be manifested, and the king would not muster them, not having need of them. But they do not approve of the king's opponent, otherwise they would not fight. Similarly a man desires the provocations to evil within himself, because God loves him who is grateful, obedient and godfearing, and that is not possible without the existence of those provocations within himself; and to desire a thing is to desire its prerequisites. But he does not approve of those provocations, for he struggles hard to banish these things from himself.

Hence it is realised that God wills evil in one way, and does not will it in another way.

The opponent says, 'God does not will evil in any way whatever.' That is impossible, that He should will a thing and not will its prerequisites. Amongst the prerequisites of God's commandment and prohibition is this headstrong soul in man which by nature longs for evil, and by nature runs away from good. The prerequisites of such a soul are all the evils that exist in this material world. Did God not will these evils, He would not have willed the soul; and if He did not will the soul, He would not will the commandment and prohibition which are attached to the soul. If however God had approved those evils, He would not have issued commandments and prohibitions to the soul. This proves that evil is willed for the sake of something other.

The opponent then says, 'If God wills all good, and amongst such good things is the averting of evil, therefore He desires the averting of evil'—and evil cannot be averted unless evil exists. Or he says, 'God wills faith'—and faith cannot exist except after unbelief, so that unbelief is a prerequisite of faith. The upshot is that the willing of evil is only reprehensible when it is willed for its own sake; when it is willed for the sake of some good, then it is not reprehensible. God most High has said:

In retaliation there is life for you.

There is no doubt that retaliation is evil, being a destruction of the edifice of God most High. But this is a partial evil, whereas the guarding of the people from killing is a total good. To will the partial evil for the sake of willing the total good is not reprehensible; whilst the partial abandonment of God's will, whilst approving total evil, is reprehensible. This is like the mother who does not desire to chide her child, because she is regarding the partial evil; whereas the father approves of chiding the child, having regard to the total evil, to nip the trouble in the bud.

God most High is All-pardoning, All-forgiving, Terrible in retribution. Does He will that different epithets should be true of Him or not? The answer cannot be other than 'yes.' Now He cannot be All-pardoning and All-forgiving without the existence of sins; and to will a thing is to will its prerequisites. Similarly He has commanded us to be forgiving, and He has commanded us to make peace and ensue it; and this commandment has no meaning without the existence of enmity.

This is paralleled by the pronouncement of Ṣadr al-Islām, that God most High has commanded us to earn and to acquire wealth, because He has said

And expend in the way of God.

Now it is impossible to expend money except by means of money; therefore it is a commandment to acquire money. When a man says to another man, 'Arise and pray,' he thereby commands him to perform the ritual ablution, and to acquire water and all the prerequisites.

48

Gratitude is a hunting and a shackling of benefits. When you hear the voice of gratitude, you get ready to give more. When God loves a servant He afflicts him; if he endures with fortitude, He chooses him; if he is grateful, He elects him. Some men are grateful to God for His wrathfulness and some are grateful to Him for His graciousness. Each of the two classes is good; for gratitude is a sovereign antidote, changing wrath into grace. The intelligent and perfect man is he who is grateful for harsh treatment, both openly and in secret; for it is he whom God has elected. If God's will be the bottom reach of Hell, by gratitude His purpose is hastened.

For outward complaining is a diminution of inward complaining. Muhammad said, peace be upon him, 'I laugh as I slay.' That means, 'My laughing in the face of him who is harsh to me is a slaying of him.' The intention of laughter is gratitude in the place of complaining.

It is related that a certain Jew lived next door to one of the Companions of God's Messenger. This Jew lived in an upper room, whence descended into the Muslim's apartment all kinds of dirt and filth, the piddle of his children, the water his clothes were washed in. Yet the Muslim always thanked the Jew, and bade his family do the same. So things continued for eight years, until the Muslim died. Then the Jew entered his apartment, to condole with the family, and saw all the filth there, and how it issued from his upper room. So he realised what had happened during the past years, and was exceedingly sorry, and said to the Muslim's household, 'Why on earth didn't you tell me? Why did you always thank me?' They replied, 'Our father used to bid us be grateful, and chided us against ceasing to be grateful.' So the Jew became a believer.

> The mentioning of virtuous men
> Encourages to virtue then,
> Just as the minstrel with his song
> Urges the wine to pass along.

For this reason God has mentioned in the Koran His prophets and those of His servants who were righteous, and thanked them for what they did unto Him who is All-powerful and All-forgiving.

Gratitude for sucking the breast is a blessing. Though the breast be full, until you suck it the milk does not flow.

Someone asked: What is the cause of ingratitude, and what is it that prevents gratitude?

The Master answered: The preventer of gratitude is inordinate greed. For whatever a man may get, he was greedy for more than that. It was inordinate greed that impelled him to that, so that when he got less than what he had set his heart upon his greed prevented him from being grateful. So he was heedless of his own defect, and heedless also of the defect and adulteration of the coin he proffered.

Raw and inordinate greed is like eating raw fruit and raw bread and raw meat; inevitably it generates sickness and begets ingratitude. When a man realises that he has eaten something unwholesome, a purge becomes necessary. God most High in His wisdom makes him suffer through ingratitude so that he may be purged and rid of that corrupt conceit, lest that one sickness become a hundred sicknesses.

And we tried them with good things and evil, that
haply they should return.

That is to say: We made provision for them from whence they had never reckoned, namely the unseen world, so that their gaze shrinks from beholding the secondary causes, which are as it were partners to God. It was in this sense that Abū Yazīd said, 'Lord, I have never associated any with Thee.' God most High said, 'O Abū Yazīd, not even on the night of the milk? You said one night, "The milk has done me harm." It is I who do harm, and benefit.' Abū Yazīd had looked at the secondary cause, so that God reckoned him a polytheist and said, 'It is I who do harm, after the milk and before the milk; but I made the milk for a sin, and the harm for a correction such as a teacher administers.'

When the teacher says, 'Don't eat the fruit,' and the pupil eats it, and the teacher beats him on the sole of his foot, it is not right for the pupil to say, 'I ate the fruit and it hurt my foot.' On this basis, whoso preserves his tongue from ascribing partners to God, God undertakes to cleanse his spirit of the weeds of polytheism. A little with God is much.

The difference between giving praise and giving thanks is that thanks are given for benefits received. One does not say, 'I gave thanks to him for his beauty and his bravery.' Praisegiving is more general.

49

A certain person was leading the prayers, and he chanted:

> *The Bedouins are more stubborn in unbelief*
> *and hypocrisy.*

By chance a Bedouin chieftain was present. He gave the chanter a good box on the ears. In the second genuflection he chanted:

> *Some of the Bedouins believe in God and the*
> *Last Day.*

The Bedouin exclaimed, 'Ha, that slap has taught you better manners!'

Every moment we receive a slap from the unseen world. Whatever we propose to do, we are kept away from it by a slap and we take another course. As the saying goes, 'We have no power of our own, it is all a swallowing up and a vomiting.' It is also said, 'It is easier to cut the joints than to cut a connexion.' The meaning of 'swallowing' is descending into this lower world and becoming one of its people; the meaning of 'vomiting' is dropping out of the heart. For instance, a man eats some food and it turns sour in his stomach, and he vomits it. If that food had turned sour and he had not vomited it, it would have become a part of the man.

Even so a disciple courts and dances service so as to find a place in the heart of the shaikh. Anything issuing from the disciple (God be our refuge!) which displeases the shaikh and is cast forth out of his heart is like the food which the man eats and then vomits. Just as that food would have become a part of the man, and because it was sour he vomited it and cast it forth, so that disciple with the passage of time would have become the shaikh, and because of his displeasing conduct he cast him out of his heart.

> Thy love made proclamation to the world
> And every heart into confusion hurled,
> Then burnt all up and into ashes turned
> And to the indifferent wind those ashes spurned.

In that wind of indifference the atoms of the ashes of those hearts are dancing and making lament. If they are not so, then who ever conveyed these tidings and who is it that every moment anew brings these tidings? And if the hearts do not perceive their very life to consist in that burning up and spurning to the wind, how is it that they are so eager to be burned? As for those hearts which have been burned up in the fire of worldly lusts and become ashes, do your hear any sound or see any lustre of them?

> Right well I know—and no wont of mine
> Is hyperbole—
> That he who is my soul's sustenance
> Will come to me.
>
> If I run after him, hard's the quest
> My love to attain;
> But let me sit quiet, and he will come
> Without my pain.

'Right well I know the rule of God's providing man's daily bread. It is no rule of mine to run about hither and thither to no purpose and to exert myself needlessly. Truly, when I renounce all thought of silver and food and raiment and the fire of lust, my daily portion will come to me. But when I run after those daily portions, the quest of them pains and wearies me and distresses me; if I sit in my own place with patience, that will come to me without pain and distress. For that daily portion is also seeking after me and drawing me; when it cannot draw me it comes to me, just as when I cannot draw it I go after it.'

The upshot of these words is this: occupy yourself with the affairs of the world to come, that the world itself may run after you. The meaning of 'sitting' in this context is sitting in application to the affairs of the world to come. If a man runs, when he runs for the sake of the world to come he is truly seated; if he is seated, if he is seated for the sake of the present world he is running. The Prophet, upon whom be peace, said, 'Whosoever makes all his cares a single care, God will suffice him as to all his other cares.' If a man is beset by ten cares, let him choose the care for the world to come and God most High will put right for him those other nine cares without any effort on his part.

The prophets cared nothing for fame and daily bread. Their only care was to seek God's approval; and they attained both daily bread and fame. Whosoever seeks God's good pleasure, such men in this world and the next will be with the prophets and be their bedfellows.

> *They are with those whom God has blessed,*
> *prophets, just men, martyrs, the righteous.*

What place indeed is there for this, seeing that they are sitting with God Himself? 'I sit with him who remembers Me.' Did God not sit with him, the yearning for God would never enter his heart. The scent of the rose never exists without the rose; the scent of musk never exists without the musk.

There is no end to these words; if there were an end to them, yet they would not be as other words.

> The night's departed; yet, my friend,
> Our story's not yet at an end.

The night and darkness of this world passes away, and the light of these words every moment becomes clearer. Even so the night of the life of the prophets departed, peace be upon them, yet the light of their discourse departed not and came not to an end, nor ever will.

People said about Majnūn, 'If he loves Lailā, what is so strange in that, seeing that they were children together and went to the same school?' Majnūn said, 'These men are fools. What pretty woman is not desirable?' Is there any man whose heart is not stirred by a lovely woman? Women are the same. It is love by which a man's heart is fed and finds savour; just as the sight of mother and father and brother, the pleasure of children, the pleasure of lust—all kinds of delight are rooted in love. Majnūn was an example of all lovers, just as in grammar Zaid and 'Amr are quoted.

> Feast on sweetmeats or on roast,
> Drink the wine that you love most:
> What's that savour on your lips?
> Water that a dreamer sips!

193

When tomorrow you arise
And great thirst upon you lies,
Little use will be that deep
Draught you've taken whilst asleep.

'This world is as the dream of a sleeper.' This world and its delights is as though a man has eaten a thing whilst asleep. So for him to desire worldly needs is as if he desired something whilst sleeping and was given it; in the end, when he is awake, he will not be profited by what he ate whilst asleep. So he will have asked for something whilst asleep, and have been given it. 'The present is proportionate to the request.'

50

Someone said: We have got to know all the circumstances of man one by one, and not so much as a single hair-tip of his temperament and nature, his hot and cold humours, has escaped our notice. Yet it has not become known, what thing it is in him that will survive.

The Master said: If the knowledge of that were attainable merely out of what other men have said, there would not be any necessity for such varied labours and efforts, and no one would put himself to such pains and sacrifice himself to the enquiry. Thus to illustrate: a man comes to the sea, and sees nothing but salt water, sharks and fishes. He says, 'Where is this pearl they speak about? Perhaps there isn't any pearl.' How should the pearl be attained merely by looking at the sea? Even were he to measure out the sea cup by cup a hundred thousand times, he will never find the pearl. A diver is needed to discover the pearl, and even then not every diver: a diver who is both lucky and nimble.

These sciences and arts are like measuring the ocean with a cup. To find the pearl calls for a different kind of approach. Many a man there is, adorned with every skill, wealthy and handsome to boot, yet this vital quality is not in him. Many a man there is who is outwardly a wreck, who has neither good looks nor elegance of speech nor elo-quence, yet there is in him that vital element which is immortal. It is by that element that man is ennobled and honoured, and by means of that he is superior to all other creatures. Leopards and crocodiles, lions and the rest of creatures, all have their peculiar skills and accomplishments; but that vital element which will survive for ever is not in them. If a man discovers that element, he has attained the secret of his own pre-excellence; if not, he remains without portion of that pre-excellence. All these arts and accomplishments are like setting jewels on the back of a mirror. The face of the mirror is destitute of them. The face of the mirror must be crystal clear. He who has an ugly face is eager for the back of the mirror, for the face of the mirror tells out every dark secret. He who has a handsome face seeks the face of the mirror with all his soul, for the face of the mirror displays his own comeliness.

A friend of Joseph of Egypt came to him from a far journey. Joseph asked, 'What present have you brought for me?' The friend replied, 'What is there that you do not possess and of which you are in need? But inasmuch as nothing exists more handsome than you, I have brought a mirror so that every moment you may gaze in it upon your own face.'

What is there that God most High does not possess and of which He is in need? It is necessary to bring before God most High a heart mirror-bright, so that He may see His own face in it. 'God looks not at your forms, nor at your deeds, but at your hearts.'

A city where you found all your desire
And naught was wanting, save men generous!

'A city in which you find everything that you desire, handsome people, pleasures, all that the natural man craves for, ornaments of every kind, but you find not one intelligent man there. Would that it had been the very opposite of this!'

That city is the human being. If there be in him a hundred thousand accomplishments but not that essential element, better it were that that city were in ruins. But if that essential element is there, though there be no outward ornament, that matters not; his secret heart must be well furnished. In every state whatsoever his secret heart is occupied with God; and that outward preoccupation hinders not his inward occupation. In the same way, in whatever state a pregnant woman finds herself, at peace or at war, sleeping or eating, the child in her womb grows all the time and receives strength and sensation, whilst the mother is wholly unaware of that. Man too is carrying that secret.

> *We offered the trust to the heavens and the earth*
> *and the mountains, but they refused to carry it*
> *and were afraid of it; and man carried it. Surely*
> *he is sinful, very foolish.*

But God most High does not leave him in sin and foolishness. Out of the physical human burden, companionship and concord and a thousand familiar friendships come. If out of that secret which man is carrying friendships and acquaintanceships also come, what is there so strange in that? What things will rise out of him after death? The secret heart must be well furnished. For the secret heart is like the root of a tree; though it is hidden, its influence is apparent on the tips of the branches. If a branch or two is broken, when the root is firm they will grow again; but if the root is damaged, neither bough nor leaf remains.

God most High said, 'Peace be upon thee, Prophet!' That is to say, 'Peace is upon thee and upon every one who is thy congener.' If this had not been the intention of God most High, Muhammad would not have countered Him and said, 'Upon us and upon all God's righteous servants.' For if 'peace' had been intended solely for him, he would not have assigned it to righteous servants; meaning, 'That peace which Thou gavest me rests on me and on all righteous servants who are my congeners.' So too the Prophet said at the time of making ablution, 'Prayer is not perfect save with this ablution.' The meaning is not that ablution specifically, otherwise it must follow that no man's prayer would ever be perfect; the condition of the soundness of the prayer would be solely the Prophet's ablution. The true intention is, that whoever performs the like of this ablution, his prayer is perfect. Similarly it may be said, 'This is a bowl of pomegranate flowers.' What does that mean? Does it mean, 'These only are pomegranate flowers'? No indeed; it means, 'This is the like of pomegranate flowers.'

A countryman came to town and became the guest of a townsman. The townsman brought him halwa, which the countryman ate with gusto. The countryman said, 'O townsman, night and day I have learned to eat carrots. Now that I have tasted halwa, the pleasure of eating carrots has shrunk away in my eyes. Now I shall not find halwa every time, and that which I formerly had has become unattractive to my heart. What am I to do?' When the countryman has tasted halwa, thereafter he yearns after the town; for the townsman has carried his heart away, so willy-nilly he comes looking for his heart.

Some men there are who, when they give greeting, the smell of smoke comes from their greeting. Some there are who, when they give greeting, the smell of musk comes from their greeting. It is the man with sensitive nostrils who smells the odour.

A man must make trial of his friend, that in the end he may not have cause to regret. This is God's rule also: 'Begin with yourself.' If the self makes claim to servanthood, do not accept its claim without making trial of it. In the act of ablution men first convey the water to the nose, and then they taste it; they are not satisfied simply to look at it. For it may be that the appearance of the water is perfectly good, but the taste and smell of it are infected. This is an examination to test the purity of the water. Then, after the test has been completed, men apply the water to their faces.

Whatever you keep hidden in your heart, be it good or evil, God most High makes it manifest in you outwardly. Whatever the root of a tree feeds on in secret, its effect becomes manifest in the bough and the leaf.

Their mark is on their faces.

God most High also says:

We shall brand him upon the muzzle.

If everyone is not to see into your thoughts, what colour are you going to make your face?

51

> Until you seek you cannot find—
>   That's true, save of the Lover:
> You cannot seek Him, being blind,
>   Until you shall discover.

The human quest consists in seeking a thing which one has not yet found; night and day a man is engaged in searching for that. But the quest where the thing has been found and the object attained, and yet there is one who is seeking for that thing—that is a strange quest indeed, surpassing the human imagination, inconceivable to man. For man's quest is for something new which he has not yet found; this quest is for something one has found already and then one seeks. This is God's quest; for God most High has found all things, and all things are found in His omnipotent power. '*Be and it is*—the Finder, the Bountiful'; for God has found all things, and so He is the Finder. Yet for all that God most High is the Seeker: 'He is the Seeker, the Prevailer.' The meaning of the saying quoted above is therefore, 'O man, so long as you are engaged in the quest that is created in time, which is a human attribute, you remain far from the goal. When your quest passes away in God's quest and God's quest overrides your quest, then you become a seeker by virtue of God's quest.'

Someone said: We have no categorical proof as to who is a friend of God and has attained union with God. Neither words nor deeds nor miracles nor anything else furnishes such a proof. For words may have been learned by rote; as for deeds and miracles, the monks have these also. They are able to deduce a man's inmost thoughts, and display many wonders by means of magic. The interlocutor enumerated a number of examples.

The Master answered: Do you believe in anyone or not?

The man said: Yes, by Allah. I both believe and love.

The Master said: Is this belief of yours in that person founded upon a proof and token? Or did you simply shut your eyes and take up that person?

The man said: God forbid that my belief should be without proof and token?

The Master said: Why then do you say that there is no proof or token leading to belief? What you say is self-contradictory.

Someone said: Every saint and great mystic asserts, 'This nearness which I enjoy with God and this Divine favour which God vouchsafes to me is enjoyed by no one and is vouchsafed to no one else.'

The Master answered: Who made this statement? Was it a saint, or someone other than a saint? If it was a saint who stated this, inasmuch as he knows that every saint has this belief regarding himself, he cannot be the sole recipient of this Divine favour. If someone other than a saint made this statement, then in very truth he is the friend and elect of God; for God most High has concealed this secret from all the saints and has not hidden it from him.

That person propounded a parable. Once there was a king who had ten concubines. The concubines said, 'We wish to know which of us is dearest to the king.' The king declared, 'Tomorrow this ring shall be in the apartment of whomsoever I love best.' Next day the king commanded ten rings to be made identical with that ring, and gave one ring to each maiden.

The Master said: The question still stands. This is no answer, and it is irrelevant to the issue. This statement was made either by one of the ten maidens, or by someone apart from the ten maidens. If it was one of the ten maidens who made the statement, then since she knew that the ring was not hers exclusively and that each of the maidens had the like of it, it follows that she had no superiority over the rest and was not the most beloved. If however the statement was made by someone other than those ten maidens, then that person was the king's favourite and beloved concubine.

Someone said: The lover must be submissive and abject and long-suffering. And he enumerated the like qualities.

The Master said: In that case the lover must be like that, alike when the beloved wishes it or no. But if he is so without the desire of the beloved, then he is not truly a lover but is following his own desire. If he accords with the desire of the beloved, then when the beloved does not wish him to be submissive and abject, how should he be submissive and abject? Hence it is realised that the states affecting the lover are unknown, only how the beloved wishes him to be.

Jesus said, 'I wonder at a living creature, how it can eat a living creature.' The literalists say that man eats the flesh of animals, and both are animals. This is an error. Why? Because man it is true eats flesh; but that is not animal, it is inanimate, for when the animal was killed animality no longer remained in it. The true meaning of the saying is that the shaikh mysteriously devours the disciple. I wonder at a procedure so extraordinary!

Someone propounded the following question. Abraham, upon whom be peace, said to Nimrod, 'My God brings the dead to life and turns the living into the dead.' Nimrod said, 'I too, when I banish a man, as good as cause him to die, and when I appoint a man to a post it is as though I bring him to life.' Abraham abandoned the argument, being compelled to yield the point. He then embarked on another line of reasoning, saying, 'My God brings the sun up from the east and sends it down in the west. Do the opposite of that!' Is not this statement manifestly at variance with the other?

The Master answered: God forbid that Abraham should have been silenced by Nimrod's argument and left without any answer to it! The truth is that he used these words to represent another idea, namely that God most High brings the foetus out of the east of the womb and sends it down into the west of the tomb. Abraham's proof, peace be upon him, was thus presented with perfect consistency. God most High creates a man anew every moment, sending something perfectly fresh into his inner heart. The first is in no way like the second, neither is the second like the third. Only man is unconscious of himself and does not know himself.

Sultan Maḥmūd, God have mercy on him, was brought a sea-horse, a fine beast with a most lovely shape. Next festival day he rode out on that horse and all the people sat on the rooftops to see him and to enjoy that spectacle. One drunken fellow however remained seated in his apartment. By main force they carried him up to the roof, saying, 'You come too and look at the sea-horse.' He said, 'I am busy with my own affairs. I don't want and don't care to see it.' In short, he could not escape. As he sat there on the edge of the roof, extremely drunk, the Sultan passed by. When the drunken fellow saw the Sultan on the horse he cried out, 'What store do I set by this horse? Why, if this very moment some minstrel were to sing a song and that horse were mine, immediately I would give it to him.' Hearing this, the Sultan became extremely angry and commanded that he should be cast into prison. A week passed. Then this man sent a message to the Sultan, saying, 'After all, what sin did I commit and what is my crime? Let the King of the World command that his servant be informed.' The Sultan ordered him to be brought into his presence. He said, 'You insolent rogue, how did you come to utter those words? How dared you speak so?' The man answered, 'King of the World, it was not I who spoke those words. That moment a drunken mannikin was standing on the edge of the roof and spoke those words, and departed. This hour I am not that fellow; I am an intelligent and sensible man.' The Sultan was delighted by his words; he conferred on him a robe of honour and ordered his release from the prison.

Whoever takes up connexion with us and becomes drunk with this wine, wherever he goes, with whomsoever he sits, with whatever people he converses, in reality he is sitting with us and mingling with this tribe. For the company of strangers is the mirror to the graciousness of the friend's company, and mingling with one who is not a congener stimulates love and commingling with the congener. 'Things are made clear by their opposites.'

Abū Bakr Ṣiddīq, God be well pleased with him, gave the name of *ummi* to sugar, that is to say, congenital sweet. Now men prize other fruits above sugar, saying, 'We have tasted so much bitterness until we attained the rank of sweetness.' What do you know of the delight of sweetness, when you have not suffered the hardship of bitterness?

52

The Master was asked concerning the meaning of the following lines:

> Yet when desire attains its utmost goal
> Love turns entirely into enmity.

He explained: The world of enmity is narrow in relation to the world of friendship, for men flee away from the world of enmity in order to reach the world of friendship. The world of friendship too is narrow in relation to that world out of which friendship and enmity come into existence. Friendship and enmity, unbelief and faith—these are all a cause of duality. For unbelief is denial, and the denier requires someone for him to deny; so too the confessor requires someone for him to confess. Hence, it is realised, concord and discord are a cause of duality; and that world transcends unbelief and faith, friendship and enmity. Since friendship is a cause of duality, and a world exists where there is no duality but only pure unity, when a man has reached that world he has come forth out of friendship and enmity. For there there is no room for two; so when he has arrived there, he has become separated from duality. Therefore that first world of duality, which is love and friendship, is degraded and inferior in relation to the world into which he has now transferred. Accordingly he does not want it, and is at enmity with it.

So, when Manṣūr's friendship with God reached its utmost goal, he became the enemy of himself and naughted himself. He said, 'I am God'; that is, 'I have passed away, God alone has remained.' This is extreme humility and the utmost limit of servanthood, for it means 'He only is.' Pretension and arrogance consists in your saying, 'Thou art God, and I am Thy servant.' For by saying this you have affirmed your own existence, and dualism ensues necessarily. If you say, 'He is God,' that too is duality; for until 'I' exists 'He' is impossible. Therefore it was God who said, 'I am God,' since other than He was not in existence and Manṣūr had passed away. Those words were God's words.

The world of phantasy is broader than the world of concepts and of sensibilia. For all concepts are born of phantasy. The world of phantasy likewise is narrow in relation to the world out of which phantasy comes into being. From the verbal standpoint this is the limit of understanding; but the actual reality cannot be made known by words and expressions.

Someone asked: Then what is the use of expressions and words?

The Master answered: The use of words is that they set you searching and excite you, not that the object of the quest should be attained through words. If that were the case, there would be no need for so much striving and self-naughting. Words are as when you see afar off something moving; you run in the wake of it in order to see it, it is not the case that you see it through its movement. Human speech too is inwardly the same; it excites you to seek the meaning, even though you do not see it in reality.

Someone was saying: I have studied so many sciences and mastered so many ideas, yet it is still not known to me what that essence in man it is that will remain forever, and I have not discovered it.

The Master answered: If that had been knowable by means of words only, you would not have needed to pass away from self and to suffer such pains. It is necessary to endure so much for yourself not to remain, so that you may know that thing which will remain.

A man said, 'I have heard that there is a Kaaba, but however far I look I do not see the Kaaba. Let me go up on the roof and look at the Kaaba.' When he goes up on the roof and stretches out his neck, still he does not see the Kaaba; so he denies that the Kaaba exists. Sight of the Kaaba is not attained merely by doing that, since it is impossible to see it from one's own abiding-place.

Similarly in the winter time you hunted for a fur jacket with all your soul; when summer is come, you fling away the fur jacket and your thoughts are averted from it. Seeking the fur jacket was in order to procure warmth, for you were in love with warmth. In the winter because of some impediment you did not find warmth and were in need of the medium of the fur jacket; but when the impediment no more remained you flung away the fur jacket.

When heaven is rent asunder, and *When earth is shaken with a mighty shaking* are a reference pointing to yourself. It means, you have experienced the pleasure of being gathered together; but a day is now coming when you will experience the pleasure of these parts being separated, when you will behold the expanse of the other world and find deliverance out of this present straitness. For instance, a man has been fettered with four nails. He thinks that he is quite comfortable in that situation, and has forgotten the pleasure of being free. When he escapes from the four nails, then he realises in what torment he was. In the same way children are swaddled and put to rest in a cradle; they feel perfectly at ease with their hands bound. But if a grown man were cribbed in a cradle, that would be a torment and a prison.

Some feel pleasure when roses have come into bloom and put forth their heads from the bud. Some feel pleasure when the particles of the rose are all scattered and rejoin their origin. So some men desire that friendship and passion and love and unbelief and faith may no more remain, so that they may rejoin their origin. For these things are all walls and a cause of narrowness and duality, whereas the other world is a cause of broadness and absolute unity.

These words are not so mighty and have no power. How should they be mighty? After all, they are merely words. On the contrary, in themselves they are a cause of weakness. Yet they influence to the truth and excite to the truth. Words are an intervening veil. How can two or three letters compounded together be a cause of life and excitement?

For instance, a man comes to visit you; you receive him politely and bid him welcome. That makes him happy and is a cause of affection. Another man you receive with two or three words of abuse; those two or three words are a cause of anger and pain. Now what connexion can there be between the stringing together of two or three words and an augmentation of affection and satisfaction, or the provocation of anger and enmity? But God most High has appointed these secondary means and veils so that no man's gaze may fall upon His beauty and perfection. Weak veils are appropriate to weak eyes. So He makes the veils as conditions and means. Bread in reality is not the cause of life; but God most High has made it the cause of life and strength. After all, it is inanimate, in the sense that it has no human life; how can it be the cause of an augmentation of strength? If it had had any life at all, it would have kept itself alive.

53

The Master was asked concerning the meaning of the following lines:

> You are that very thought, my brother:
> Those bones and nerves are something other.

He said: You too consider this idea. 'That very thought' is a reference to that peculiar 'thought' which I have expressed by means of that word in an extended sense. In reality however that is not 'thought' at all, and if it is, it does not belong to the kind of thought which men understand by the term. By using the word 'thought' my intention was this idea or essential element. If any one desires to interpret this 'idea' in a more humdrum way so that the common people may understand, let him say 'Man is a speaking animal.'

Speech is thought, whether concealed or expressed. The rest is animal. So it is perfectly correct to say that man consists of thought, and the rest is 'bones and nerves.' Speech may be compared with the sun. All men derive warmth and life from the sun, and the sun is always there, existing and present. All men are always warm through the sun; yet that sun is invisible, and they do not know that they derive life and warmth from it. However, when that thought is spoken through the medium of a word or an expression, be it of thanks or complaint, be it good or evil, then the sun becomes visible; just as the celestial sun which is always shining, but its rays are invisible until they shine upon a wall. Even so the rays of the sun of speech do not appear save through the medium of letters and sounds. Though it is always in being—for the sun is subtle, and *He is the All-subtle*—some element of grossness is required, through the medium of which it may become visible and apparent.

A certain man said that God had no meaning for him; the word left him bewildered and frozen. When they said, 'God did this, and God commanded this and forbade that,' he became warm and saw. So although God's subtlety existed and shone on that man, he did not see; until they explained it to him through the medium of command and prohibition, creation and omnipotent power, he was unable to see.

Some people there are who on account of infirmity cannot take honey; yet through the medium of some food, such as rice dressed with turmeric and halwa and the like, they are able to eat it, until their recovery reaches the point where they can eat honey without any medium.

So we realise that speech is a subtle sun shining continually and without ceasing; but you require some gross medium in order to see and enjoy the rays of that sun. When things reach the point where you are able to see those rays and that subtlety without the gross medium and you have grown accustomed to it, then you become bold in your inspection of it and wax strong. In the depths of that sea of subtlety you see marvellous colours and marvellous spectacles. Yet what is so marvellous in that? For that speech is always within you, whether you actually speak or no, even though at the moment no speech is even in your thoughts.

We say that speech is always in being, just as the philosophers have said that 'Man is a speaking animal.' This animality is always in you so long as you are living. Hence it follows necessarily that speech too is always with you. Thus, chewing is a means of manifesting animality and not a condition, and so speaking and chattering is a means of 'speech' but not a condition.

Man has three spiritual states. In the first he pays no heed to God at all, but worships and pays service to everything, woman and man, wealth and children, stones and clods; God he does not worship. When he acquires a little knowledge and awareness, then he serves nothing but God. Again, when he progresses farther in this state he becomes silent; he does not say, 'I do not serve God,' neither does he say, 'I serve God,' for he has transcended these two degrees. No sound from these people issues into the world.

'Your God is neither present nor absent, for He is the Creator of both'—that is, of presence and absence. Hence He is other than both of these. For if He were present, it must be that absence does not exist. But absence exists, and He is not present, for 'in presence absence exists.' Therefore He is not qualified by either presence or absence; otherwise it would necessarily follow that opposite proceeds out of opposite. For in the state of absence it would follow that He created presence, and presence is the opposite of absence; and similarly with regard to absence. So it is not right to say that opposite proceeds out of opposite, or that God should create the like of Himself; for He says, 'No like has He.' For if it were possible for the like to create the like, then it would necessarily follow that there was a giving of precedence without any to be preferred, and it would likewise follow that a thing could create itself; and both of these propositions are untenable.

When you have reached this point, halt and apply yourself no more. Here reason has no further control. Once it reaches the margin of the sea it halts, notwithstanding that even to halt no more remains in its power.

All words, all sciences, all skills, all professions derive their flavour and relish from this speech. If that were not so, no flavour would remain in any employment or profession. The end of what is in the chapter is unknown, and knowing is not a condition. This is illustrated by the man who sought in marriage a wealthy woman possessing flocks of sheep and horses and other things. This man looks after the sheep and horses and waters the orchards. Though he is occupied with those services, the flavour of those tasks derives from the existence of the woman; for if the woman were to disappear, those tasks would lose their flavour and become cold and appear lifeless. Even so all professions and sciences in the world and so forth derive life and pleasure and warmth from the ray of the gnostic's 'relish', but for his 'relish' in those things, all tasks would be utterly without relish and enjoyment.

54

The Master said: When I first began to compose poetry it was a great urge that compelled me to compose. At that time the urge had much effect; now the urge has grown weaker and is declining, but still it has its effect. Such is the way of God most High. He fosters things in the time of their rising, and great effects and much wisdom are produced therefrom; in the state of declining his fostering still has its force. *The Lord of the East and the West* means, 'He fosters the urges both rising and declining.'

The Mu'tazilites hold that a man creates his own acts, and that every act that issues from him is of his own creation. That cannot be so. For each act that issues from man does so either through the medium of the instrument he possesses—such as reason, spirit, faculty and body— or without any medium. He cannot be the creator of acts performed through the medium of these things, for he is not capable of assembling them; therefore he is not the creator of acts performed through the medium of such an instrument, since the instrument is not subject to his control. It is also impossible that he should create an act without such an instrument, for it is out of the question that any act should come from him without such an instrument.

Hence we realise absolutely that the creator of man's acts is not man but God. Every act that proceeds out of a man, whether it be good or evil, he performs intentionally and with a purpose, but the wisdom of that deed is not limited to the extent that he conceives. The extent of the meaning and wisdom and advantage which appeared to him in that deed—the advantage of that is limited to the extent that that action comes into being from him. Only God however knows the total advantage of that deed, what fruits he will discover therefrom. For instance, you pray with the intention that you shall be rewarded in the next world and acquire a good name and safety in the present world. But the advantage derived from that prayer will not be limited to that; it will confer a hundred thousand advantages which do not pass into your understanding. Those advantages are known only to God, who moves a man to perform such an act.

Man is like a bow in the hand of the grip of God's omnipotence. God most High employs him upon various tasks, and the agent in reality is God, not the bow. The bow is the instrument and the medium, but it is unaware and unconscious of God, that the world's order may be maintained. Mighty indeed is the bow that is aware in whose hand it is! What am I to say of a world whose maintenance and columns rest on heedlessness? Do you not see that when a man is awakened, he becomes indifferent to the world also and grows cold; he also melts and perishes. From his very childhood, when he first began to wax and grow, man has done so out of negligence; else he would never have grown up and become a man. Since therefore his growing into manhood has been accomplished through negligence, God most High imposes upon him willy-nilly many pains and labours that He may wash those acts of negligence away from him and make him clean. Only then is he able to become acquainted with the other world.

The human being is like a dunghill, a heap of manure. But if this manure-heap is precious, it is because in it is the seal-ring of the King. The human being is like a sack of corn. The King cries out, 'Where are you carrying that corn? For my cup is in it.' Man is heedless of the cup, being absorbed in the corn. If he were aware of the cup, how would he pay attention to the corn? Now every thought which draws you towards the supernal world, making you cold and indifferent to this lower world, is a reflection of the ray of that cup flashing out. So man comes to yearn for the other world. When contrariwise he yearns after this lower world, that is a sign that that cup has become hidden in the veil.

55

Someone said: Qāḍī 'Izz al-Dīn sends his greetings, and always speaks of you in the most approving terms.

The Master said:

> Whoso remembers us, and speaks us well,
> Long may the world of his high merit tell.

If any man speaks well of another, that good appraisal reverts again to himself, and in reality it is himself that he is praising and applauding. It is like a man who sows round his garden flowers and aromatic herbs; whenever he looks out, he sees flowers and aromatic herbs and is always in Paradise, inasmuch as he has formed the habit of speaking well of other men. Whenever a man has engaged himself in speaking well of another, that person becomes his friend; when he remembers him, he brings to mind a friend; and bringing to mind a friend is like flowers and a flower-garden, it is refreshment and repose. But when a man speaks ill of another, that person becomes hateful in his eyes; whenever he remembers him and his image comes before him, it is as though a snake or a scorpion, a thorn or a thistle has appeared in his sight.

Now since you are able night and day to see flowers and a flower-garden and the meadows of Iram, why do you go about amidst thorns and snakes? Love every man, so that you may always dwell amongst flowers and a flower-garden. When you are a foe of every man, the image of your foes appears before you and it is as if day and night you are going about amidst thorns and snakes. It is for this reason that the saints love all men and think well of all men. They do that not for another but solely for themselves, lest haply a hateful or loathsome image should appear before them. Since in this world one cannot escape mentioning men and encountering their image, the saints strove their utmost that everything in their mind and memory should be amiable and desirable, so that the unpleasantness of a hateful image should not confound their way.

So it is that whatsoever you do unto other men, whenever you make mention of them whether for good or ill, all that reverts to yourself. It is of this that God most High declares:

> *Whoso does righteousness, it is to his own gain,*
> *and whoso does evil, it is to his own loss.*

> *And whoso has done an atom's weight of good shall see it,*
> *and whoso has done an atom's weight of evil shall see it.*

Someone proposed the following question. God most High declares:

> *I am setting in the earth a viceroy.*

The angels said:

What, wilt Thou set therein one
who will do corruption there, and shed blood,
while we proclaim Thy praise and call Thee holy?

Now Adam had not as yet come into the world. How then did the angels judge beforehand that man would do corruption and *shed blood?*

The Master answered: There are two ways of explaining this matter, one traditional and the other rational. The traditional version is that the angels had read on the Preserved Tablet that a people would come forth whose description would be such, and so they made that statement. The rational version is that the angels deduced by reasoning that that people would come forth from the earth; they would necessarily be animals, and such conduct certainly comes from animals. Though this essential element would be in them, namely that they would be speaking, yet inasmuch as animality would also be in them, inescapably they would be ungodly and shed blood, these being the prerequisites of being human.

Other people offer still another explanation. They say that the angels are pure reason and goodness unalloyed, and have no choice in any matter. Just as when you do something in a dream you have no choice in the matter, so that of course you cannot be criticised, whether you utter unbelief in your sleep or declare God is One, or if you then commit adultery, the angels are in a like case in the waking state. Men are the reverse of that; they have freewill and are lustful and passionate and desire all things for themselves, being ready to shed blood to secure everything for themselves. That is the attribute of animals. So the state of those others, being angels, is the opposite of the state of men.

It is therefore perfectly feasible to report of them that they spoke in this fashion, even though in their case there was neither speech nor tongue. This is the suppositional situation, that if those two mutually opposite states were to be endowed with words and gave an account of themselves, this is how it would be. Similarly the poet will say,

'The pool said, I am full.' Pools of course do not really speak; the meaning is, that if the pool had had a tongue, in such a situation that is what it would have said.

Every angel has within him a tablet, and from that tablet, according to the degree of his own powers, he reads aforetime all that is to happen in the world and everything that is going to transpire. When the time comes that what he has read and got to know actually comes into being, then his belief in God most High becomes all the stronger and his love and mystic intoxication increase. He marvels at God's majesty and clairvoyance. That increase of love and faith, that wordless and unexpressed wonder, is the angel's proclamation of God's praise.

Thus, a builder informs his apprentice, 'In this house which they are making so much wood will go, so many bricks, so many stones, so much straw.' When the house is completed and exactly that amount of materials has been used, neither less nor more, the faith of the apprentice increases. The angels too are in a like case.

Someone asked the Master: The Prophet Muhammad, with all his majesty—so that God said, 'But for thee I would not have created the heavens'—yet said, 'Would that the Lord of Muhammad had not created Muhammad.' How can this be?

The Master answered: The statement will become clear through a comparison. Let me propound to you a comparison for this, so that you may realise the meaning. In a certain village a man fell in love with a certain woman. The two dwelt close together and lived happily and pleasurably one with the other, so that they grew fat and thrived on one another. They lived by each other, just as a fish keeps alive in water. Some years they were together. Then suddenly God most High made them wealthy, bestowing on them many sheep and oxen and horses, wealth and gold and servants and slaves. Because of their extreme magnificence and prosperity they set out for the city. Each purchased a great royal palace and there took up residence with horse and retinue, she in one part of the city and he in another. When things had reached this pitch they were no longer able to enjoy each other's company as before; their hearts smouldered away within them and they uttered secret lamentations, being unable to speak. The consuming fire in them became so violent that they entirely perished in the flames of separation. The conflagration of their grief finally passed all bounds. Then their lamentation was heard by God. Their horses and sheep began to vanish; little by little they were restored to their former situation. So after a long while they were reunited in that village of old and resumed full enjoyment of their life together. Then they recalled the bitterness of their separation; and the cry went up, 'Would that the Lord of Muhammad had not created Muhammad.' So long as Muhammad's soul was dwelling apart in the world of holiness in union with God most High, it grew and thrived, plunging about in that sea of compassion like a fish. Though in this earthly world he was endowed with the rank of prophet and guide to men, greatness and majesty and fame and a large following, yet on returning to that former joyous life he says, 'Would that I had never been a prophet and never come into the world, which in comparison with that absolute union is all burden and torment and suffering.'

All these sciences and exertions and acts of devotion, in comparison with the merit and majesty of the Creator, are as though a man bowed to you, performed a service, and departed. If you were to set the whole earth upon your heart in serving God, it would amount to the same as bowing your head once to the ground. For God's merit and graciousness preceded your existence and your service. Whence did He bring you forth and give you existence and make you capable of service and worship, that you should boast of serving Him? These services and sciences are just as if you had made little shapes of wood and leather, then come and offer them up to God, saying, 'I like these little shapes. I made them; but it is Your business to give them life. If you give them life, You will have made my works to live; and if You give them not— the command is Yours entirely.'

Abraham said, 'God is He who *gives life, and makes to die.*' Nimrod said, '*I give life and make to die.*' When God most High gave him the kingship he deemed himself also omnipotent, not attributing the merit to God. He said, 'I too make alive and cause to die, and my desire out of this kingdom is knowledge.' When God most High bestows upon man knowledge and sagacity and shrewdness, he attributes all actions to himself, saying, 'I myself by means of this deed and this action give life to all actions and attain ecstatic joy.' Abraham said, 'No, it is He who *gives life and makes to die.*'

Someone said to our great Master: Abraham said to Nimrod, 'My

God is He who brings up the sun out of the east and sends it down into the west. *God brings the sun from the east.* If you make claim to God-head, do the reverse.' It follows necessarily from this that Nimrod compelled Abraham to abandon the point; for he abandoned his first argument and left Nimrod's rejoinder unanswered, embarking upon another proof.

The Master answered: Others have talked nonsense over this, and now you are also talking nonsense. This is one and the same argument presented in two forms. You are mistaken, and so are they. There are many meanings underlying this statement. One meaning is this, that God most High shaped you out of the concealment of non-entity in your mother's womb. Your 'east' was your mother's womb; from there you rose, and went down into the 'west' of the tomb. This is precisely the first statement, only expressed in another way: *He gives life, and makes to die.* 'Now, if you are able, bring forth from the west of the tomb and convey back to the east of the womb.' That is one meaning; another is the following. Inasmuch as through obedience and strenuous effort and noble actions the gnostic attains illumination and spiritual intoxication, refreshment and ease, and in the state of abandoning such obedience and effort that happiness goes down like the sinking sun, these two states of obedience and abandoning obedience have been for him his 'east' and 'west.' 'So if you are able, by bringing to life in this state of apparent setting, which is ungodliness and corruption and dis-obedience, now in this state of setting make manifest that illumination and ease which rose up out of obedience.'

That is not the business of the servant, and the servant will never be able to do it. That is God's business; for if He wishes He causes the sun to rise from the west, and if He wishes from the east; for

My Lord is He who gives life, and makes to die.

The unbeliever and the believer both proclaim the praises of God. For God most High has stated that every man who goes on the right road and practises righteousness, following the sacred law and the way of the prophets and the saints, shall be vouchsafed such happiness and illumination and life. If he does the reverse, he will be vouchsafed such darkness and fear, such pits and sufferings. Since both believer and unbeliever practise accordingly, and that which God most High

213

has promised comes to pass precisely, neither more nor less, it follows then that both proclaim the praises of God, the one with one tongue and the other with another. How great is the difference between the one praiser and the other praiser!

For instance: a thief has committed a theft, and is hung on the gallows. He too is a preacher to the Muslims, saying, 'Whosoever commits a theft, such is what becomes of him.' Upon another man the king has bestowed a robe of honour on account of his righteousness and trustworthiness: he likewise is a preacher to the Muslims. But the thief preaches with that tongue, and the trusty servant with this tongue. Yet do you consider the difference between those two preachers!

56

The Master said: You are happy in mind. How is that? Because the mind is a precious thing; it is like a snare that must be properly set to catch the prey. If your mind is unhappy, the snare is torn and useless.

It therefore behoves one not to go to excess in one's love or enmity towards another, since by both of these the snare becomes torn. One must be moderate. Now this love which must not be excessive—I mean by that love for other than God. As for what appertains to the Creator, God most High, excess there is inconceivable: the greater the love, the better. Because when love directed towards other than God is excessive— and all men are subject to the wheel of heaven, and heaven is a circling wheel, and men's circumstances also revolve like a wheel—when love for a certain person is excessive, one always desires that good fortune may attend him. But that is impossible, and so the mind becomes disturbed. Similarly when enmity is excessive one always desires that that person may be unlucky and unfortunate; but since the wheel of heaven is ever turning and his circumstances too are revolving, so that now he is lucky now unlucky, it is likewise impossible that he should always be unlucky; and so the mind becomes disturbed. But love for the Creator is latent in all the world and in all men, be they Magians, Jews or Christians, indeed in all things that have being. How indeed should any man not love Him who gave him being? Love is latent in every man, but impediments veil that love; when those impediments are removed that love becomes manifest.

Why indeed should I speak only of things that have being? Not-being too is in commotion, expectant that He will give them being. Non-entities are just like four persons ranged before a king. Each one desires and expects that the king will confer on him a special rank, and each one feels shy of the other because his expectation is contrary to the other. So the non-entities, being ranged in expectation of being brought into being by God—'Make me to be!'—and desiring of the Creator each to be the first to be brought into being, therefore feel shy of one another. If the non-entities are in such a case, how should the things which have being be?

Nothing there is, that does not proclaim His praise.

This is not remarkable; what is remarkable is that 'there is not no-thing that does not proclaim His praise.'

Both unbelief and faith are seeking Thee
And shout Thy undivided Unity.

This house was built out of forgetfulness. All bodies and all the world are maintained in being by forgetfulness. This full-grown body too has grown out of forgetfulness. Forgetfulness is unbelief; and faith cannot exist without the existence of unbelief, for faith is the forsaking of unbelief. Therefore there must be an unbelief which can be forsaken. Therefore both of these are one and the same thing, since this does not exist without that and that does not exist without this. They are indivisible; and their Creator is one, for if their Creator had not been one they would have been divisible. Each creator would have created a separate thing, so that they would have been divisible. So since the Creator is One, He is alone and has no partner.

They said: Saiyid Burhān al-Dīn discourses very well, but he quotes Sanā'ī frequently in his discourse.

The Master answered: What they say is quite true: the sun is excellent, but it gives light. Is that a fault? Introducing Sanā'ī's words casts light on that discourse. The sun casts light on things, and in the light of the sun it is possible to see. The purpose of the light of the sun is to show things up. After all, this sun in heaven shows things which are of no use. That is the real sun, which shows things up that are of use. The sun in heaven is derivative and metaphorical; that sun is the true sun. Do you also, according to the degree of your partial intellects, yearn after this sun and seek the light of knowledge, that you may behold something other than sensibilia, and that your knowledge may ever increase. Be expectant of understanding and comprehending something from every teacher and every friend.

So we realise that there is another sun, apart from the sun of physical form, through which realities and inner truths are revealed. This partial knowledge to which you fly and in which you feel pleasure is a branch of that great knowledge, and a ray of it. This ray is calling you unto that great knowledge and original sun.

Those—they are called from a far place.

You draw that knowledge towards yourself. It says, 'I cannot be contained here, and you are tardy in arriving there. It is impossible for me to be contained here, and it is difficult for you to come there.' To bring about the impossible is impossible; but to bring about the difficult is not impossible. So, though it is difficult, strive to attain the great knowledge; and do not expect that it will be contained here, for that is impossible. Even so the wealthy ones out of their love for the wealth of God collect penny by penny, grain by grain, so that they may attain the attribute of wealth from the ray of wealth. The ray of wealth says, 'I am calling to you out of that great wealth. Why are you drawing me here? For I cannot be contained here. Do you come unto this great wealth.'

In short, the root of the matter is the end: may the end be praiseworthy! What is the praiseworthy end? That the tree whose roots are fixed firm in that spiritual garden, and whose branches and boughs and fruits have become suspended in another place, and its fruits have scattered—that in the end those fruits should be carried back into that garden, for there its roots are. If the contrary should be the case, though that tree in outward form proclaim God's praises and cry Him alleluia, inasmuch as its roots are in this world, all its fruits are carried back into this world. If however both are in that garden, that is *Light upon Light.*

57

Akmal al-Dīn said: I love our Master and am desirous to see him. Even the world to come is blotted out of my mind. I find comfort in the image of the Master without these ideas and propositions; I take repose in his beauty, and pleasure accrues to me from his very mien, or from the mental picture of him.

The Master answered: Though the world to come, and God, do not enter your thoughts, yet all is implicit and remembered in love. A beautiful dancing-girl was once playing the castanets in the presence of the Caliph. The Caliph said, 'Your art is in your hands.' She replied, 'No, in my feet, Caliph of God's Messenger!' 'Excellence is in my hands because excellence of foot is implicit in it.' Though the disciple does not remember the world to come in every detail, yet his delight in seeing the shaikh and his fear of being separated from him comprehend all those details, and the whole of them are implicit in that. Similarly with a man who cherishes and loves a child or a brother, though the thoughts of sonship and brotherhood, the hope of fidelity, compassion and fondness and his love for himself, the issue of the affair, and all the other benefits which kinsmen hope for from kinsmen—though these thoughts do not enter his mind, yet all these details are implicit in that degree of encounter and contemplation. In the same way, air is implicit in wood even though the wood be in earth or in water; were there not air in the wood, fire would never have any effect on it.

For air is the fuel of fire and the life of fire. Do you not see how a breath of air puts life into a fire? Though the wood may be in water or earth, yet air is latent in it. If air were not latent in it, it would never come to the surface of the water. So again with the words you speak: though many things are the prerequisites of these words, such as intelligence and brain, lips and mouth, throat and tongue and all the parts of the body which are the controllers of the body, as well as the elements and temperaments, the spheres, and the hundred thousand secondary causes on which the world depends, and so on until you come to the world of attributes, and then essence—though all these realities are not expressed in words and are not disclosed, yet the whole of them are implicit in the words as I have already mentioned.

Every day five or six times something undesired and painful happens to a man without his freewill. Certainly these things do not proceed from him, but from other than he. He is under the control of that other, and that other watches over him. For many an evil act gives him pain, if there is no opportune watcher watching over him when the act operates. Nevertheless despite these unwanted contingencies, his nature does not acknowledge and is not secure in the thought that 'I am under the control of somebody.'

'God created Adam in His own image.' In your attribute divinity, which is the opposite of servanthood, is deposited on loan. So often man is beaten about the head, yet he does not let go that borrowed obstinacy. He forgets these unwanted contingencies, but it profits him nothing. Until the time when that borrowed element becomes his very own, he will not escape from slapping.

58

A certain gnostic once said: I went into the bath-stove that my heart might be dilated, for it had been the place of retreat of certain of the saints. I saw that the master of the stove had an apprentice who was working with girded loins. The master was telling him, 'Do this and do that.' The apprentice was labouring briskly, and the stove gave off a fine heat on account of the nimbleness with which he obeyed his orders.

'Fine,' said the master. 'Be nimble like this. If you are always energetic and mind your manners, I will give you my own position and appoint you in my own place.'

I was overcome with laughter, and my knot was resolved, for I saw that the bosses of this world all behave like this with their apprentices.

59

Someone said: That astronomer says, 'You claim that there is something without, apart from the heavens and the terrestrial ball which I see. In my view, apart from that nothing exists. If it exists, then show me where it is!'

The Master answered: That demand is invalid from the very start. For you say, 'Show me where it is'; and that Thing has no place. Come then, tell me, whence and where is your objection? It is not in the tongue, it is not in the mouth, it is not in the breast. Search through all of these; divide them piece by piece, atom by atom, and see that you will not find this objection and thought in all of these. So we realise that your thought has no place. Since you have failed to discover the place of your own thought, how will you discover the place of the Creator of thought?

So many thousands of thoughts and moods come over you without your having any hand in them, for they are completely outside your power and control. If you only knew whence these thoughts arise, you would be able to augment them. All these things have a passage over you, and you are wholly unaware whence they come and whither they are going and what they will do. Since you are incapable of penetrating your own moods, how do you expect to penetrate your Creator?

The whoreson says, 'That is not in heaven.' You cur, how do you know That is not? Yes, you have measured heaven span by span; you have gone about all of it, and you pronounce that That is not in it. Why, you do not know the whore you have in your own home; how then should you know heaven? Oh yes, you have heard of heaven, and the names of the stars and the spheres. You say that is something. If you really penetrated the depths of heaven or mounted a single span towards heaven, you would never utter such nonsense.

What do I mean when I say that God is not over heaven? My intention is not, that He is not over heaven; my meaning is, that heaven comprehends Him not, whilst He comprehends heaven. He has an ineffable link with heaven, even as He has established an ineffable link with you. All things are in the hand of His omnipotence and are His theatre and under His control. Hence He is not without heaven and the universe, neither is He wholly in them. That is to say, these comprehend Him not, and He comprehends all.

Someone said: Before earth and heaven and the Throne existed, pray where was He? We said: This question is invalid from the start. For God is He who has no place. You ask, 'Where was He before all this?' Why, all your things are without place. Have you discovered the place of these things which are in you, that you are searching for His place? Since your moods and thoughts have no place, how should a place for Him be conceivable? After all, surely the Creator of thought is subtler than thought. For instance, the builder who has constructed a house is subtler than this house, for that builder, a man, is able to make and plan a hundred such buildings other than this, each different from the other. Therefore he is subtler and more majestic than any fabric; but that subtlety cannot be seen save through the medium of a house, some work entering the sensible world, that that subtlety of his may display beauty.

This breath of yours is visible in winter, but in summer it is invisible. That does not mean that in summer the breath is cut off and there is no breath; but summer is subtle, and the breath is subtle and does not appear, contrary to the winter. In like manner all your attributes and essential elements are subtle and cannot be seen save through the medium of some act. For instance, your clemency exists, but it cannot be seen; only when you forgive an offender, then your clemency becomes visible. Similarly your vengefulness cannot be seen; only when you take vengeance upon a criminal and beat him, then your vengefulness is seen; and so on *ad infinitum*.

God most High by reason of His extreme subtlety cannot be seen. He created heaven and earth, so that His omnipotence and His handiwork might be seen. Therefore He declares:

> *What, have they not beheld heaven above them,*
> *how We have built it?*

My words are not in my control, and therefore I am pained: because I desire to counsel my friends, and the words do not come as I would have them come, therefore I am pained. But inasmuch as my words are higher than I and I am subject to them, I am happy; for the words which God speaks bring to life wherever they reach, and make a mighty impression.

> *And when thou threwest, it was not*
> *thyself that threw, but God threw.*

The arrow which leaps from the bow of God, no shield or breast-plate can repel it. Therefore I am happy.

If all knowledge were within a man, and ignorance were wholly absent, that man would be consumed and cease to be. So ignorance is desirable, inasmuch as by that means he continues to exist; and knowledge also is desirable, in that it is a means to the spiritual knowledge of God. So each is an ally of the other, and both at the same time are opposites. Though night is the opposite of day, yet it is the ally of day and both do the same work. If night lasted forever, no work would ever be produced and result; while if day lasted forever, eye and head and brain would remain dazzled and would go mad and cease to function. Therefore men rest and sleep in the night, and all the implements —brain, thought, hand and foot, hearing and sight—all gather strength; and by day they expend those powers.

So all things, though appearing opposite in relation to their opposites, in relation to the wise man are all performing the same work and are not opposed. Show me the evil thing in this world wherein no good is contained and the good thing wherein no evil is contained! For instance, a man was intent on murder, then busied himself with fornication, so that he shed no blood. Inasmuch as it is fornication, it is evil; but inasmuch as it prevented murder, it is good. So evil and good are one and indivisible. That is the substance of our quarrel with the Magians. They say there are two Gods, one the creator of good and one the creator of evil. Now show me good without evil, that I may acknowledge that there is a God of evil and a God of good! This is impossible, for good does not exist apart from evil. Since good and evil are not two and there is no separation between them, therefore it is impossible that there should be two creators. Do we not confute you? By all means, be sure that it is so.

We have spoken few words, because the thought may occur to you that perhaps it is as the Magians say. Granted that you are not sure that it is as I have said, yet how can you be sure that it is not so? Wretched infidel, God declares:

> *Do those not think that they shall be raised up*
> *unto a mighty day?*

'Has not the thought also occurred to you that those threats which We have made may also come true, and that punishment will be visited upon the unbelievers in such wise as you have never imagined? Why then did you not take precautions and seek after Us?'

60

'Abū Bakr was not deemed your superior on account of much praying and fasting and almsgiving, but on account of something that was fixed in his heart.' The Prophet says that Abū Bakr's superiority over others was not by reason of much praying and much fasting, but because God's special favour was with him, namely the love of God. On the resurrection day when men's prayers are brought, they will be put in the balance, and likewise their fastings and almsgivings; but when love is brought, it will not be contained in the balance. So the root of the matter is love.

When therefore you perceive love to be in you, augment it that it may become greater. When you perceive the principal sum to be in you, namely the quest of God, increase it by ever questing, for 'In movement is blessing'; if you do not increase it, your principal will go away from you. You are not less than the earth. Men change the earth by movement and by turning it with the hoe, and it yields crops; when they abandon it, it becomes hard. So when you perceive the quest to be in you, be always coming and going, and do not say, 'What use is there in this going?' Keep going, and the use will appear of itself. The use of a man going to the shop is simply to present his requirements. God most High bestows provisions; but if a man sits at home, pretending to be self-sufficient, then the provisions do not arrive.

Consider the little child who cries, and his mother gives him milk. If he were to think, 'What use is there in my crying, and what is the cause of her giving milk?' he would get no milk. So we see that the crying is the reason why he gets the milk. After all, if anyone is absorbed in asking, 'What use is there in this bowing and prostrating? Why should I do it?'—when you do obeisance before a prince or a chieftain, bowing and kneeling, why, the prince has compassion on you and gives you a sop. What makes compassion in the prince is not the prince's skin and flesh. After death that skin and flesh are still there, as also when the prince is asleep and insensible, but then this obeisance before him goes to waste. So we realise that the compassion which is in the prince is not something that can be perceived and seen. So if it is feasible for us to do obeisance to something which we cannot see which is contained in skin and flesh, surely it is feasible also in the case of That which is without skin and flesh. If that thing which is contained in skin and flesh were not invisible, Abū Jahl and Muhammad would have been one and the same, and so there would have been no difference between them. The ear to outward appearance is just the same whether it is deaf or hearing, there is no difference; the one and the other are the same material shape; but that in which hearing is contained is invisible and cannot be seen.

So the root of the matter is that Divine grace. You, being a prince, have two slaves. One has performed many services and made many journeys on your behalf; the other is idle in your service. Yet we see that your love for the idle one is greater than for the active one; though you do not let the active one go unrewarded, yet such is the case. It is impossible to determine in the matter of God's grace. This right eye and this left eye are both one and the same from the external viewpoint; why, what service has the right eye performed which the left eye has not performed? And the right hand—what work has it done that the left hand has not done, and so with the right foot? Yet the Divine favour has fallen on the right eye. So too Friday has been preferred over the rest of the days. 'God has certain portions to bestow other than those inscribed for a man on the Tablet, so let him seek for them on Friday.' Now what service has this Friday performed which the other days have not performed? Yet God bestowed His grace and special mark of honour upon Friday.

If a blind man should say, 'I was created blind like this, it is not my fault,' it will do him no good to say 'I am blind' and 'It is not my fault.' That will not relieve him of his suffering. Those infidels who are fixed in unbelief—after all, they suffer because of their unbelief. Yet when we look at the matter again, that suffering too is itself a Divine grace. When the unbeliever is left at ease he forgets the Creator; so God reminds him by means of suffering. Therefore Hell is a place of worship, and is the mosque of the infidels, for there the unbeliever remembers God; just as in prison and suffering and toothache—when the pain comes, it tears away the veil of forgetfulness. The sufferer acknowledges God and makes lamentation, saying, 'O Lord, O Compassionate One, O God!' He is healed; then the veils of forgetfulness descend again and he says, 'Where is God? I cannot find him. I cannot see Him. What should I look for?'

How is it that when you were suffering you saw and found, and now you do not see? Since therefore you see when you suffer, suffering is made to prevail over you to the end that you may recollect God. The inmate of Hell was forgetful of God in the time of his ease and did not remember God; in Hell he recollects God night and day. God created the world, heaven and earth, moon and sun and stars, good and evil, that they might remember Him and serve Him and proclaim His praise. Inasmuch as the unbelievers in the time of their ease do not do this, and since their purpose in being created was to recollect God, therefore they go to Hell in order that they may remember Him. Believers however have no need to suffer; in their time of ease they are not unmindful of that suffering and see that suffering constantly present. In the same way once an intelligent child has had its feet put in the stocks that is enough, he never forgets the stocks. The stupid child however forgets, and must therefore be put in the stocks every moment. So too the clever horse, once it has felt the spur, does not require the spur again; he carries the rider for many leagues and does not forget the sting of the spur. The stupid horse however requires the spur every moment; he is not fit to carry a man, so they load him with dung.

61

Successive hearsay does the same work as actual seeing and exercises the same authority. Thus, you were born of your father and mother; you have been told that you were born of them; you have not seen with your own eyes that you were born of them, but by being stated so often it comes to be accepted by you as the truth, so that if you were now told that you were not born of them you would not listen. Similarly you have heard successively from many people that Baghdad and Mecca exist; if they were now to say and swear an oath that they do not exist, you would not believe it. So we realise that when the ear has heard successively, it exercises the same authority as the eye.

In the same way, from the external standpoint a statement when made successively is given the same authority as actual seeing. It may be that the statement of a certain person has the authority of being handed down successively, so that it is not a single statement but a hundred thousand; so one statement of his will be a hundred thousand statements. What is so surprising in this? The external king exercises the authority of a hundred thousand, though he is only one; if a hundred thousand should speak nothing would happen, but when he speaks something happens.

Since this happens in the external world, it follows all the more so in the world of spirits. Though you have gone about the world, inasmuch as you have not gone about it with God in mind, it is necessary for you to go about the world again.

> Say: 'Journey in the land, then behold
> how was the end of them that cried lies.'

'That journey was not on My account, it was for the sake of garlic and onions. Since you did not go about for His sake, it was for another purpose and that other purpose became a veil to you, not allowing you to see Me.' It is the same when you search earnestly for a person in the bazaar; you see nobody, or if you see people you see them as shadows. Or you are hunting up a problem in a book; your ears and eyes and mind are full of that one problem; you turn the pages, and you see nothing. Since therefore you had an intention and object in view other than this, wherever you went about you were full of that object and did not see this.

In the time of 'Umar, God be well pleased with him, there was a certain man who had grown so old that his daughter used to give him milk and looked after him like a child. 'Umar, God be well pleased with him, said to that daughter, 'There is no child to compare with you in these times in dutifulness to your father.' She replied, 'What you say is true. But there is a difference between me and my father. Though I fall not short in my service to my father, yet when my father was bringing me up and serving me he used to tremble for me, lest any harm should come to me; while I serve my father, and pray night and day asking of God that he may die, that the trouble he causes me may end. If I serve my father, whence can I get that trembling of his for me?' 'Umar said, 'This woman is wiser than 'Umar.' He meant, 'I judge by externals, whilst you spoke of the core.'

The truly wise and learned man is he who penetrates into the core of a thing so that he diagnoses the truth of it. God forbid that 'Umar should not have been apprised of the truth and secret of things; but such was the Companions' way, that they dispraised themselves and commended others.

There are many who have not the strength for 'presence'; they find 'absence' a pleasanter state to be in. In the same way, all the brightness of day is from the sun; but if a man stares at the sun's orb all day and every day it does him no good, and his eyes get dazzled. It is better for him to be occupied with some task or other, which is absence from staring at the sun's orb. Similarly, to mention tasty dishes in the presence of a sick person excites him to acquire strength and appetite, but the actual presence of those dishes does him harm.

Hence it is realised that trembling and passionate love are necessary in the quest for God. Whoever trembles not himself must wait upon tremblers. No fruit ever grows on the trunk of a tree, for trunks do not tremble; the tips of the branches tremble; yet the trunk of the tree strengthens the tips of the branches, and because of the fruit is secure from the blow of the axe. Since the trembling of the trunk of the tree will end in ruin, it is better for the trunk not to tremble, and it suits the trunk to be quiet so that it may serve the tremblers.

Since he is Mu'īn al-Dīn, he is not 'Ain al-Dīn ('Essence of the Faith') because of the M which has been added to the 'Ain. 'Any addition to perfection is a diminution.' That addition of M is a diminution. In the same way, though six fingers are an addition, yet they are a diminution. Aḥad ('One') is perfection, and Aḥmad is not yet in the station of perfection; when that M is removed it becomes complete perfection. That is to say, God comprehends all; whatever you add to Him is a diminution. The number one is in all numbers, and without it no number can be.

Saiyid Burhān al-Dīn was discoursing learnedly. A fool interrupted him as he was speaking to say, 'We need some words without likenesses.' The Saiyid answered, 'You who have no likeness, come and listen to words without likeness!' After all, you are a likeness; you are not this of your own self, this person is the shadow of you. When anyone dies, people say, 'So-and-so has departed.' If this body was he, then whither has he departed? So it is realised that your external form is the likeness of your internal being, that men may be guided by your external to your internal. Every thing that is visible is visible because of density. Thus, the breath in hot weather cannot be perceived; but when it is cold, it becomes visible out of density.

It is incumbent upon the Prophet, peace be upon him, to manifest the power of God, and by preaching to waken men. It is not incumbent upon him, however, to bring a man to the stage of being ready to receive God's truth; that is the work of God. God has two attributes: wrath and lovingkindness. The prophets are theatres of both; to believers they are a theatre of God's lovingkindness, and to unbelievers they are a theatre of God's wrath.

Those who acknowledge the truth see themselves in the prophet and hear their own voice proceeding from him and smell their own scent proceeding from him. No man denies his own self. Therefore the prophets say to the community, 'We are you, and you are we; there is no strangeness between us.' A man says, 'This is my hand'; nobody asks him to furnish proof, for it is a conjoined part of him. But if he says, 'So-and-so is my son,' proof is demanded of him, for that is a disjoined part.

62

Some have said that love is the cause of service. This is not so. Rather it is the inclination of the beloved that is the requisite of service. If the beloved desires that the lover should be occupied with service, then service proceeds from the lover; if the beloved does not desire it, then the lover abandons service. The abandonment of service is not contrary to love; after all, even if the lover does no service, love does service in him. No; on the contrary, the root of the matter is love, and service is the branch of love.

If the sleeve moves, that happens because the hand moves. On the other hand it does not necessarily follow that if the hand moves the sleeve also moves. For instance, a man has a large gown, so that he rolls about in his gown and the gown does not move. That can happen; but what is not possible is that the gown should move without the person himself moving.

Some people have deemed the gown itself a person, have considered the sleeve a hand and imagined the boot and breeches a foot. This hand and foot are the sleeve and boot of another hand and foot. They say, 'So-and-so is under the hand of So-and-so,' and 'So-and-so has a hand in so many things,' and 'You have to hand it to So-and-so when he speaks.' Certainly what is meant by that hand and foot is not this hand and foot.

That prince came and assembled us, and himself departed. In the same way the bee united the wax with the honey and itself departed and flew away. Because his existence was a condition, after all his continuance is not a condition. Our mothers and fathers are like bees, uniting the seeker with the sought and assembling together the lover and the beloved. They then suddenly fly away. God most High has made them a means for uniting the wax and the honey, and then they fly away; but the wax and honey remain, and the garden. They themselves do not go out of the garden; this is not such a garden that it is possible to go out of it; but they depart from one corner of the garden to another corner of the garden.

Our body is like a beehive in which are the wax and honey of the love of God. Though the bees, our mothers and fathers, are the means, yet they too are tended by the gardener; the gardener also makes the beehive. God most High gave those bees another form; at the time when they were doing this work they had another garment appropriate to that work, but when they departed into the other world they changed garment, for there another work proceeds from them. Yet the person is the same as he was in the first place. Thus for example: a man went into battle, and put on battledress, girded on armour and placed a helmet on his head, because it was the time of combat. But when he comes to the feast he puts off those garments, for he will be occupied with another business. Yet he is the same person. But since you have seen him in that garment, whenever you bring him to mind you will picture him in that shape and that garment, even though he may have changed garments a hundred times.

A man has lost a ring in a certain place. Though the ring has been transported from that place, nevertheless he circles around that place, implying, 'It was here that I lost it.' So a bereaved person circles around the grave and ignorantly circumambulates about the earth and kisses it, implying, 'I lost that ring here'; yet how should it be left there?

God most High has performed so many wonderful works to display His omnipotence. It was here for the sake of Divine wisdom that He composed for a day or two spirit with body. If a man should sit with a corpse in a tomb even for a moment, there is fear that he may go mad. How then, when he escapes from the trap of form and the ditch of the bodily mould, how should he remain there? God most High has appointed that to strike fear into men's hearts and as a token to renew that striking of fear again and again, so that a terror may be manifest in the hearts of men because of the desolation of the tomb and the dark earth. In the same way, when a caravan has been ambushed in a certain place on the road, two or three stones are placed together there to act as a waysign, as much as to say, 'Here is a place of danger.' These graves too are a visible waysign indicating a place of danger.

Fear makes its mark on men; though it does not necessarily follow that it should be realised. For instance if people say to you, 'So-and-so is afraid of you,' without any act issuing from him, an affection manifests in you in regard to him without doubt. If on the contrary they say, 'So-and-so is not in the least afraid of you,' and 'There is no terror of you in his heart,' by the mere fact of this being said an anger towards him appears in your heart.

This running about is the effect of fear. All the world is running; but the running of each one is appropriate to his state. The running of a man is of one kind, the running of a plant is of another kind, the running of a spirit is of another kind. The running of the spirit is without step and visible sign. After all, consider the unripe grape, how much it runs until it attains the blackness of the ripe grape; the moment it has become sweet, at once it reaches that station. Yet that running is invisible and imperceptible; but when it reaches that stage, it becomes realised that it has run very much until it arrived there. Similarly a man enters the water, and nobody has seen him go; when suddenly he brings his head out of the water, then it is realised that he entered the water, for he has reached this point.

63

Lovers have heartaches which no cure can mend, neither sleeping nor faring abroad nor eating, only the sight of the beloved. 'Meet the friend and your sickness will end': this is true to such an extent, that if a hypocrite sits in the company of believers, under their influence he becomes a believer that very instant. So God most High declares:

When they meet those who believe, they say, 'We believe.'

How then, when a believer sits with a believer? Since that has such an effect on a hypocrite, consider what benefits it confers on the believer! Consider how wool, through being in the vicinity of an intelligent man, has become a figured carpet; and this earth, through the vicinity of an intelligent man, has become such a fine palace! The society of an intelligent man has had such an effect on inanimate things; consider then what effect the society of a believer has on the believer!

Through the society of a partial soul and a miniature intellect inanimate things have attained this rank, and these are all the shadow of a partial intellect. One can deduce a person from his shadow. Now deduce from this what manner of intellect and reason is required for yonder heavens, and the moon and sun, and the seven layers of the earth to become manifest through it, and all that lies between earth and heaven. All these existing things are the shadow of the Universal Intellect. The shadow of the partial intellect is proportionate to the shadow of its person; the shadow of the Universal Intellect, which is the whole of existing things, is proportionate to That.

The saints of God have beheld other heavens besides these heavens; for these heavens are disregarded by them and appear lowly before them; they have set their foot upon them and transcended them.

Heavens there are in the province of the soul
That hold our worldly heaven in their control.

What is there so wonderful in the fact that a certain man out of the whole of mankind should discover this particular quality, that he can set his foot upon the head of the seventh heaven? Were we not all congeners of the earth? Yet God most High implanted in us a faculty whereby we became distinguished from our genus, we in control of that and that under our control. We control that in whatever manner we desire, now lifting it up and now setting it down; now we fashion it into a palace, now we make it a cup and a goblet; now we stretch it out, now we shorten it. If in the first place we were this very earth and its congener, God most High distinguished us by means of that faculty. In like manner, what is there so wonderful in the fact that out of the midst of us, who are all congeners, God most High should distinguish a certain one, in relation to whom we are as some inanimate thing, he controlling us, we being unaware of him whilst he is aware of us?

When I say 'unaware,' I do not mean utterly unaware. On the contrary, everyone who is aware of one thing is unaware of another thing. Even earth, inanimate as it is, is aware of what God has given it. For if it were unaware, how would it have been receptive to water, and how would it have nursed and nourished every seed accordingly? When a person applies himself earnestly and attentively to a particular task, his attentiveness to that task means that he is unaware of any other. But by this inattention we do not mean total inattention. Some people wanted to catch a cat, but found it impossible to do so. One day that cat was preoccupied with hunting a bird, and became inattentive through hunting the bird; so they caught it.

So it is not necessary to become wholly preoccupied with worldly affairs. One must take them easily, and not be in bondage to them, lest this should fret and that should fret. The treasure must not fret; for if these things should fret, that will transform them; whereas if that frets (we seek refuge with God!) who then will transform that? If for instance you have many kinds of cloth of every sort, when you are absorbed, why, which of them will you clutch? Though all are indispensable, yet it is certain that in the bundle you will lay hands on something precious and to be treasured; for with one pearl and a single ruby one can make a thousand decorations.

From a certain tree sweet fruit materialises; though that fruit is a part of it, yet God most High has chosen and distinguished that part above the whole, for in it He deposited a sweetness that He did not deposit in the rest; and by virtue of that, that part became superior to that whole, and proved the pith and purpose of the tree. So God most High declares:

Nay, but they marvel that a warner has come to them from among them.

231

A certain man said, 'I have a certain state in which neither Muhammad nor the angel near the Throne is contained.' The shaikh replied 'Is it so amazing that a man should have a state in which Muhammad is not contained? Muhammad does not have a state in which a stinking creature like you is not contained!'

A certain jester desired to restore the king to his humour. Every one engaged with him for a certain sum, for the king was greatly vexed. The king was walking angrily along the bank of a river. The jester was walking on the other side level with the king. The king paid not the slightest attention to the jester; he kept staring in the water. The jester, becoming desperate, said, 'O king, what do you see in the water, that you are staring so?' The king replied, 'I see a cuckold.' The jester said, 'Your slave is also not blind.'

So now, since you have a time when Muhammad is not contained, why, Muhammad does not have a state in which such a stinking creature is not contained! After all, this degree of spiritual state which you have discovered is due to his blessing and influence. For in the first place all gifts are showered on him, then they are distributed from him to other men. Such is the rule. God most High said, 'O Prophet, peace be upon thee, and God's mercy and blessings!' 'We have scattered all gifts upon thee.' Said Muhammad, 'And upon God's righteous servants!'

God's way is exceeding fearful, blocked and full of snow. He was the first to risk his life, driving his horse and pioneering the road. Whoever goes on this road, does so by his guidance and guarding. He discovered the road in the first place and set up waymarks everywhere, posting pieces of wood to say, 'Do not go in this direction, and do not go in that direction. If you go in that direction you will perish, even as the people of 'Ad and Thamud; and if you go in this direction you will be saved, like the believers. All of the Koran expounds this, for *therein are clear signs*—that is to say, upon these ways We have given waymarks. If any man attempts to break any of these pieces of wood, all attack him, saying, 'Why do you destroy the road for us, and why do you labour to accomplish our destruction? Perchance you are a highwayman.'

Know now that Muhammad is the guide. Until a man first comes to Muhammad he cannot reach unto Us. Similarly, when you wish to go to a certain place, first reason leads the way, saying, 'You must go to a certain place, that is in your best interests.' After that the eyes act as a guide, and then the limbs begin to move, all in that order; though the limbs have no knowledge of the eye, neither the eye of the reason.

Though a man is inadvertent, others are not unaware of him. If you labour strenuously in pursuit of the world, you become unaware of your real concern. It is necessary to seek God's approval, not the approval of men; for approval and love and affection are only on loan in men, being placed there by God. If God so wishes, He gives no composure or enjoyment; with all the means of ease and bread and luxury provided, everything becomes pain and affliction. Therefore all secondary means are as it were a pen in the hand of God's omnipotence; God is the mover and the writer. Until He wishes, the pen does not move. You fix your eye on the pen; you say, 'There must be a hand to this pen.' You see the pen, but you do not see the hand. You see the pen and remember the hand; where is that which you see, and that which you say? They however always see the hand, and they say, 'There must also be a pen'; but beholding the beauty of the hand, they do not care to behold the pen. They simply say, 'Such a hand cannot be without a pen'; whilst you are so delighted with beholding the pen that you do not care for the hand, they are so delighted with beholding the hand, how could they care for the pen? Whilst you find such pleasure in barley bread that you do not remember wheaten bread, since they have wheaten bread how could they remember barley bread? Since He has bestowed upon you such joy upon earth that you have no desire for heaven, which is the true place of joy, and since earth derives its life from heaven, how should the inhabitants of heaven remember earth?

So do not regard happiness and pleasure as coming from secondary causes, for those realities are merely on loan to the secondary causes. It is He who hurts and profits, for all hurt and profit come from Him. Why do you cling so to secondary causes?

'The best words are those which are few and telling.' The best words are those which convey a lesson, not those which are many. Though the Sura *Say, He is One* is little in form, yet it is superior to the Sura of the Cow though that is very long, from the standpoint of conveying a message. Noah preached for a thousand years and forty persons rallied to him; it is well known how long Muhammad preached, yet so many climes believed in him, so many saints and 'pegs' appeared because of him. Much and little therefore are no criterion; the true object is the conveying of a lesson.

With some men it may be that few words convey the lesson better than many. In the same way, when the fire of a stove is extremely fierce you cannot derive any benefit from it and are unable to go near it; whereas you derive a thousand advantages from a feeble lamp. Hence it is realised that it is benefit gained which is the true objective. With some men it is beneficial not to hear any words at all; it is enough for them to see; that is what profits such a man, and if he hears any words it actually harms him.

A certain shaikh from India was seeking to come to a great saint. When he reached Tabriz and came to the door of the saint's cell, a voice came to him from within the cell, saying, 'Return! In your case the benefit is that you have come to the door. If you see the saint, that will harm you.'

A few words which convey a lesson are like a lit lamp which kissed an unlit lamp and departed. That is enough for him, and he has attained his purpose. After all, the prophet is not that visible form; that form is the steed of the prophet. The prophet is that true love and affection, and that is immortal; just as the she-camel of Salih, his form is the she-camel. The prophet is that true love and affection, and that is eternal.

Someone asked the question, 'Why do they not praise God only upon the minaret? Why do they also mention Muhammad?' He was answered, 'Well, praising Muhammad is praising God. It may be compared with a man saying, "God give the king a long life, and him who showed me the way to the king, or told me of the king's name and attributes!" Praising the man is in reality praising the king.'

This Prophet says, 'Give me something. I am in need. Either give me your cloak, or your wealth, or clothes.' What would he do with your cloak and wealth? He desires to lighten your garment, so that the warmth of the sun may reach you.

And lend to God a good loan.

He does not want wealth and cloak only. He has given you many things besides wealth—knowledge, and thought, and wisdom, and vision. He means, 'Expend on Me a moment's regard and thought and consideration and reason; after all, you have acquired wealth by means of these instruments which I have given.' God desires alms alike from bird and snare. If you are able to go before the sun naked, that is better; for that Sun does not burn black, it makes a man white. Or at least make your clothes lighter, that you may enjoy the feel of the Sun. You have become accustomed for a while to bitterness; at least make trial of sweetness too!

64

Every science that is acquired in this world by study and application is the science of bodies; that science which is acquired after death is the science of religions. To know the science of 'I am God' is the science of bodies; to become 'I am God' is the science of religions. To see the light of the lamp and the fire is the science of bodies; to burn in the fire or in the light of the lamp is the science of religions. Everything that is sight is the science of religions; everything that is knowledge is the science of bodies.

You may say that the only verity is seeing and vision; all the other sciences are the science of fantasy. For instance, an architect has thought and pictured the building of a school; however much that thought may be right and correct, yet it is a fantasy. It becomes reality when he actually raises and constructs the school.

Now there are differences between fantasy and fantasy. The fantasy of Abū Bakr and 'Umar and 'Uthmān and 'Alī is superior to the fantasy of the Companions. Between fantasy and fantasy there is a great difference. The expert architect built a house, and a man who was not an architect also conceived a fantasy; the difference is great, because the architect's fantasy is closer to reality. Similarly on the other side, in the world of realities and vision, there are differences between vision and vision, and so on *ad infinitum*.

So when it is said that there are seven hundred veils of darkness and seven hundred of light—all that belongs to the world of fantasy is a veil of darkness, and all that belongs to the world of realities is veils of light. But between the veils of darkness, which is fantasy, no difference can be made or seen because of their extreme subtlety; and despite a vast and enormous difference in realities, that difference also cannot be comprehended.

65

The inhabitants of Hell will be happier in Hell than in the world, for in Hell they will be aware of God whereas in the world they are not aware; and nothing can be sweeter than the awareness of God. So their desire to return to the world is in order that they may do something whereby they may become aware of the manifestation of Divine grace, not because the world is a happier place than Hell.

Hypocrites are consigned to the lowest reach of Hell because faith came to the hypocrite, but his unbelief was strong and so he did nothing; his punishment will be more severe so that he may become aware of God. To the unbeliever faith did not come; his unbelief is weak, and so he will become aware through a less punishment. So as between the breeches with dust upon them and the carpet with dust upon it, in the case of the trousers it is sufficient for one person to shake them a little for them to become clean, whereas it takes four persons shaking the carpet violently for the dust to leave it.

When the inhabitants of Hell cry:

Pour upon us water, or of that God
has provided you—

God forbid that they should desire foods and drinks; it means, 'Pour upon us too of that thing which you have found and which shines on you.'

The Koran is as a bride who does not disclose her face to you, for all that you draw aside the veil. That you should examine it, and yet not attain happiness and unveiling, is due to the fact that the act of drawing aside the veil has itself repulsed and tricked you, so that the bride has shown herself to you as ugly, as if to say, 'I am not that beauty.' The Koran is able to show itself in whatever form it pleases.

But if you do not draw aside the veil and seek only its good pleasure, watering its sown field and attending on it from afar, toiling upon that which pleases it best, it will show its face to you without your drawing aside the veil.

Seek the people of God, for

> *Enter thou among My servants!*
> *Enter thou My Paradise!*

God does not speak to every one, just as the kings of this world do not speak to every weaver; they have appointed a vizier and a deputy to show the way to the king. God most High also has chosen a certain servant, so that whosoever seeks God, God is in him. All the prophets have come for this reason, that only they are the way.

56

Sirāj al-Dīn said: I spoke on a problem, but something within me ached.

The Master answered: That is something put in charge of you which does not allow you to speak. Though that controller is imperceptible to you, yet when you feel yearning and compulsion and pain you know that there is a controller. For instance, you enter the water; the softness of the flowers and fragrant herbs reaches you. When you go to the other side, thorns prick into you. It thus becomes known to you that on that side is a thorn-bed, and discomfort and pain, whilst on the other side is a flower-bed and ease; though you perceive neither. This is called emotion, and it is more apparent than anything perceptible. For instance, hunger and thirst, anger and happiness—all these things are imperceptible, yet they are more apparent than anything percept-ible. For if you close your eyes you do not see the perceptible, whereas you cannot by any device drive hunger away from yourself. Similarly hotness in hot dishes, and coldness, sweetness and bitterness in foods, these are imperceptible, yet they are more apparent than anything perceptible.

Why now do you regard this body? What connexion have you with this body? You subsist without it. You are always without it. If it is night, you have no care for the body; while if it is day, you are pre-occupied with your affairs. You are never with the body. So why do you tremble over this body, seeing that you are not with it for a single hour, but are always elsewhere? Where are you, and where is the body? 'You are in one valley, and I am in another.' This body is a great deception; it thinks that it is dead, and it is dead too. Why, what connexion have you with the body? It is a great hoodwink. Pharaoh's magicians, inasmuch as they had paused like a mote, sacrificed their bodies, for they perceived themselves to be subsisting without this body and that the body had no connexion with them. In the same way Abraham and Ishmael and all the prophets and the saints, having paused, were indifferent to the body and whether it existed or no.

Ḥajjāj, having taken beng, had rested his head against the door and was shouting, 'Do not move the door or my head will fall off!' He had supposed that his head was separate from his body and only subsisted through the medium of the door. Our situation and that of all men is like this: they suppose that they are connected with the body or subsist through the body.

67

'He created Adam in His likeness.' All men are seeking manifestation. There are many women who are veiled, but they uncover their faces to try the object of their desire, as you try a razor. The lover says to the beloved, 'I have not slept and I have not eaten, I have become like this and that without you.' The meaning of this would be, 'You are seeking a manifestation; I am your manifestation, to which you may vaunt your belovedness.' In the same way all scholars and learned men are seeking manifestation. 'I was a hidden treasure, and I desired to be known.'

'He created Adam in His likeness,' that is, in the likeness of His rules. His rules are manifest in all creation, because all things are the shadow of God, and the shadow is like the person. If the five fingers are spread out, the shadow too is spread out; if the body bows, the shadow also bows; if it stretches out, the shadow also stretches out. So all men are seeking after a sought-for and beloved One, for they desire all to be His lovers and humble ones, enemies to His enemies and friends of His friends. All these are the rules and attributes of God which appear in the shadow.

To sum up, this shadow is unaware of us, but we are aware. But this awareness of ours in relation to God's knowledge is in the predicament of unawareness. Not everything that is in the person shows in the shadow, only certain things. So not all the attributes of God show in this shadow, only some of them show, for

> *You have been given of knowledge nothing*
> *except a little.*

68

Jesus, upon whom be peace, was asked, 'Spirit of God, what is the greatest and most difficult thing in this world and the next?' He replied, 'The wrath of God.' They asked, 'And what shall save a man from that?' He answered, 'That you master your own wrath and suppress your rage.'

That is the proper way: that when the soul desires to complain, a man should go contrary to it and give thanks and exaggerate the matter to such a degree that he acquires within himself a love of the other. For to give thanks lyingly is to seek love of God.

So says our great Master, God sanctify his spirit: To complain of the creature is to complain of the Creator. He also said: Enmity and rage in your unconsciousness are hidden from you. It is as if you see a spark leaping from a fire: extinguish it, so that it may return to non-existence whence it came. If you assist with the match of an answering word and the expression of a reprisal, it will find the way and move again and again out of non-existence, and then only with difficulty can you send it back to non-existence.

> *Repel thou the evil with that which is fairer*

so that you may triumph over your enemy in two ways. One way is this: that your enemy is not his flesh and skin, it is the evil thought; when that is repelled from you by an abundance of thanks, it will inevitably be repelled from him also. The first way is in accordance with instinct, for 'A man is the slave of beneficence.' The second is that he sees no advantage. So it is with children: when they shout names at one of them and he calls bad names back, they are all the more encouraged, saying, 'Our words have had an effect.' But if the enemy sees no change and no advantage, no inclination remains in him. The second way is this: that when the attribute of forgiving appears in you, it becomes realised that the other man's reproaches were a lie and that he saw crooked, not seeing you as you truly are. It also becomes realised that he is the one to be reproached, not you; and no proof puts an adversary to shame more than that, that his lying should become manifest. So by praising and giving thanks to him you are administering poison to him; for whilst he is manifesting your deficiency, you have manifested your perfection. For you are beloved of God—

and pardon
the offences of their fellow-men; and God
loves the good-doers.

He who is loved by God can hardly be defective. Praise him, so that his friends may conceive the idea, 'Perhaps he is at odds with us, for there is so much agreement with him.'

Though they are powerful, pluck out their beards politely;
Firmly break their necks, though they are high and mighty.

May God assist us to that!

69

Between a man and God there are just two veils, and all other veils manifest out of these: they are health, and wealth. The man who is well in body says, 'Where is God? I do not know, and I do not see.' As soon as pain afflicts him he begins to say, 'O God! O God!' communing and conversing with God. So you see that health was his veil, and God was hidden under that pain. As much as a man has wealth and resources, he procures the means to gratifying his desires, and is preoccupied night and day with that. The moment indigence appears, his spirit is weakened and he goes round about God.

Drunkenness and emptyhandedness brought Thee to me;
I am the slave of Thy drunkenness and indigency!

God most High granted to Pharaoh four hundred years of life and
rule and kingship and enjoyment. All that was a veil which kept him
far from the presence of God. He experienced not a single day of
disagreeableness and pain, lest he should remember God. God said,
'Go on being preoccupied with your own desire, and do not remember
me. Goodnight!'

King Solomon grew weary of his reign,
But Job was never sated of his pain.

70

The Master said: This that men say, that in the human soul there is an
evil which does not exist in animals and wild beasts—it is not from the
standpoint that man is worse than they; it is explained by the fact that
that evil character and wickedness of soul and the vilenesses which are
in man are according to a secret essential element which is in him.
Those characteristics and vilenesses and evil are a veil over that
element. The more precious and venerable and noble that element is,
the greater are its veils. So vileness and evil and bad character are the
cause of the veil over that element; and these veils cannot be removed
save with great strivings.

Those strivings are of various kinds. The greatest of them is to
mingle with friends who have turned their faces to God and turned
their backs on this world. For there is no more difficult striving than
this, to sit with righteous friends; for the very sight of them dissolves
and naughts that carnal soul. It is for this reason that they say that when
a snake has not seen a man for forty years it becomes a dragon; that is,
because it sees no one who would be the means of dissolving its evil
and vileness.

Wherever men put a big lock, that is a sign that there is to be found
something precious and valuable. So you see, the greater the veil the
better the element. Just as a snake is over the treasure, so do you not
regard our ugliness, but regard the precious things of the treasure.

71

> 'On what,' My darling cried,
> 'Does So-and-so abide?'

The difference between birds and their wings, and the wings of the aspirations of intelligent men, is that birds fly on their wings towards a certain direction, whereas intelligent men fly on the wings of their aspirations away from all directions.

Every horse has its stable, every beast its pen, every bird its nest. And God knows best.

NOTES

I

Is it permissible for a scholar to visit princes, in view of the fact that the Prophet Muhammad is reported to have condemned the practice? Rūmī argues somewhat captiously that a true scholar, even if *formally* he goes to visit a prince, because of the independence of his outlook is *in fact* visited by the prince who wishes to consult him.

The discussion turns to a famous event in the early history of Islam, when the Prophet's uncle 'Abbās whilst yet an infidel was taken prisoner by the victorious Muslim forces and the Prophet laughed. Muhammad tests his uncle's profession of faith, and then accepts him as a true convert.

Rūmī explains the relevance of his discourse to the situation of the Parvāna of Rūm, whom he had chided for siding with the Mongols against the Syrians and Egyptians and urged to make common cause with the latter in defence of Islam. He concludes with expressing gratification that the Parvāna had accepted his advice, to be bold in God's cause and to have good hope in Divine assistance.

The final section enables us to assign this discourse to the last years of Rūmī's life, in any case after 1268.

p. 13. 'The worst of scholars': this Tradition of the Prophet is given by al-Ghazzālī in *Ihyā'*, vol. I, p. 51.

p. 14. 'We have learned': a similar saying is attributed to the Angel of Death in conversation with the Prophet Abraham, see al-Tirmidhī, *Nawādir al-uṣūl*, p. 377.

'O Prophet, say': the quotation is from Koran VIII 70, a passage explained as referring to events which followed the victory of Badr in A.D. 624.

'And laughed': Rūmī refers to this incident in the *Masnavi* III, lines 4473 ff.

p. 15. 'He makes the night': Koran XXXV 13.

'He brings forth': Koran XXX 18.

'Of God's comfort': Koran XII 87.

p. 16. 'Easy it is': the verses are in Persian, and of course are not meant to have been actually spoken by the Prophet.

p. 17. The Amir Parvāna: for a brief account of his career, see the Introduction to this book.

p. 18. 'God is a great deviser': a reminiscence of Koran II 47, VIII 30.

'Lord, show me things as they are': this Tradition, which is not to be found in the usual collections, was a great favourite with Rūmī, who refers to it repeatedly in the *Masnavi*.

2

The discourse opens with a topic often discussed by Rūmī, the kind of telepathic communication between true mystics which renders speech superfluous. Thought is the attractive force, and not the expression of thought. Expressions are multitudinous, but the controlling thought is one. For thought to be pure and true it is necessary for a man to keep his discriminative faculty clear of all ulterior objects, and to concentrate his purpose on seeking a true friend in the Faith.

Rūmī reverts to a subject treated in Discourse I, the placing of all one's hope in God. This leads him to speak of the danger inherent in associating with princes, that the desire to please them may corrupt the purity of the believer's faith and lure him away from the Divine Beloved. In the concluding section Rūmī speaks of man as the astrolabe of God. Just as the astrolabe is useless save to an astronomer, so man's special relationship to God avails him nothing unless he knows his true self.

p. 19. 'The element of congeneity': this is frequently referred to in the *Masnavi*, see especially IV 2671.

'A hundred thousand miracles': the same point is made in *Masnavi* VI 1176.

'Upon the day': Koran LXXXVI 9, a reference to the Last Day.

'And their number': Koran LXXIV 31.

p. 20. 'Few in the numbering': quoted inaccurately from the famous Arab poet al-Mutanabbī (d. 965), see his *Dīwān* (Cairo 1930) I, p. 237.

p. 21. 'The bird that perched': this quatrain occurs in Muḥammad ibn al-Munawwar's *Asrār al-tauḥīd*, p. 122, a biography of the mystic Abū Saʿīd ibn Abi 'l-Khair written before 1200.

'Whosoever assists an oppressor': this Tradition of Muhammad is quoted in ʿAbd al-Raʾūf al-Munāwī, *Kunūz al-ḥaqāʾiq*, p. 123.

p. 22. 'Decked out fair': Koran III 13.

'Man is the astrolabe of God': see *Masnavi* VI 3140 f.

'He who knows himself': this famous Tradition, frequently cited by Sufi writers, is also sometimes assigned to the caliph ʿAlī.

'We have honoured': Koran XVII 72.

p. 23. 'Figured silks': quoted from al-Mutanabbī, *Dīwān* II, p. 158. Aflākī states that Rūmī was particularly fond of reading al-Mutanabbī, and was reproved on that account by Shams al-Dīn of Tabrīz. He quotes al-Mutanabbī a number of times in the *Discourses*.

3

The theme of this discourse is preoccupation and absorption. The scene opens with an anonymous visitor, evidently the Parvāna, excusing himself for remissness in his religious duties owing to preoccupation with Mongol affairs. Rūmī replies that inasmuch as those preoccupations are in defence of Islam, the Parvāna's work counts as religious service. Other visitors arrive, and Rūmī now excuses himself for inattention to them, his plea being that he was preoccupied with prayer. This leads into a discussion of the nature of prayer, and Rūmī distinguishes between the 'body' or 'form' (physical acts) of (formal) prayer, and the 'soul' of prayer which is a state of complete absorption with God.

p. 24. 'I have a time': this Tradition of Muhammad is a favourite of the Sufis though not admitted as genuine by the orthodox. For other discussions of 'absorption' see *Masnavi* VI 4630 ff. and below, Discourse II.

Bahā' al-Ḥaqq wa'l-Dīn: Rūmī's father, for whom see the Introduction. This anecdote is also related in the *Risāla* of Farīdūr Sipahsālār, p. 16.

Khvājagī: a disciple of Bahā' al-Dīn Valad who accompanied him on his flight from Balkh.

'Die before you die': a Tradition beloved of the Sufis but rejected by the orthodox, quoted by Rūmī several times in the *Masnavi*.

4

Stimulated by the casual remark of a visitor that he had forgotten something, Rūmī discourses on the one task which men must never forget to discharge, namely to fulfil the high trust which man in the beginning of the world accepted from God, to serve Him only in utter devotion.

Rūmī quotes a remark of his teacher Burhān al-Dīn when he was told that a certain man had sung his praises; he declared himself indifferent until he should know whether his admirer applauded him out of true knowledge and not from mere hearsay. The only knowledge worth possessing is self-knowledge.

p. 26. 'We offered the trust': Koran XXXIII 72.

p. 27. 'And We honoured': Koran XVII 72.

'God has bought': Koran IX 112.

p. 28. 'You are more precious': quoted from the *Ḥadīqat al-ḥaqīqa* of Sanā'ī (fl. 1140), a poem on the mystical life which Rūmī studied deeply and frequently quoted.

'Sell not yourself': quoted from Rūmī's own poetry, see his *Ghazalīyāt* (Teheran 1956), p. 565.

'I pass the night': a Tradition of Muhammad accepted as genuine by al-Bukhārī and Muslim.

p. 29. 'Even so when Majnūn': the desert romance of Majnūn and Lailā is cited frequently by the mystics as a prototype of perfect devotion. The present anecdote is retold by Rūmī in *Masnavi* IV 1533 ff.

'My camel's desire': quoted from the Bedouin poet 'Urwa ibn Ḥizām, cited by Rūmī again in *Masnavi* IV 1533.

Burhān al-Dīn Muḥaqqiq: for further details of Rūmī's teacher see the Introduction. The same anecdote occurs in Farīdūn's *Risāla*, p. 121.

5

An unnamed admirer, doubtless the Parvāna, thanks Rūmī fulsomely for the honour of a visit. Rūmī replies by applauding his lofty aspirations which move him to such humility and a sense of unworthiness. Form has its importance as well as spirit. Yet man's true destiny lies far beyond mere worldly things; the ascetic sees into the hereafter, but God's elect transcends both this world and the next, having his eyes fixed on the First Thing, God.

Rūmī turns to discourse on pain, which is a spur to action. Unless there is a burning desire, an ache within the soul for higher things, those loftier aims will remain unattainable.

p. 31. 'Two inclinations': this Tradition of Muhammad is given in al-Munāwī, *Kunūz*, p. 67.

'A dervish entered': this story is told of the ascetic al-Fuḍail ibn 'Iyāḍ speaking to Hārūn al-Rashīd, see Ibn Khallikān, *Wafayāt al-a'yān*, no. 504. Other versions are given in 'Aṭṭār, *Tadhkirat al-auliyā'*, I, p. 251; Sanā'ī, *Ḥadīqa*, p. 645.

p. 32. 'Whithersoever you turn': Koran II 109.

'God brought him into existence': for the idea of the 'ascent of man' see *Masnavi* III 3901 ff, IV 3637 ff., and compare R. A. Nicholson, *Rumi, Poet and Mystic*, p. 187, n.1.

'You shall surely ride': Koran LXXXIV 19-20.

p. 33. 'And the birthpangs': Koran XIX 23.

'The soul within you': quoted from the poet Khācānī (d. about 1200).

6

Words are spoken for the sake of those who need words; the man who understands without words hears the message of heaven and earth proclaiming God their Creator. Rūmī tells a story of a Turkish king who applauded the work of an Arab poet though he knew no Arabic; it was not the words themselves but the purport of the words that really signified. Phenomena are many; the ultimate Object is one.

A bystander interrupts with a confession of remissness. This moves Rūmī to discourse on the Divine purpose in reproach and self-criticism, and the sense in which one man is a mirror to another enabling him to see in the other his own faults. From this Rūmī returns to the thesis that multiplicity and duality vanish in the presence of God; a man must sacrifice his own self in order that God may be revealed in all His glory.

Why do the saints and prophets seek worldly fame? So that the light which they brought may shine forth upon all men. Men reject their message, saying that they have heard plenty of such words before, but that is because they do not understand those words.

'Be! and it is': Koran XXXVI 82.

p. 35. 'Love continues': quoted from an unknown Arab poet.

'The believer is the mirror': this Tradition of Muhammad is a favourite with the Sufis when they discuss clairvoyance. The theme is elaborated several times in the *Masnavi*, especially IV 2137 ff.

p. 37. 'Simurgh of the Mount Qaf': the simurgh is a legendary bird nesting in Mount Qaf on the rim of the earth, used by the Sufi poets as a symbol of the Divine Presence.

'There was a servant of God': Aflākī tells a closely similar story of Shams al-Dīn of Tabriz.

'A bore came': said to have been Shaikh Sharaf al-Dīn Haravī, one of the leading ulema of Konia. The 'great saint' is identified with Chelebi Husām al-Dīn, favourite disciple of Rūmī and his successor.

p. 38. 'And they say, Our hearts': Koran II 83.

'God has set a seal': Koran II 6.

p. 39. 'He kneaded the clay': a well known Tradition of Muhammad.

7

The entry of the Atabeg's son causes Rūmī to speak of the multiplicity of religions and of men, a multiplicity inherent in the nature of things and not to vanish until the resurrection. It is a Divine mercy that men are all occupied with their diverse interests. Nevertheless certain men, the mystics, have attained the vision of the One God already in this world.

Rūmī resumes the topic of the use of words, enunciating the principle that they are measured to the capacity of the hearers; some men require a multitude of words, others penetrate the meaning from the merest hint.

'The son of the Atabeg': evidently Majd al-Dīn Atabeg, son-in-law of the Parvāna, mentioned as a disciple of Rūmī by both Farīdūn and Aflākī.

p. 40. 'Even were the veil removed': a saying frequently attributed to 'Alī.

p. 41. 'Naught there is': Koran XV 21.

p. 42. 'Majnūn and Farhād': Majnūn wandered in the desert for love of Lailā, Farhād enamoured of Shīrīn haunted the mountains. Both romances are told by Niẓāmī and other poets.

8

Rūmī resumes the topic of prayer, with which he had dealt in Discourse 3. Then he passes again to the theme of words and the hearer. A verse he quotes leads him to speak of the disciple and his dependence upon his preceptor. The prophets and saints are sent to remind men of their original purity when they were spirits; men recognise the truth of the message only if they are congeners of the prophets and saints.

p. 43. 'Someone asked': said to be Nūr al-Dīn Jīcha, mentioned by Aflākī as a disciple of Rūmī.

p. 44. 'O would that I were dust': Koran LXXVIII 41.

'And the unbelievers': Koran II 259.

p. 45. 'This is that wherewithal': Koran II 23.

'Those spirits which recognise': a Tradition of Muhammad recognised by both al-Bukhārī and Muslim.

'Now there has come': Koran IX 129.

p. 46. 'The colour is the colour of blood': part of a Tradition of Muhammad describing the Last Day when the martyrs will be revealed by the fragrance of their blood.

9

The report that a certain man desired to see Rūmī leads to a discussion of the true nature of desire, that all human cravings spring from the one overriding desire, to see God. Mundane desires are veils over God's beauty to save man from the annihilation which would follow the unveiled epiphany of the Divine. The use made by Rūmī of the parallel of the sun draws him on to explain the difference between 'likeness' and 'comparison'; comparisons are instituted to stimulate and assist the reason in its quest for truth.

p. 47. 'And when his Lord': Koran VII 139.

'Neither camel nor sheep': the Persian has *jamal* (camel) and *ḥamal* (sheep), a half-pun not reproducible in English.

'Likeness is one thing': the same point is made in *Masnavi* III 1155, 1942, 3407, III 419 ff.

10

The Parvāna reports to Rūmī that the latter's son Bahā' al-Dīn (Sulṭān Valad) had said that Rūmī did not wish the Parvāna to visit him since he was subject to varying moods and was not always available to see visitors; it was better that Rūmī should himself go to visit his friends. The Parvāna explains that he does not come in order that Rūmī may converse with him, but just to have the honour of waiting on him. Rūmī has kept him waiting so as to teach him what it feels like to be kept waiting.

Rūmī answers that his purpose was quite otherwise. He kept the Parvāna waiting not to teach him a lesson, but because he so loved him that he wished to enjoy his company as long as possible. This leads to a discourse on friendship and love; those who have been close friends in this world will at once resume their friendship in the next world. It is the essential substance of a man and not any accidental attributes which forms the basis of such friendship; and the substance survives death. Nevertheless form (as opposed to substance) has its own value, as giving a partial revelation of the nature of reality.

Rūmī passes on to explain the meaning of 'God says' in the mouth of the Prophet Muhammad. God's speech is wordless and soundless, but through the mouths of the prophets and saints He gives it word and sound. A man may be known by his words. Rūmī then illustrates the nature of clairvoyance. After touching on the mystery of the 'unseen' saints of God, he returns to the original topic and explains why the Parvāna should be pleased to have been kept waiting.

p. 48. 'The Parvāna said': Aflākī also reports this incident in very similar words.

Bahā' al-Dīn: Rūmī's eldest son Sulṭān Valad, born in 1226, married the daughter of Shams al-Dīn Farīdūn Zarkūb, succeeded Chelebī Ḥusām al-Dīn as head of the Mevlevi Order, and died in 1312.

p. 49. 'It is related that God Most High declares': this Tradition of Muhammad is close to one reported by al-Tirmidhī in his *Nawādir al-uṣūl*. p. 368.

'That Joseph-like form is changed': because Joseph's brothers pretended to Jacob that Joseph had been killed by a wolf, see Koran XII 17.

p. 51. 'The Prophet was asked': both question and answer are a pure invention.

'Nor speaks he out of caprice': Koran LIII 3–4.

p. 52. Shaikh Sar-razī: this person is mentioned in *Maṯnavi* V 2667, 2779. A similar story is told of him by Bahā' al-Dīn Valad in his *Maʿārif*, p. 264.

p. 53. 'Certain men said to Jesus': this and the following story are reminiscences of Matthew 8:20, a favourite topic with Muslim writers, see Ibn Qutaiba, *'Uyūn al-akhbār* II, p. 271; al-Ghazzālī, *Iḥyā'* III, p. 141.

11

A discussion is initiated by the proverbial saying 'Hearts bear witness one to another.' Rūmī explains that when the heart is absorbed (compare Discourse 3) all other parts of the body including the tongue are atrophied. In absorption the senses become a unity; the person absorbed loses his freedom of action. This explains Ḥallāj's famous utterance 'I am God' which, so far from being (as is alleged) a blasphemy, is in reality the acme of humility, being a confession that only God exists. Absorption is accompanied by a fear of God, which is different from all other fears; it is a realisation that all human states come from God, and is an actual experience and not a logical proof of God's existence. In absorption the mystic passes away into God. The terms obedience and disobedience, righteousness and sin then become irrelevant.

Rūmī turns to discuss the difference between the 'knower' and the 'gnostic' and to compare the merits of knowledge and asceticism. Whereas primary knowledge (theory) is inferior to asceticism, secondary knowledge (direct cognition of God) is its superior. To arrive is better than to travel hopefully; the man who has arrived has transcended hope and fear.

Which is better, to laugh or to weep, to fast or to pray, to be alone or in company? The answer is that this depends upon the requirements of the individual soul, to know which calls for the assistance of a wise counsellor; though it remains true that self-knowledge and self-revelation lie at the roots of the matter.

The presence of the Amir stimulates Rūmī to utter great truths. That is because of the unison between their hearts, which indeed dispenses with the need for uttered communication.

p. 54. 'Hearts bear witness': a proverb.

Amīr Nā'ib: presumably Amīn al-Dīn Mīkā'īl, deputy to the Sultan of Rūm from 1260 to 1278.

p. 55. 'Your name is upon my tongue': a similar verse is ascribed to the martyr-mystic al-Ḥallāj (executed in 922), see L. Massignon, *Le Dīwān d'al-Ḥallāj*, p. 106.

'Take the famous utterance': the much-discussed *Ana 'l-Ḥaqq* of al-Ḥallāj which led to his execution.

p. 57. 'But for thee I would not have created': a well known Tradition of Muhammad.

p. 58. 'Nothing is, that does not': Koran XVII 46.

'Even were the veil': see Discourse 7.

p. 60. 'And We have raised some': Koran XLIII 31.

'And whoso has done an atom's weight': Koran XCIX 7.

'This world is the seed-plot': a Tradition of Muhammad, see al-Munāwī, *Kunūz*, p. 64.

p. 61. 'I am where My servant': a Tradition of Muhammad, see al-Tirmidhī, *Nawādir al-uṣūl*, p. 85; al-Ghazzālī, *Iḥyā'* III, p. 269.

'Take counsel of your heart': a Tradition of Muhammad, see al-Sarrāj, *Kitāb al-Luma'*, p. 16, 45; Abū Nu'aim, *Ḥilyat al-auliyā'* VI, p. 255.

'Show me things': see Discourse 1.

p. 62. 'A raven': Koran V 34.

12

Who is the wrongdoer in the case of a man justly striking another? The example of the Prophet Muhammad gives the clear answer: he was the wronged party even when he defeated his enemies. The Parvāna then asks whether the good resulting from a human action is due to the action itself, or a gift of God. Rūmī answers it is the latter, though God assigns the merit to man. The Parvāna comments that in that case every seeker is bound to find; Rūmī rejoins that for all that a guide is still needed. The body's guide is the intellect; humanity's guide is the saint.

God's providential care can draw a man to serve His will, nevertheless man is given the power to exert himself. First comes grace, which is like a spark setting afire a mass of tinder. Rūmī compares his own words with such a spark, and prays that they may find response in the hearts of his hearers.

Rūmī then defines the difference between soul and spirit, discoursing on the well known definition of man as a 'rational animal.' He returns to the theme of the preacher's words, and discusses the nature of thought. Thoughts exercise a tremendous influence for good or evil, and act independently of the body. Physical delights are mere accidents, the scent of the heavenly musk; it behoves a man to transcend the accidental and to reach after the substance, which is the eternal presence of God.

p. 64. 'Islam began a stranger': this famous Tradition of Muhammad, which goes on 'and will return a stranger as it began,' is recognised by Muslim and other orthodox collectors.

'In your present state of bondage': a reference to Koran VIII 70, see Discourse 1.

p. 65. 'No soul knows': Koran XXXII 17.

'The Night of Power': Koran XCVII 3.

p. 66. 'One tugging from God': this saying is quoted anonymously in the *Asrār al-tauḥīd*, p. 247. Rūmī discusses 'Divine tugging' several times in the *Masnavi*, see especially VI 1475 ff.

'He said, Lo': Koran XIX 31.

John the Baptist: see *Masnavi* II 3602 ff.

'Is he whose breast': Koran XXXIX 22.

p. 67. 'For man was created': Koran IV 32.

'Surely thou art upon': Koran LXVIII 4.

'To God belong the hosts': Koran XLVIII 4.

Nimrod: for his killing by a gnat see *Masnavi* I 1189.

Abraham: the miracle of the furnace turning into a rose-garden is based on Koran XXI 69.

p. 68. 'What though a man': quoted from Sanā'ī, *Ḥadīqa*.

p. 69. 'Who shall succeed': this verse, which is repeated in Discourse 17, is quoted by Rūmī in his *Majālis*, p. 121.

p. 70. 'We have returned from the lesser struggle': a well known Tradition of Muhammad, see al-Munāwī, *Kunūẓ*, p. 90. Rūmī comments on this Tradition in *Masnavi* I 1373 ff.

13

This discourse is a sermon on the text of a Tradition of Muhammad, the theme being the struggle against the inward enemy, the carnal soul.

p. 71. 'The night is long': this Tradition is not recorded in any of the canonical collections.

p. 72. 'Say, He is God': Koran CXII 1.

'Take not My enemy': Koran LX 1.

p. 73. 'But as for him who feared': Koran LXXXIX 40–41.

14

The present world is as it were a collection of samples of the other world. Man's origin is from the Beyond, and to the Beyond he must return. The eternal attributes, infinite in variety, are in themselves invisible; they only become visible through their association with matter.

p. 73. Shaikh Ibrāhīm: a disciple of Shams al-Dīn of Tabriz, mentioned again in Discourse 46.

Saif al-Dīn Farrukh: unknown.

'Naught there is': Koran XV 21.

'The bald man of Baalbek': the text presents a crux, and I owe this interpretation to Dr Ṣādiq Gauharīn.

p. 74. 'Surely we belong to God': Koran II 151.

15

This discourse ranges over many topics and clearly records an actual scene in the life of Rūmī enacted certainly after 1260.

The restlessness within the human soul, which men seek vainly to satisfy in various ways, is a symptom of the universal quest for God.

The question is asked whether it is lawful to accept property from the Mongols. Rūmī gives an affirmative answer, developing an explanation of the reason why God first allowed the Mongols to prosper and is now slowly destroying them. He rebuts the rumour that the Tartars believe in the resurrection. From this he passes on to argue that the resurrection is enacted daily in the lives of men. God occupies His prophets in various ways.

Is there any changing God's eternal decrees? Rūmī replies in the negative; except that the measure of the Divine reward and punishment varies according to men's individual actions.

Does a broken vow to fast on a certain day require expiation? Rūmī states the views of the Shāfi'ī and Ḥanafī jurists, and gives his own verdict. He then answers a question on the meaning of the formulae of blessing the Prophet, that these are Divine and not human acts. He distinguishes between secondary causes and actualities; the former are apparent acts, the latter the Divine cause of those acts.

All men, prophets and saints and ordinary mortals, descend into this world from the Beyond; but they differ in the degree of their recollection of the other world, and the extent to which they are stimulated by the Word of God. The mystic must not reveal to other men truths vouchsafed to him which transcend the understanding of the uninitiated.

p. 75. 'There is no monkhood': a well known Tradition of Muhammad, see *Masnavi* V 574.

'The congregation is a mercy': a famous Tradition of Muhammad, see *Masnavi* I 3017.

p. 76. 'Certain of them came as merchants': Rūmī refers to the events leading up to the Mongol invasion, see *Encyclopaedia of Islam* III, p. 1014.

p. 77. 'Because he turned a ring upon his finger': see al-Ghazzālī, *Iḥyā'* I, p. 51, 120.

'What, did you think': Koran XXIII 118.

p. 78. 'And whoso has done': Koran XCIX 7–8.

p. 79. 'Thou createdst me': Koran VII 11.

Shāfi'ī . . . Abū Ḥanīfa: founders of two of the four orthodox schools of Islamic jurisprudence.

p. 80. 'A camel came forth': Koran XI 64–71.

'Lord, said Zachariah': Koran III 35.

p. 81. 'Am I not your Lord': Koran VII 171, a passage frequently quoted by Sufi writers as referring to the Primaeval Covenant between God and man.

'Impart not wisdom': this saying, seemingly based on Matthew 7:6, is quoted again in Discourse 41.

p. 82. 'The earth has its share': these anonymous verses are quoted by al-Ghazzālī in *Iḥyā'* IV, p. 71.

'The inhabitants of the Fire': Koran VII 48.

'Cover up your vessels': for this Tradition see Muslim, *Ṣaḥīḥ* VI, pp. 105 ff. Rūmī interprets the injunction after his own fashion.

16

This discourse again touches on a variety of topics. First Rūmī discusses the theme of love and beauty; it is love which makes things to appear desirable, therefore the mystic must cultivate a spiritual yearning so that 'in all being and space you may see the Beloved.' The ultimate quest behind all quests is God. From this Rūmī passes to speak again about absorption, as in Discourse 3. The prophet and the saint are totally absorbed with God; men's attitude to them determines their attitude to God.

Rūmī explains why he composes poetry, a thing extremely distasteful to him personally; but people in Rūm like poetry, and he wishes to accord with their desire. A remark by the Parvāna moves him to discuss the nature of action; he denies that action is fundamental; 'the root principle of all things is speech.' Thus, prayer is ineffective unless it is uttered.

In answer to a question Rūmī justifies again the attitude of hope, as in Discourse 1. He then speaks about the Perfect Man, who is a microcosm representing faithfully the macrocosm.

p. 83. 'In Majnūn's time': this story is retold in *Masnavi* V 3286 ff.

p. 84. 'The abiding things': Koran XVIII 44.

p. 85. 'Whosoever sees him': this is based on a saying of Abū Yazīd al-Bisṭāmī describing his mystical ascension into heaven, see al-Sahlajī, *al-Nūr min kalimāt Abī Ṭaifūr*, p. 139.

'None but the purified': Koran LVI 79.

'It is a habit with me': this section is reproduced word for word in Farīdūn, *Risāla*, pp. 68 ff. See further, Discourse 54.

p. 87. 'His command, when He desires': Koran XXXVI 82.

p. 88. 'All game is in the belly': a famous Arabic proverb.

'All, good and evil': Rūmī quotes from his own poetry, see *Dīvān* (ed. Furūzānfar) I 4476.

'Thyself a true transcription art': this quatrain has been attributed to Najm al-Dīn Dāya, Bābā Afḍal and others.

17

The Nā'ib of Rūm having remarked that the Muslims in serving the Mongols are no better than idolaters, Rūmī rejoins that they are superior in that they are conscious of the unworthiness of such an attitude. He goes on to discourse of man as midway between the angels and the beasts, with the prophets and saints waiting to lead men back to God. Man's first step is to struggle; then God's grace supervenes to bring him to the end of the journey. The principle of opposites applies only to form, necessary for the display of God's power; in reality all things are one.

p. 89. The Nā'ib: see Discourse 11.

'Things are made clear by their opposites': quoted from al-Mutanabbī, *Dīwān*, I, p. 15.

'The bird flies with its wings': see *Marʒubān-nāma*, p. 137.

p. 90. 'He whose intelligence': this saying is variously attributed to ʿAlī and Muhammad; for the latter attribution see *Masnavi* III 1497 ff., a passage closely modelled on the present discussion.

'The angel is saved': Rūmī quotes himself, see *Dīvān* (ed. Furūzānfar) II 9669.

'No fear shall be on them': Koran X 63.

'We desire this': see p. 69.

'When comes the help of God': Koran CX.

p. 92. 'I was a hidden treasure': a famous Tradition often quoted by Sufi writers, rejected by later critics.

'Go forth with My Attributes': quoted from al-Bisṭāmī, see al-Sahlajī, *al-Nūr*, p. 139.

Abū Jahl: the bitter enemy of Muhammad.

'They desire to extinguish': Koran LXI 8.

'The moon sheds light': closely similar to some verses by Ḥasan Ghaznavī, see his *Dīvān*, p. 32.

p. 93. 'A dervish saw': according to Farīdūn, *Risāla*, p. 124, the dervish was Shams al-Dīn of Tabrīz.

18

A comment on a Koran reciter leads to a discussion of the difference between 'form' and 'meaning'. The Koran is not the whole of God's Word. It is God's will that some men should be heedless, in order that the world may continue to exist. Rūmī declares that he speaks as he does out of compassion and not out of envy, to draw his listeners on to higher truths.

p. 93. Ibn Muqrī: Furūzānfar identifies with Ṣāʾin al-Dīn Muqrī, mentioned by Aflākī in a number of anecdotes.

'Say, if the sea were ink': Koran XVIII 109.

p. 94. 'Many a Koran-reciter': this saying is attributed to Anas ibn Mālik by al-Ghazzālī, *Ihyāʾ* I, p. 195.

'God has closed in heedlessness': the topic is repeated in Discourse 25 and is developed in *Masnavi* I 2063 ff., IV 1323 ff., 2608 ff., etc.

p. 95. 'Since greatness never once': quoted from the satire on Maḥmūd of Ghazna attributed to Firdausī.

'A great caravan': Furūzānfar states that this story occurs in a prose

Iskandar-nāma of early date, a manuscript of which is in the possession of Professor Sa'īd Nafīsī.

19

This brief discourse reports a remark by Tāj al-Dīn Qubā'ī, and speaks on the topic of hypocrisy. Longwindedness is no substitute for sincerity.

p. 96. Tāj al-Dīn Qubā'ī: unknown.

p. 97. 'So woe to those that pray': Koran CVII 4-7.

20

Women are intended for the purification of men, who by enduring their absurdities learn to control themselves. That is why the Prophet forbade celibacy. It is useless to argue with a woman.

The claim by certain men to have seen Shams al-Dīn of Tabriz provokes a statement on the 'veiled' saints of God. Some remarks on the relationship between lover and beloved lead on to the remark that the lover of God must forsake his own identity and become wholly absorbed in God.

p. 98. 'There is no monkhood': see p. 75.

'Surely thou art upon': Koran LXVIII 4.

'It is related that the Prophet': after the raid on Tabuk in 630.

p. 100. 'Man is passionate for what he is denied': a Tradition of Muhammad, see al-Munāwī, *Kunūz*, p. 31.

'While we proclaim Thy praise': Koran II 28.

p. 101. 'This time you will experience': Furūzānfar sees in this a reference to the return of Shams al-Dīn from Damascus, and so dates the discourse among the earliest in the collection.

'Thou whose form is fairer far': untraced.

Bahā' al-Dīn: either Rūmī's son Sulṭān Valad, or Bahā' al-Dīn Baḥrī who is mentioned many times by Aflākī as a member of Rūmī's circle.

21

Rūmī quotes with disapproval some verses describing God as indifferent to the world. After a brief comment on a saying which appears to promote Moses over Muhammad, he ridicules the claim of a certain man to have proved the existence of God by logical reasoning. Rūmī takes up again the theme of negligence being allowed by God to some men in order that the world may continue. Every man has his appointed task; the saints' part is the supreme role of contemplation. Rūmī then answers those who complain when he is silent that he is running away from them; their charge reflects that precise thought within themselves. He concludes by recommending gradualness in mastering the Sufi discipline.

p. 102. Sharīf Pāy-sūkhta: unknown.

p. 103. 'The Verse of Self-sufficiency': a reference to Koran XCII 8.

Shaikh-i Maḥalla: a gloss names him as Fakhr-i Akhlāṭī.

'Moses enjoyed converse': see Koran VII 138–9.

p. 104. 'Nothing there is'; Koran XVII 46.

'Our great Master': Rūmī's father Bahā' al-Dīn Valad, see his *Ma'ārif*, p. 388.

p. 105. Shaikh Ṣalāḥ al-Dīn: Ṣalāḥ al-Dīn Farīdūn Zarkūb, for whom see the Introduction.

'And those you fear': Koran IV 38.

22

This discourse, which is entirely in Arabic, is a reprocf to a disciple for backbiting against a certain member of the circle.

p. 106. Ibn Chāvish: Najm al-Dīn ibn Khurram Chāvish, addressee of a letter from Rūmī, see his *Maktūbāt* (Teheran 1957), p. 56.

Ṣalāḥ al-Dīn: Farīdūn Zarkūb, see Discourse 21.

p. 108. 'Yet it may happen': Koran II 213.

23

This somewhat diffuse discourse begins with the theme of reacting to the spirit of spoken words though ignorant of their formal meaning, the main topic of Discourse 6. Though the ways to God are various, the ultimate goal is one, since God is the fashioner of all and is therefore beloved of all. At this level no difference exists between infidelity and faith; thoughts only differ when they are clothed in expression. God controls the world of ideas but is Himself beyond that world.

Rūmī then discusses the formula 'If God wills,' which he interprets as a token of absorption in God. He passes to speak of the vision granted by

God to Muhammad, and of visions and dreams in general. The mystic's vision is revealed in the other world. Rūmī repeats that God is the ultimate quest beyond all quests. Then he touches on the doubts which beset the human soul, saying that in love they all vanish away. Finally he reminds his listeners that his words are attuned to their degrees of understanding.

p. 108. Tuqat: a town to the north-west of Konia.

p. 110. 'We judge by outward profession': a saying attributed to Muhammad, see al-Ghazzālī, *Iḥyā'* IV, p. 251.

p. 111. 'If out of the veil appeared': Rūmī quotes himself.

'God has indeed fulfilled': Koran XLVIII 27.

'If God wills': Rūmī discusses this matter in *Masnavi* I 49 ff., VI 3667 ff.

'The pen reached thus far': quoted from Khāqānī.

p. 112. 'This world is as the dream': a saying of Muhammad according to al-Ghazzālī, *Iḥyā'* III, p. 148. The idea is developed in *Masnavi* III 1300 ff., 1736 ff.

p. 113. 'Your love for a thing': a Tradition of Muhammad, see al-Ghazzālī, *Iḥyā'* III, p. 25.

'Thou createdst me of fire': Koran VII 12.

p. 114. 'Speak to men according to the degree': a similar saying of Muhammad is admitted by al-Bukhārī, *Ṣaḥīḥ* I, p. 24; see also al-Ghazzālī, *Iḥyā'* I, p. 74.

24

The true mystic is indifferent to worldly advancement; like God himself, he is independent of all directions. Men's motives in building mosques and writing religious books may differ from God's purpose, but it is God's purpose that prevails.

p. 114. 'If a lamp desires': see Discourse 6.

'Do not prefer me above Jonas': see Muslim, *Ṣaḥīḥ* VII, pp. 101 f. Rūmī comments on this Tradition in *Masnavi* III 4512 ff.

p. 115. Zamakhsharī: the famous grammarian and Koran commentator, a native of Khvarizm, born 1075, completed the *Kashshāf* in 1134, died in 1144.

Kiblah: the direction of Mecca towards which the faithful turn in their prayers.

25

The Prophet Muhammad was a humble man, and humility is a great virtue yet he was the foundation of the world, comparable with the reason which controls all the body's members. The caliph exercises the same function in his time, though he is liable to error. Reason is the congener of the angels; man is a compound of angel and beast.

Rūmī explains how the body's members will 'speak' at the resurrection, quoting the views of the philosophers and the theologians respectively. This leads him to discourse on his theory of the nature of speech. God gives to every man according to his needs. Some men have been created heedless, to secure the maintenance of the physical world.

p. 116. 'No man ever preceded': see al-Ghazzālī, *Ihyā'* II, p. 250.

p. 117. 'But for thee I would not have created': see p. 57. The theme is common among the Sufis; Rūmī treats of it in *Masnavi* I 589 (see R. A. Nicholson's note), II 974.

'Reason is a congener of the angel': see Discourse 17, and compare *Masnavi* III 3193 ff.

p. 118. 'Reason lent to Jesus pinions': quoted from Sanā'ī *Dīvān*, p. 497.

p. 119. 'God gave us speech': Koran XLI 21, the context for the ascription of speech at the resurrection to the body's members.

'He inculcates wisdom'; this uncanonical Tradition is also quoted in *Masnavi* VI 1656 (heading).

'I am the shadow of a man': Rūmī quotes himself, see *Dīvān* (Teheran 1958) II, p. 90.

p. 120. 'Do not suppose no travellers': untraced.

26

This long and diffuse discourse covers a wide variety of topics. The connecting theme appears to be that there is One to whom all should be addressed, for He is the source of all Good and Power.

p. 121. Shaikh Nassāj of Bukhara: Rūmī mentions him again in *Dīvān* (ed. Furūzānfar) I 1534.

p. 122. Shaikh al-Islām Tirmidhī: this anecdote is repeated in Farīdūn, *Risāla*, p. 121.

Burhān al-Dīn: Rūmī's teacher Burhān al-Dīn Muhaqqiq.

'These words are Syriac': i.e. unintelligible except to the initiated.

p. 123. Their mark is on their faces': Koran XLVIII 29.

'The man who has read the *Wasīt*': by the *Wasīt* Rūmī evidently means al-Ghazzālī's 'middle' treatise on Shāfi'ī jurisprudence. The reference to *Mutawwal* ('Extensive') is not clear. The *Tanbīh* is presumably the Shāfi'ī manual by Abū Ishāq al-Shīrāzī (died 1083).

'Did We not expand': Koran XCIV 1.

p. 124. 'In the time of the Prophet': this story is retold in *Masnavi* III 3055 ff. Rūmī's source was his father's *Ma'ārif*, p. 77.

'Every day He is upon some labour': Koran LV 29.

p. 125. 'It is We who have sent down': Koran XV 9.

'A certain man came to Muhammad': see al-Ghazzālī, *Iḥyā'* IV, p. 209.

'In the time of Muhammad': see al-Wāḥicī *Asbāb al-nuẓūl*, p. 231.

'None but the purified': Koran LVI 78.

p. 127. 'I am amazed at a people': see Discourse 1, where the Prophet's words are paraphrased in Persian.

'Take him, and fetter him': Koran LXIX 30.

'God grasps, and outspreads': Koran II 246.

p. 128. 'The believer is sagacious': a Tradition of Muhammad, see al-Munāwī, *Kunūẓ*, p. 136.

p. 129. 'Just as at first you were earth'; see above, Discourse 5. Koran XXIII 11 ff. is the ultimate authority.

'A bowl full of poison': the story is retold in *Masnavi* V 4238 ff.

p. 131. The world subsists on a phantom': see *Masnavi* I 70.

28

The prayers of God's elect are so exalted that they pass the understanding of ordinary mortals, who have their own stations according to their spiritual rank.

p. 132. 'We are the rangers': Koran XXXVII 165–6.

'Postpone them': a Tradition of Muhammad, see al-Munāwī, *Kunūẓ*, p. 5.

p. 133. 'Whom none knows but God': Koran XIV 10.

'And thou seest men': Koran CX 2.

'And the angels shall enter': Koran XIII 23.

'Take on the characteristics': see al-Ghazzālī. *Iḥyā'* IV, p. 218.

'I am for him hearing and sight': part of a famous Tradition beloved of the Sufis.

'Kings, when they enter a city': Koran XXVII 34.

'Only in ruins': quoted from Sanā'ī, *Ḥadīqa*, p. 347.

p. 134. 'I hold it unlawful': quoted from Muhammad ibn al-Munawwar, *Asrār al-tauḥīd*, p. 26.

29

This discourse is wholly in Arabic. It is a refutation of a statement made by a Christian, that Muslims secretly believe that Jesus was God. Rūmī goes on to condemn those who stubbornly adhere to their fathers' religion though the truth has been revealed to them.

p. 134. Shaikh Ṣadr al-Dīn: Ṣadr al-Din al-Qonawī, famous Sufi author, commentator on Ibn 'Arabī, who died in 1273.

p. 135. Yūtāsh: Shams al-Dīn Yūtāsh Beglerbeg, Saljuq prince, who died in 1258, mentioned by Rūmī in his *Maktūbāt*, p. 252.

p. 136. 'To clothe the Kaaba': quoted from Sanā'ī, *Sair al-'ibād*, p. 101. The reference is to the custom of covering the Black Stone with a curtain.

'To apply eye-black to the eyes': quoted from al-Mutanabbī, *Dīwān* II, p. 72.

30

The main topic of this discourse is that good and evil are one and indivisible, being the creation of the one God. This paradox leads on to other paradoxes.

p. 137. 'And God is with the patient': Koran II 250.

'Everything We have numbered': Koran XXXVI 12.

p. 138. 'I laugh as I slay': also quoted in Discourse 48. For the Prophet laughing, see p. 14.

31

A saying of Abū Yazīd is quoted approvingly to argue that the absence of all desire is the high objective of the mystic in his progress towards God. The common statement that Divine revelation ceased with Muhammad is not strictly true; the mystic enjoys revelation, only it is called by another name. An anecdote of the caliph 'Uthmān proves that silence can be as effective as any speech or action. Nothing is harder to endure than stupidity in a disciple; but the exercise is good for the saint, discipline being the high-road to victory over desire and the attainment of Divine detachment.

p. 138. 'God most High said to Abū Yazīd': see al-Sahlajī, *al-Nūr*, p. 96.

p. 139. 'Say, the Truth has come': Koran XVII 84.

'Enter, O believer': a Tradition of Muhammad referring to the day of resurrection, see al-Suyūṭī, *al-Jāmi' al-ṣaghīr* I, p. 132.

'The believer sees with the light of God': a favourite Tradition with the Sufis, see *Masnavi* I 1331; al-Ghazzālī, *Iḥyā'* II, p. 201.

'When 'Uthmān became caliph': see al-Jāḥiẓ, *al-Bayān wa'l-tabyīn* I, p. 272; *Masnavi* IV 487 ff.

p. 140. 'My Companions are as stars'; for this Tradition see al-Munāwī, *Kunūz*, p. 13, and compare *Masnavi* I 2925 f.

'So let who will regard me': quoted from al-Mutanabbī, *Dīwān* II, p. 132.

p. 141. 'Greater struggle': see the Tradition quoted on p. 70.

'What eye has not seen': a famous Tradition of Muhammad admitted by both al-Bukhārī and Muslim, evidently a reminiscence of I Corinthians 2:9.

32

This short discourse discusses the certainty of faith which characterises the perfect mystic, and how it banishes all doubts.

p. 142. 'If the faith of Abū Bakr': this Tradition occurs in al-Ghazzālī, *Iḥyā'* I, p. 35.

'In their hearts is a sickness': Koran II 9.

'What, do they not consider': Koran LXXXVII 17.

'Save him who repents': Koran XIX 61.

'Those, God will charge': Koran XXV 70.

33

Rūmī quotes snatches of an old poem on the topic of an old man still yearning for amorous play. He applies this profane theme to the mystic life.

p. 143. 'They said, Keep away': these verses, like the others quoted in this discourse, come from an ancient Arabic poem, see Ibn Qutaiba, *'Uyūn al-akhbār* IV, p. 53.

p. 144. 'Over eighty': in the original version, 'over thirty.'

34

This strange account, which is in Arabic apart from the first five words, appears to represent an actual mystic experience in which Rūmī saw a rebellious disciple in the form of a wild animal.

p. 144. Jalāl al-Tibrīzī: unknown.
p. 145. 'And God's earth is wide': Koran XXXIX 13.
    'And they comprehend not': Koran II 256.
    'The moaning pillar'; see *Masnavi* I 2113, with R. A. Nicholson's note.
    'Iron in David's hand': see Koran XXXIV 10.
    'The Kaaba, when you pray': quoted from Sanā'ī, *Ḥadīqa*, p. 112.
    'The unbeliever eats in seven stomachs': part of a Tradition admitted
by both al-Bukhārī and Muslim, see *Masnavi* V 64 ff.

35

This brief discourse describes the marvellous subtlety of the Koran, locked
away from the enemies of religion.
p. 147. 'And obey thou not': Koran LXVIII 10.
    'Backbiter': Koran LXVIII 11–12.
    'God has set a seal': Koran II 6.

36

Form is a branch or derivative of love; need is the root, the thing needed is
the branch.
    For a similar discussion in the *Masnavi*, see IV 4440 ff.

37

Rūmī refutes an allegation brought against a certain girl (thought by
Furūzānfar to be the wife of Shams al-Dīn of Tabriz). He passes on to
speak of the nature of imagination. Then he discusses the old controversy
whether the world is eternal or created in time, one of the principal quarrels
between the philosophers and the theologians in Islam.

38

A reminiscence of an incident in the Prophet's struggle against the unbelievers leads to a discussion of the relationship between the partial (or
human) intellect and the universal intellect, which is the source of all in-

spiration. Rūmī then turns to elaborate further the topic raised in Discourse 36.

p. 151. 'Unlettered': Rūmī's interpretation of the much-discussed epithet *ummī* given to Muhammad in Koran VII 156, 158.

'The partial intellect': see also *Masnavi* IV 1295 ff., which is closely similar to the present passage.

p. 152. 'The story of the raven': Koran V 34, see *Masnavi* IV 1301 ff.

'There is no prayer without the heart': this Tradition of Muhammad is quoted by al-Ghazzālī, *Ihyā* I, p. 110.

'And these continue at their prayers': Koran LXX 23.

39

Disputation is set aside when one becomes a dervish. The way of poverty leads to the attainment of all one's desires; the Prophet's life is an example of this. Rūmī declares that his words as a Sufi, are true coin, whereas other men's words are a spurious imitation; discrimination is needed to distinguish between the two.

p. 153. Ḥusām al-Dīn Arzanjānī: unknown.

'It takes another love': a quotation from Fakhr al-Dīn Gurgānī, *Vīs u Rāmīn*, cited also in the rubric to *Masnavi* V 2228.

'Whoever desires to sit with God': an alleged Tradition of Muhammad, see al-Suyūṭī, *al-La'ālī' al-maṣnū'a* II, p. 264, and compare *Masnavi* I 1529 ff.

'The present life is naught': Koran XLVII 38.

p. 154. 'Thou seest their eyes': Koran V 86.

p. 156. 'The believer is shrewd': see p. 128.

'Water unstaling': Koran XLVII 16.

'Water of the eyes': see *Masnavi* V 1265–70, a passage based on this paragraph.

p. 157. Abū Yazīd: there is a serious anachronism in this story, since Abū Yazīd died in about 877 whereas al-Junaid died in 910.

'There was a certain Shaikh': see al-Qushairī, *Risāla*, p. 129; 'Aṭṭār, *Tadhkirat al-auliyā* I, p. 326.

40

What is a question and what is an answer? These need not be spoken, action being itself vocal. The answer received is appropriate to the question asked;

the world indeed is like a mountain which echoes back the speech of the speaker.

p. 158. Jauhar: unknown.

p. 159. 'The crucible tells you': quoted from Sanā'ī, *Ḥadīqa*, p. 382.

'Do you not know': see *Masnavi* III 1490, heading.

'A king read a letter': this story is retold in *Masnavi* III 1490 ff.

'If only when Our might': Koran VI 43.

'And Satan decked out fair': Koran VI 43.

p. 160. 'A man said, Why': retold in *Masnavi* II 776 ff.

'Everything is from God': Koran IV 80.

'That is like the story': retold in *Masnavi* V 3077 ff.

'Speak pleasantly': quoted from Sanā'ī, *Ḥadīqa*, p. 145.

'The azure sky sends back': quoted from Sanā'ī, *Dīvān*, p. 51.

41

Men are compared with bowls carried about on the surface of a river; the mystic surrenders himself to the direction of God and does not dispute. Rūmī distinguishes between true and false ecstasy.

p. 161. 'The heart of the believer': for this Tradition, admitted by Muslim, see al-Ghazzālī, *Iḥyā'* I, p. 76.

'The All-Merciful has taught': Koran LV 1–2.

'Who created the heavens and the earth': Koran VI 1.

p. 162. 'Impart not wisdom': see p. 81.

'O monarch of all truthful men': Rūmī quotes himself, see *Dīvān* (Teheran 1958) II, p. 13.

p. 163. 'Abraham was a man who sighed': Koran IX 115.

42

Rūmī rebuts the charge that attendance at his discourses destroys the good results of orthodox studies. His teachings give a soul to formal learning. Knowledge is based not on words and sounds but derives from the other world; God does not speak by words and sounds. Men yearn after the ineffable, provided that they are spiritually healthy; in sickness they crave for what will increase their distemper. It is better that women should unveil before mystics, to deliver them out of temptation.

p. 164. 'And unto Moses God spoke': Koran IV 162.

'I was sent as a teacher': this Tradition of Muhammad is quoted by al-Ghazzāli, *Ihyā'* I, p. 8.

p. 166. Ḥasan and Ḥusain: sons of the caliph 'Ali.

Qāḍi Abū Manṣūr Harawī: a leading literary figure of Khurasan in the eleventh century, dying in 1048; see Yāqūt, *Muʿjam al-udabā'* VII, no. 107.

Manṣūr: i.e. al-Ḥallāj.

43

This section, which appears to commemorate the departure of a disciple, is in Arabic. Rūmī speaks of the 'mirror' which the true believer is to his brother in the faith, and the reverence due to spiritual directors.

p. 167. Saif al-Bukhārī: unknown.

44

This long discourse ranges over a variety of Rūmī's favourite topics, the connecting thread being the mystic's journey to the object of his desire.

p. 169. 'Ignoring Fate': Rūmī quotes himself, see *Dīvān* (ed. Furūzānfar) II 6800.

p. 170. 'God stands between': Koran VIII 24.

Ibrāhīm ibn Adham: the story of the conversion of the Prince of Balkh, who died in 783, is a favourite theme of the Sufi writers.

'Before becoming a Muslim': this story has no historical foundation.

'Ta Ha': Sura XX 1.

p. 172. 'Omar, the Prophet for to slay': Rūmī quotes himself, see *Dīvān* II 6303.

'And when We appointed': Koran II 118-9.

'My covenant shall not reach': Koran II 117.

p. 174. 'God has likened His light': a reference to Koran XXIV 35.

p. 175. 'I pray that moon-faced idol': this quatrain occurs in Rūmī's *Rubā-ʿiyāt* (Istanbul edition), p. 130.

p. 176. 'Not equal are the blind': Koran XXXV 20.

p. 177. 'The leanness of my body': quoted from al-Mutanabbī, *Dīwān* II, p. 434.

p. 178. 'I said to my heart': see Rūmī, *Rubāʿiyāt*, p. 354.

'Your name is upon my tongue': see p. 55.

45

The discourse begins with a pun on the name of a certain man. Rūmī passes to the theme of the mystic quest, and declares that God is very near to man and that man should always be begging of God; indeed He is invisible because of His extreme propinquity, yet the evidence of His omnipotence is to be seen on every side.

p. 179. 'Begin with yourself': this Tradition of Muhammad is given by al-Suyūṭī, *al-Jāmi' al-ṣaghīr* I, p. 4.

'He has not begotten': Koran CXII 3.

'God is the All-sufficient': Koran XLVII 40.

p. 181. 'Call upon Me': Koran XL 61.

p. 182. 'When the mother of Mary bore Mary': see Koran III 31 ff.

p. 183. 'They continue at their prayers': Koran LXX 23.

'Light upon Light': Koran XXIV 35.

46

Personal effort is useless unless it is accompanied by Divine favour; yet even those apparently rejected by God may be rejected for a good purpose and may in fact be under Divine favour. God's purpose is revealed in all men's acts. All believers are as a single soul in their devotion to God and to one another.

p. 183. Shaikh Ibrāhīm: see p. 73.

p. 184. I was a hidden treasure': see p. 92.

p. 185. 'The believers are as it were': see al-Ghazzālī, *Iḥyā'* II, p. 228.

p. 186. 'They said, There is no harm': Koran XXVI 50.

'Poison is right good to sup': not traced.

47

God wills both good and evil, but approves only the good. This discussion of the problem of evil is spoken in Arabic.

p. 188. 'In retaliation there is life': Koran II 175.

Ṣadr al-Islām: probably the man intended is Abu 'l-Yusr al-Pazdāwī, famous Ḥanafī jurist, teacher of al-Nasafī, who died in 1100.

'And expend in the way of God': Koran II 191.

48

This discourse which is partly in Arabic and partly in Persian touches on the merits of gratitude to God and the causes of ingratitude.

p. 189. 'I laugh as I slay': see p. 138.

'The mentioning of virtuous men': quoted from Sanā'ī, *Ḥadīqa*, p. 582.

p. 190. 'And We tried them': Koran VII 166.

49

The unseen world intervenes at every moment of our lives to keep us from disaster. The mystic should surrender himself in confidence to God's care and attend only to those things which appertain to eternal life.

p. 191. 'The Bedouins are more stubborn': Koran IX 98.

'Some of the Bedouins believe': Koran IX 100.

'Thy love made proclamation': not traced.

p. 192. 'Right well I know': Arabic verses by the Umayyad poet 'Urwa ibn Adhīna, see Abu 'l-Faraj, *al-Aghānī* XXI, p. 107.

'Whosoever makes all his cares': a favourite Tradition with the Sufis.

p. 193. 'They are with those whom God': Koran IV 71.

'I sit with him who remembers Me': see al-Ghazzālī, *Iḥyā'* II, p. 141.

'The night's departed': part of a quatrain ascribed to Rūmī, *Rubāʿīyāt*, p. 170.

'Feast on sweetmeats': not traced.

p. 194. 'This world is as the dream': see p. 112.

50

It is the essential element in man which survives death, being the element by virtue of which man is superior to all the animals. The secret heart must be kept occupied with the remembrance of God. Though the thoughts are secret, God manifests them on a man's face and in his actions.

p. 195. 'A friend of Joseph': this story is retold in *Masnavi* I 3158 ff.

'God looks not at your forms': a Tradition admitted by Muslim, *Ṣaḥīḥ* VIII p. 11.

'A city where you found': quoted from al-Mutanabbī, *Dīwān* II, p. 341.

p. 198. 'We offered the trust': Koran XXXIII 72.

'Begin with yourself': see Discourse 45.

p. 197. 'Their mark is on their faces': Koran XLVIII 29.
'We shall brand him': Koran LXVIII 16.

51

Man's quest is for a thing not yet found, whereas God's quest is for that which has already been found. What is the proof that a man has attained union with God? The proof is that he is in perfect accord with God's will. Rūmī answers a question about Abraham's argument with Nimrod.

p. 197. 'Until you seek you cannot find': quoted from Sanā'ī, *Dīvān*, p. 466.
p. 198. 'Be and it is': Koran II 3, etc.
p. 199. Abraham said to Nimrod: see p. 179.

52

The quotation of a verse leads to the statement that friendship and enmity, like all dualities, become one and the same in the state of union with God. Rūmī then answers a question on the function of words, which he sees as a veil over God's insupportable beauty.

p. 202. Manṣūr: al-Ḥallāj and his famous utterance *Ana 'l-Ḥaqq*.
p. 203. 'When heaven is rent': Koran LXXXIV 1.
'When earth is shaken': Koran XCIX 1.

53

Rūmī comments on a couplet of his own in which he expresses the idea that thought is the true substance of a man. He proceeds to discuss the nature of speech in relation to thought.

p. 204. 'You are that very thought': quoted from *Masnavi* II 277.
p. 205. 'He is the All-Subtle': Koran VI 103.

54

God is the creator of men's acts, contrary to the doctrine of the heterodox Mu'tazilites.

p. 207. 'The Lord of the East': Koran XXVI 28.
p. 208. 'Man is heedless of the cup': a reminiscence of Koran XII 70 ff.

55

To praise another man is to praise oneself; to speak ill of another is to surround oneself with evil thoughts; good and evil actions revert upon oneself. A quotation from the Koran leads to a discussion of the nature of the angels. A saying attributed to Muhammad is explained as meaning that the Prophet regretted ever being separated from God. Abraham's argument with Nimrod is rehearsed and explained. Believer and unbeliever alike proclaim God's praise.

p. 208. Qāḍī 'Izz al-Dīn: vizier to Kai-Kā'ūs II, who built a mosque in Konia for Rūmī, died in 1256 or 1258.

p. 209. 'Meadows of Iram': see Koran LXXXIX 6.

'Whoso does righteousness': Koran XLI 46.

'And whoso has done': Koran XCIX 7–8.

'I am setting in the earth': Koran II 27.

p. 210. 'What, wilt Thou set therein': Koran II 27.

'But for thee I would not have created': see p 57.

p. 212. 'Gives life, and makes to die': Koran II 260.

'I give life, and make to die': Koran II 260.

p. 213. 'God brings the sun from the east': Koran II 261. See p. 200.

56

Happiness consists in keeping a wise moderation in one's earthly relationships. All things are in love with God, who in His wisdom suffers some men to be forgetful of Him so as to maintain the world in being. God created both belief and unbelief. The physical sun is a symbol of that eternal Sun towards Whom all creatures are returning.

p. 215. 'Nothing there is': Koran XVII 45.

'Both unbelief and faith': quoted from Sanā'ī. *Hadīqa*, p. 60.

Saiyid Burhān al-Dīn: Rūmī's teacher, who in fact quotes often from the poems of Sanā'ī in his *Ma'ārif*.

p. 216. 'Those—they are called': Koran XLI 44.

'Light upon Light': Koran XXIV 35.

57

Love is all-comprehending and all things are implicit in love. Man is under the complete control of God, but stubbornly refuses to acknowledge the fact.

p. 127. Akmal al-Dīn: Akmal al-Dīn Ṭabīb, prominent physician and disciple of Rūmī who treated him in his last illness.

'A beautiful dancing-girl': see Ibn Qutaiba, *'Uyūn* IV, p. 111.

p. 218. 'God created Adam': a famous Tradition, theme of Discourse 67.

59

Rūmī answers the astronomer's challenge. God, though invisible, exists beyond and transcending heaven; He becomes visible in the effects of His creative power. Ignorance is good as well as knowledge; evil and good are one thing and the creation of one Creator.

p. 220. 'What, have they not beheld': Koran L 6.

'And when thou threwest': Koran VIII 17, a reference to Divine intervention in the battle of Badr.

p. 221. 'Do those not think that they': Koran LXXXIII 4–5.

60

The superiority of Abū Bakr over the other Companions was owing to God's grace and love within him. Rūmī urges his disciples to augment the love within them and to be ever in quest of God; for grace does not dispense with the necessity of effort. Suffering too is a Divine grace, in that it reminds men of the existence and power of God.

p. 222. 'Abū Bakr': a famous Tradition, see al-Ghazzālī, *Iḥyā'* I, p. 17.

'In movement is blessing': a well-known proverb.

61

Statements transmitted by a succession of reliable informants have the same authority as actual witnessing of the event reported. The quest blinds a man to all other considerations; passionate love is necessary in the quest for God. Rūmī then touches briefly on a variety of familiar topics.

p. 225. 'Say: Journey in the land': Koran VI 11.

p. 226. 'Since he is Muʿīn al-Dīn': evidently a criticism of the Parvāna, playing on his name.

'Any addition to perfection': a well-known proverb.

Burhān al-Dīn: Rūmī's teacher Muḥaqqiq.

62

The lover's service to the beloved springs not from love but from the inclination of the beloved. So it is in the relationship between man and God. God joined the soul with the body, which may be compared with a beehive, in order to display His omnipotence. Physical death was designed by God to strike fear into men's hearts.

Rūmī speaks of the powerful influence of the society of a true believer. The saint, who is accorded a special vision, controls his fellow-men though they may be unaware of the fact. Men should not be wholly occupied with mundane affairs. Muhammad is the guide of mankind, having pioneered the fearful way to God. All earthly pleasures and joys derive from secondary causes, and the mystic will therefore not cling to them. A few words are sometimes more effective than long speeches.

p. 229. 'Meet the friend': an Arabic proverb.

p. 230. 'When they meet those who believe': Koran II 14.

'Heavens there are': quoted from Sanā'ī, cited also in Masnavi I 2035, heading.

p. 231. 'Nay, but they marvel': Koran L 2.

p. 232. 'A certain jester': repeated from Discourse 6.

'Therein are clear signs': Koran III 91.

p. 233. 'The best words': a well-known proverb.

'Say, He is One': Koran CII.

'Sura of the Cow': Koran II.

p. 234. 'The she-camel of Salih': see Koran XI 64 ff.

'And lend to God a good loan': Koran LXXIII 20.

p. 236. 'Pour upon us water': Koran VII 47.

p. 237. 'Enter thou among My servants': Koran LXXXIX 29–30.

p. 237. Sirāj al-Dīn: presumably Rūmī's disciple Sirāj al-Dīn 'Mathnavī-khvān'; possibly Sirāj al-Dīn Maḥmūd ibn Abī Bakr Urmawī.

p. 238. 'You are in one valley': an Arabic proverb.

'Pharaoh's magicians': see *Masnavi* III 1721 ff.

Ḥajjāj: unlikely to be intended as the famous governor of Iraq.

67

p. 238. 'He created Adam': this Tradition is admitted by Muslim and al-Bukhārī.

'I was a hidden treasure': see p. 92.

p. 239. 'You have been given of knowledge': Koran XVII 87.

68

p. 239. 'Repel thou the evil': Koran XXIII 98.

p. 240. 'And pardon the offences': Koran III 128.

'Though they are powerful': quoted from Sanā'ī, *Dīvān*, p. 151.

69

p. 241. 'Drunkenness': not traced.

'King Solomon grew weary': Rūmī quotes himself, see *Dīvān* (ed. Furūzānfar) II 11178.

71

p. 242. 'On what': not traced.

'The difference between': see *Masnavi* VI 134.